Richard Rawlinson

For Nigel,
from the new Director
of the Richard Rawlinson
Center of Anglo-Saxon Studies
and Manuscript Research
in Michigan,
with love,
Milly

May 1994

Dr. Richard Rawlinson, Lane Poole No. 256. Reproduced by permission of the Bodleian Library.

Richard Rawlinson

A Tercentenary Memorial

by

Georgian R. Tashjian
David R. Tashjian
Brian J. Enright

Georgian Rawlinson Tashjian
David R. Tashjian

New Issues Press

WESTERN MICHIGAN UNIVERSITY

1990

Library of Congress Cataloging-in-Publication Data

Tashjian, Georgian Rawlinson.
    Richard Rawlinson : a tercentenary memorial / by Georgian R.
Tashjian, David R. Tashjian, Brian J. Enright.
       p. cm.
    Includes bibliographical references.
    ISBN 0-932826-23-7
    1. Rawlinson, Richard, 1690-1755. 2. Antiquarians—Great Britain—
Biography. 3. Book collectors—Great Britain—Biography. 4. Book
collecting—Great Britain—History—18th century. 5. English
philology—Old English, ca. 450-1100—Study and teaching—England—
Oxford—History. I. Tashjian, David R. II. Enright, Brian J.
III. Title.
DA93.R38T37   1990
002' .074'092—dc20
[B]   89-13858
                                                   CIP

Cover design by Elizabeth King

Armorial book plate used on the cover is one of seven (Rawlinson copperplates g. 107-114) that Rawlinson had made for his own use. Reproduced
by permission of the Bodleian Library.

The illustration of buildings in Williamsburg, Virginia used on the end
papers is reproduced by permission of the Colonial Williamsburg Foundation.

Printed in the United States of America

Contents

Foreword   vii

Preface   xi

Introduction   xiii

Chronology   xvii

Richard Rawlinson: A Biographical Study   1
    Georgian R. Tashjian

Richard Rawlinson and the Non-juring Movement   69
    David R. Tashjian

Richard Rawlinson and the Anglo-Saxon Professorship at Oxford   83
    Georgian R. Tashjian

Publications on Anglo-Saxon Studies by Rawlinsonian and   99
Rawlinson-Bosworth Professors

A Selection of Illustrations from Manuscripts   113
Collected by Richard Rawlinson

Richard Rawlinson and the Chandlers   121
    Brian J. Enright

The Later Auction Sales of Thomas Rawlinson's Library: 1727-34   133
    Brian J. Enright

Bibliographies   169

Appendix 1:
At the Three Sugar Loaves and Crown: The Origin of the Firm   179
    Owen Rutter

Appendix 2:
The Rawlinson Family and its Language Scholars   193
    Georgian R. Tashjian

Appendix 3:
Eighteenth-Century Copperplates Discovered in   201
Richard Rawlinson's Collection
    Pearce S. Grove

Appendix 4:
Daniel Rawlinson, the Mitre Tavern, and Samuel Pepys   207
    David R. Tashjian

Appendix 5:
Rawlinson Family Genealogies   211

Index   215

Foreword

The holder of the Rawlinson and Bosworth Professorship of Anglo-Saxon in the University of Oxford is not required to know anything about the history of his Chair or about its pious founder. To the latter he will look back with pleasure and gratitude, gladly recalling Sir James Murray's definition of *Pious founder*, in the *OED* entry for *Pious*, as "the founder of a college or other endowment for the glory of God and the good of his fellow-men." The history of the Rawlinsonian Professorship, as it used to be called before it became the Rawlinson and Bosworth Professorship in 1916, is long, but not all of glory, and false piety might seek to conceal the lack of distinction of some of its occupants. I admire among the earlier Rawlinsonian Professors Conybeare and Earle. It saddens me that the excellent Miss Anna Gurney gave up her projected edition of the Saxon Chronicle because Dr. Ingram, the Rawlinsonian Professor, expressed his wish to edit it. At least, he did edit it (in 1823): many Rawlinsonian Professors of that leisured age—and later—published little or nothing on Anglo-Saxon. And Miss Gurney brought out (in 1819) for private circulation her admirable translation of the Chronicle.

I have known three of my predecessors: J. R. R. Tolkien, who, by the time I knew him, had ceased to be the Rawlinson and Bosworth Professor and Professorial Fellow of Pembroke College, and held the Merton Professorship; C. L. Wrenn, the Rawlinson and Bosworth Professor when I was an undergraduate; and my immediate predecessor, Alistair Campbell, who was my tutor when he was attached to Balliol College and I was an undergraduate at University College.

I greatly admired Tolkien as a scholar, and liked him as a person. He was, when I was an undergraduate, the philologist of English at Oxford with the most ideas. He did not always trouble to present them in polished form; but they burst forth from him, and required of us, who were privileged to attend his lectures and seminars, that we should underpin them with examples of our own finding, and that we should establish for ourselves connections barely adumbrated by him. He was a technical philologist; for example, he explained convincingly why the verb *wind* is pronounced differently from the homograph noun, and he found the evidence in the *Ayenbite of Inwyt*. I believe the explanation remains unpublished still; there never seemed to him any need to rush into print with vulgar haste every fact or likely theory. He taught us how many different English vowels spring from short Germanic *a*. He explained better than anyone I ever knew the workings of that aspect of analogy called in German *Systemzwang*, especially the *Systemzwang* of the English verbal system.

Wrenn was dogmatic: he was the clearest expositor of difficulties in *Beowulf*, and a dominating lecturer. I remember well how, having just learnt not without difficulty the art, or science, of scanning Old English verse, I went to one of his lectures on *Beowulf* and heard him say, "and now I shall propose an emendation." I looked at it; I knew with all the doubtlessness of a newly-acquired mastery that his emended line would not scan, and I never went to another lecture of his. The loss was mine; and I now often relate that example of undergraduate arrogance as I tell my undergraduate and graduate pupils to expect a measure of error from me when I lecture to them: why, the system of weeks, it seems to me, has been invented so that in a series of lectures I can correct each week the errors of the preceding lecture. Wrenn believed, as was then (and may still be) generally accepted by Anglo-Saxonists, that the philological, dialectal analysis of text could reveal the secrets of an Ur-*Beowulf*. His assurance left me suspicious. After he had retired and I used to meet him at parties in the University of London, I got to like him better, and to relish his wit and the acerbity as well as the acumen of his judgement of many academic matters.

Alistair Campbell was my tutor. He made me work. From the first, he taught me to venerate Luick's *Historische Grammatik der englischen Sprache:* "Luick must be a bible to you." I thought I had learnt my assigned pages of Luick fairly well for the week's exercise; but it did not take Campbell long to find that I had failed to understand an *Anmerkung* to which he attached importance. I hear him still: "There are some people, Stanley, who, when they learn something, know it: you're clearly not one of those." Yet I liked him greatly. I always knew that he would never say as badly of me behind my back as to my face; and I was justified in my trust, for I have seen kind, though honest, references written by him for pupils whom, I know, he assailed—with good humor, no doubt—in tutorials.

Years later, in the 1960s, Campbell had a Canadian graduate student, a Rhodes Scholar who rowed for Jesus College: Angus Cameron. After leaving Oxford he took up his first post at Toronto, and there, within a year or two of his arrival, he founded the *Dictionary of Old English*. My first contact with Angus Cameron was when I was appointed his examiner for his higher degree at Oxford. After Campbell's death and my appointment to the Rawlinson and Bosworth Professorship, I took Campbell's place, alongside Helmut Gneuss and Fred C. Robinson, on the International Advisory Committee of the Cameron dictionary. After Angus Cameron's tragically early death, the editorship went to Ashley Crandell Amos, who had been an undergraduate and graduate student taught and directed by Fred Robinson at Stanford University and at Yale, and taught a little also by me at Yale, joint-editor now with Antonette di Paolo Healey at about the same time our colleague at Yale, and before that Angus Cameron's graduate student at Toronto. Anglo-Saxonists have become, like others in English studies, involved with the scholarship of their subject wherever it flourishes; and for a Rawlinson and Bosworth Professor it is a special pleasure to find throughout the world men and women taught by a Rawlinson and Bosworth Professor, or taught by someone who has been taught by a Rawlinson and Bosworth professor. Wrenn loved travel; he loved giving lectures, for example, in the Soviet Union, where, a sound Conservative, he was welcome when not many scholars from Great Britain were; and he loved travel to North America, and taught there with much pleasure, and with less ferocity than we had experienced. But Campbell never visited the *Dictionary* offices at Toronto; I do not know that he ever travelled to North America. And as for a new dictionary, he thought that on the whole Anglo-Saxonists were well served by the two best existing dictionaries, Bosworth-Toller and Grein-Köhler. When, at a dinner in University College, London—I believe it was the last time I saw him—I suggested, as I praised the Toronto *Dictionary of Old English* with which, at that time, I had only the slightest connection, that too often the references in Bosworth-Toller were to obscure or inaccessible editions, he replied, "It teaches a young man his trade."

I saw Sir William Craigie only once in my life, at a meeting at Oxford of the Philological Society in the 1950s. He was in his late eighties. My other tutor at Oxford was Stefanyja Ross, and to her and to Campbell—as well as, and especially, to Geoffrey Shepherd, unconnected with Oxford but my colleague at the University of Birmingham—I owe most. She had known Craigie's work in detail when she served under Dr. C. T. Onions on the staff of the first *Supplement* to the *Oxford English Dictionary*. I got the impression from her that she thought little of Craigie as a lexicographer on *OED*. I thought myself too junior to speak to him unintroduced, and probably concealed my inhibitions from myself by judging him too harshly and at second hand. His little editions of Old English texts are admittedly not much good.

Nevertheless, I regret now that I did not speak to him that day over tea, or I should have been able to claim at least acquaintance with all four of my predecessors in the Rawlinson and Bosworth Professorship. But thirty years ago I no more thought that I should be elected to succeed them than that solemn conclave should elect me pope of Rome.

Now, by reading the book to which this is to serve as Foreword, I have learnt a great deal about my Chair and its founder. I have not made any attempt to check, correct, or modify any of it, though, inevitably, there are things here and there that one might wish to change. Not, however, its piety of Dr. Richard Rawlinson, familiar piety as Mrs. Tashjian's middle name reveals and her Introduction confirms, which is very pleasing to the latest of the long line of beneficiaries of Dr. Richard Rawlinson's generosity.

Let me pay tribute, in conclusion, to one relatively recent and happy innovation. In Rawlinson's time such chairs as the one he founded were not attached to a particular college, but now the Rawlinson and Bosworth Professorship is attached to Pembroke College. We may no longer be the nest of singing birds we were in Rawlinson's day, as Dr. Johnson bore witness in fond retrospect. In Tolkien's time there were so few Fellows that he could stand his colleagues' faces no longer, and he migrated to Merton with few regrets. It is different now; there are many of us, in the Humanities and in Science, and it has become a place of more varied learning than in Tolkien's day, with a Senior Common Room in which one is soon made to feel at home. I did not know Pembroke when, about ten years ago, coming from Yale where I was very happy, I became a Professorial Fellow of Pembroke College. That Dr. Rawlinson's Professorship is now attached to Pembroke College seems proof to me that Fortune smiles on his foundation to this day.

Eric Gerald Stanley
26 May 1988
The Feast of Bede
in Anglo-Saxon times,
and of St. Augustine of Canterbury

Preface

One of the Oxford graduates whom Richard Rawlinson approached for autobiographical information to be included in his continuation of Anthony Wood's *Athenae Oxonienses* implored him to make no mention of him: "a busy Curacy for above 20 years has almost effaced those small Marks of Literature impressed upon me in the University." After submitting my doctoral thesis on Richard Rawlinson towards the end of 1956 I moved from the staff of the Bodleian Library to a post in the House of Commons Library, from there to reorganize the British Broadcasting Corporation Television Film Library, and then to the headships of three university libraries during the expansion of higher education in Great Britain. It would therefore be justifiable to claim that a series of busy bibliothecal "Curacies" over the past thirty years has prevented me from pursuing research into Rawlinson or of contemplating publishing a complete biography, or even further papers concerning aspects of his life and interests. The demanding tasks of the present, when higher education has ceased expanding and when, like Rawlinson, the problem of a working librarian seems to lie in the field of what is now referred to as "damage limitation"—to preserve as much as possible "for posterity without regard to the ungrateful age"—makes it unlikely that there will be an opportunity for the scale of revision which a youthful work requires.

Nevertheless the spell of the "ingenious and learned" doctor, his relentless and successful lifework in carrying out the injunction of his non-juring episcopal motto—"I Collect and I Preserve"—and the years I spent teasing out information about his life and collections which he was not particularly anxious to reveal, has left its mark. It was therefore a great pleasure to receive a telephone call in 1982 from Georgian and David Tashjian who, with characteristic zeal and determination, had traced me to Newcastle and told me of their interest in Richard Rawlinson.

Since then their dedication has been an inspiration. They have been indefatigable in pursuing Rawlinson and his family connections throughout England, from the family origins in Cumbria and their estates in Warwickshire to Richard's activities in London and Oxford. It has been a delight to meet them regularly, to correspond and to discuss Rawlinson problems and issues; surprising to have so much which has subliminally been lurking in the memory revived; and exciting to hear about their new discoveries. In particular, their mature interpretation of the Rawlinson family background, the Grand Tour, and the non-juring movement has provided new insights and put flesh on the bare bones of the thesis sketch, while the chapter on Rawlinson and the Anglo-Saxon professorship opens up new and previously neglected ground.

Over sixty years ago, Henry Broxap, writing the history of the later Non-jurors from the point of view of the Usagers, explained that "it has not been possible always to depict the character of Richard Rawlinson in the most amiable light," yet he nevertheless maintained that "the University of Oxford and the College of the 'Forerunner' never held in thrall a more devoted lover, and all who have to any degree come under the charm of the 'sweet city' will unite to honour the memory of one of her greatest benefactors." It is fitting that the tercentenary of Rawlinson's birth should be marked by this work, and it is a great satisfaction to me that research undertaken many years ago has been of some assistance for, as Rawlinson wrote about his own manuscript collections to Browne Willis a month before he died: "As I follow you in years, and in my Grand Climaterick, I must leave them to Posterity to find them in Bodley…and trust…to some future Editors. Sic vos non vobis."

Brian J. Enright
Newcastle Upon Tyne
1988

Introduction

This collection of essays is intended as a tercentenary memorial to mark the birth of Richard Rawlinson (1690-1755). He is little known to the general reader, but his enduring contributions to the academic life of his country and of the English-speaking people deserve wider fame. He bequeathed to the Bodleian Library a collection of books and manuscripts so monumental that the cataloguing took more than a hundred years to complete. To the Ashmolean Museum he left collections of medals, rare coins, statuary, portraits, and paintings. To his college at Oxford, St. John's, he left extensive properties in Warwickshire. Hertford College also enjoyed his generosity with the gift of an estate in London. He established and endowed the Chair of Anglo-Saxon Study at Oxford, which was known as the Rawlinsonian Professorship until 1916 when, combined with a bequest from Dr. Joseph Bosworth, it became the Rawlinson and Bosworth Professorship.

Rawlinson was a contemporary of Isaac Newton (1642-1727) and Edmund Halley (1656-1742) and a member of the Royal Society in London, as they were. At one time a room in the Bodleian Library was named for him, and in north Oxford, not far from St. Giles's Church where he is buried, there is a Rawlinson Road. But he is best remembered by students of English literature and English history, who continue to benefit from his legacy. As recently as 1986, for example, the Oxford University Press published a new edition of the works of Shakespeare that included a previously unattributed poem which had been found in the Rawlinson collections; and in the 1930s strikes from a copperplate engraving from his collections were used for precise architectural details by the Rockefeller Foundation during the reconstruction of Colonial Williamsburg in Virginia.

This work is not meant to be a panegyric, a work of undiluted praise. Rawlinson was a complex individual who sometimes responded with wrath and resentment to the rebuffs he received, some of which he invited because of his recalcitrance and his inability to move with the times. He could be coldly uncaring of the needs of his close relatives and, simultaneously, enormously proud of his family history. Like many bibliophiles, he may have placed his collections above his own flesh and blood, but he brought honor and lustre to his ancient name.

I have felt drawn to this agreeable labor not only because my family name is Rawlinson but also because the study of Anglo-Saxon, as well as the body of critical literature surrounding it, has been a lasting pleasure. The unlocking of that winsome word-hoard for me began with the outstanding instruction of Dr. William R. Brown during my undergraduate days at Western State Teachers College in Kalamazoo, Michigan. Those were good hours gladly spent and gladly remembered.

Throughout the years of research needed to produce this volume, my husband, whose essays included here are a departure from his professional life in the field of communications and space technology, has participated actively. (Also he has spent countless hours at the word-processor.) Our initial efforts at research were slowed by the daunting mass of materials relating to Rawlinson held at the Bodleian Library; then, fortunately, on visiting the Society of Antiquaries in London, we were directed by the librarian there to Dr. Brian J. Enright, who while at Oxford had written his doctoral thesis on Rawlinson. Although we were total strangers to him, Dr. Enright greeted us as friends of long standing. With a spirit of scholarly generosity, he invited us to draw freely on his carefully documented thesis, which proved to be an invaluable guide through the wealth of Rawlinson manuscripts. On two occasions he interrupted his heavy schedule as Librarian at the University of Newcastle upon Tyne to travel to London and discuss problems and various possibilities that we encountered during the course of our investigations. Like Rawlinson, who with great cordiality "plundered" his own collections to assist his friends, Dr. Enright has lent us books and other materials. We are grateful for his assistance; without it the biographical study, admittedly only a partial treatment of Rawlinson's long and productive life, could not have been accomplished. We are additionally grateful in that he has permitted us to reprint two of his previously published essays on Rawlinson and allowed copies of his thesis to be deposited in the libraries of San Jose State University, San Jose, California; Western Michigan University, Kalamazoo, Michigan; and the Colonial Williamsburg Foundation Library, Williamsburg, Virginia. Readers interested in the documentation on which the biographical study and non-juring essay are based may consult Dr. Enright's thesis.

We are grateful to the members of the staff of Duke Humfrey's Library who provided ready access to the Rawlinson papers; to the Librarian of St. John's College at Oxford, who made the papers of that college available to us; to the staff of the Henry E. Huntington Library in San Marino, California, who kindly directed our use of a collection which includes publications of Richard Rawlinson, a medieval charter once in the collection of his brother Thomas, and other rare eighteenth century books pertaining to our subject; to members of the English Department at San Jose State University for many helpful suggestions; and in particular to Dr. Allison Heisch for attention, support, and encouragement since the first days of the present work. We want also to express deep gratitude to our editor, Dr. Thomas H. Seiler, for his exceptional scholarship, his regard for precision, and his personal commitment to this work; to some extent the book has become his as well as ours.

xv

Finally, we thank Richard Rawlinson for being what he was. *The Battle of Maldon* is Bodleian MS. Rawlinson B. 203. Although he may never have read the poem, inasmuch as he himself, to his stated regret, was not a Saxon scholar, he learned from his many private battles the necessity of brandishing the ash-spear, hearth companions hewn down, heroes in the hall, he by no means a slack one to seek safety in the forest, but, fighting to the finish, saying with Byrhtwold

> Hige sceal þe heardra,   heorte þe cenre,
> mod sceal þe mare,   þe ure mægen lytlað.

Georgian Rawlinson Tashjian
Palo Alto, California
1988

Chronology

1690   January 3: Richard Rawlinson born in London to Sir Thomas and Lady Rawlinson, *née* Mary Taylor.

1697   Rawlinson is admitted to St. Paul's School as a day pupil.

1702   Rawlinson is admitted to Eton.

1705-06   Sir Thomas Rawlinson, Richard's father, becomes Lord Mayor of London.

1708   March 9: Rawlinson matriculates at St. John's College, Oxford. November: Sir Thomas Rawlinson dies.

1711   Rawlinson receives his B.A. degree.
Rawlinson publishes *The Life of Anthony Wood*.
Lady Rawlinson marries her second husband, Stephen Hutchinson (d. October 1712).

1713   May 30: Lady Rawlinson marries her third husband, Michael Lister.
July 5: Rawlinson is awarded his M.A. degree.

1713-19   Rawlinson publishes a number of antiquarian and topographical studies.

1714   July: Rawlinson is elected to the Royal Society.

1716   Rawlinson is ordained a non-juring priest and later a deacon; moves to Gray's Inn.

1719   Rawlinson travels to France and the Low Countries; in June returns to receive the degree of D.C.L. at Oxford.

1720-26 Rawlinson travels on the Continent, leaving England on 12 June 1720.

1720 November: The South Sea Company fails; the Bubble bursts.

1725 January 23: John Hannam, the Rawlinson family banker, dies in London.
February 21: Rawlinson's mother dies in London.
July 9: Rawlinson begins the trip toward England.
August 6: Rawlinson's elder brother, Thomas, dies in London.

1726 April: Rawlinson returns to England.

1726-49 Rawlinson works to free the family properties from debt and to re-establish the family fortunes. His activities during these years include involvement with the Society of Antiquaries, the Freemasons, and the Royal Society, and his duties as a bishop among the Non-jurors.

1727 May: Rawlinson elected to membership in the Society of Antiquaries.
June: Rawlinson becomes a member of the Freemasons.

1728 March: Rawlinson is consecrated as a non-juring Bishop.

1734 Rawlinson moves from Gray's Inn to London House.

1749 Rawlinson at last becomes free from debt.

1750 Rawlinson makes provisions for the Anglo-Saxon Professorship at Oxford.

1752 Rawlinson makes his will.

1755 February: The ailing Rawlinson travels to the spa at Islington, a suburb of London, to recuperate.
April 6: Rawlinson dies at Islington.

Richard Rawlinson: A Biographical Study

To the Continent and Back

To young Englishmen of position in the eighteenth century, the Grand Tour of the Continent was not an unusual event. Sometimes travelling alone, but more often in the company of another man or a tutor, they spent years, not just months, in these travels which were intended to put the finishing touches onto a young man's education. Dr. Johnson, who was never able to make the Tour, confesses "A man who has not been in Italy is always conscious of an inferiority."

As it was evolving, the Grand Tour had been described by Sir Francis Bacon more than a century earlier:

> The things to be seen and observed are the courts of princes, especially when they give audience to ambassadors; the courts of justice...the churches and monasteries, with the monuments which are therein extant; the walls and fortifications...havens and harbors, antiquities and ruins, libraries, colleges, disputations and lectures...shipping and navies...armouries, arsenals, magazines, exchanges, bourses, warehouses, exercises of horsemanship, fencing, training of soldiers, and the like; comedies, such whereunto the better sort of persons do resort; treasuries of jewels and robes; cabinets and rarities....

Among other attractions which one would not fail to observe as a matter of routine practice, continues Bacon, are masques, feasts, weddings, funerals, "capital executions and such shows."

Richard Rawlinson's European travels began in 1720 and ended in 1726. During these years he saw much more than the attractions noted above. He visited a king in exile, was present at the birth of the son of that king, ministered as priest to a dying Englishman, saw four popes, peered into the crater of Vesuvius, registered at three universities, and visited many hospitals. He became adept at the Italian language, so adequate in it that, as he records in his journal, he passed as an Italian; furthermore, while in Pisa, he translated from the Italian a book which he later published in England.

Rawlinson, thirty years of age when he left London, was older than the usual student tourist. Seven years earlier he had completed his studies at Oxford with the usual Bachelor's and Master's degrees. In 1719 he had been awarded the degree of Doctor of Civil Law. His Church had made him a deacon as well as a priest. He had spent several years touring England, searching out material for topographical studies which he later published. In addition he had been elected to membership in the Royal Society, and during these early years he served as governor of the Bethlem and Bridewell Hospitals. It was, therefore, as a mature man that he visited the continent. The greatest enthusiasm of Rawlinson's life was collecting, and one of his objectives while abroad was to add to his already substantial collections of all things that were old or rare or curious. As the son of a wealthy and recognized London family and with letters of credit to foreign bankers, he was able to indulge his acquisitive inclination and to purchase freely. It is to his credit and to posterity's gain that he exercised an educated taste, as during his six years in Europe he accumulated and shipped back to England manuscripts, books, statuary, paintings, coins, and other such rich stores. Inasmuch as his searches were time-consuming and an almost primary occupation, it is understandable that his tour covered a longer period of time than one that was merely for the advantages of education—much longer, for instance, than that of John Evelyn, Joseph Addison, or Horace Walpole.

He would have been content to remain longer in Italy, but in 1725 he received word of the death of his banker, who was a long-time family friend and who was also the holder of the mortgages on the Rawlinson properties. In addition, Richard had been named as the executor of his friend's will. He decided to return to England and planned a homeward route which would allow him to visit areas previously neglected. While in Genoa Rawlinson learned from an English newspaper of the death of his brother Thomas, who was a well-known collector; it was he who had introduced Richard to the excitement and satisfaction of collecting. In the distant city of Rome, Richard had heard of his brother's business reverses, but, removed as he was, he was not alarmed until he actually returned and found that the situation was desperate; the family fortune had been dissipated, and Thomas was seriously in debt. Furthermore, to the disapproving astonishment of his intimates in London, he had married his servant and had left a will which deprived Richard and the other family members of their hereditary rights. The total estate had been willed over in trust to a lawyer, William Ford, in exchange for his agreement as trust officer to pay the debts which amounted to £10,000, to honor two legacies, and to secure a comfortable annuity for his widow. To Richard and the other members of the family, nothing was left; it was incomprehensible to him that such a state of affairs could have come about.

It is from Thomas Hearne, the untiring Oxford diarist, antiquary, and publisher of medieval chronicles, that we are able to learn much that is known about the Rawlinson brothers, who were his close friends. In his pages he recorded that Thomas died after a languishing illness, on August 6, 1725, in London House, in Aldersgate Street, where he had lived for many years. Thomas, Hearne said, died of a distemper caused by his great concern on account of his debts. London House had been in earlier times a home for the bishops of London. Large and commodious with an inner courtyard and numerous staircases serving different apartments, it presented to Thomas Rawlinson the ideal place for his residence; there he could live with his accumulations of books, manuscripts, and paintings. He had moved there in 1716 from his rooms in Gray's Inn where his vast collections compelled him to sleep in a passageway. Dibdin's *Bibliomania,* in referring to London House and Thomas, says that there "among dust and cobwebs and bulwarks of paper" he used to "regale himself with the sight and scent of innumerable black-letter volumes, arrayed in sable garb and stowed three deep from the bottom to the top of the house." This is the house in which Thomas lived and died—and to which Richard returned in 1726 to face financial disaster. He himself resumed his quarters in Gray's Inn which he had retained during his time abroad and which had been lent to his younger brother John in his absence.

At the end, according to Hearne, Thomas had suffered the loss of his good name when he married his servant, Amy Frewin. Up to that time his financial standing (even though for several years he had been seriously in debt) was fairly stable and reputable. The marriage enraged his creditors who, as Hearne wrote,

> united to give him trouble, particularly Dr. Mead (whom he owed upon bond £100) was very clamorous...[But] I am of the opinion that [they] should have been less violent towards him, especially Booksellers, for whom he had done eminent service. For, being a man of brave, noble Spirit, and being a great lover of books, in which I never knew anyone whatsoever better skilled, he took all opportunities of being present at, or at least giving commissions at, Sales and Auctions, and by his high bidding, he strangely advanced the Prices of Books, which he likewise did in Bookseller's shops, so that I have heard it said...that the Booksellers ought to erect a statue to him. And yet so ungrateful were they that one of them arrested him for an inconsiderable sum (and yet he was a person

that Mr. Rawlinson had particularly obliged), which was the beginning of his troubles, and occasioned him to keep in, so that he hath hardly been out,...[and] wore his beard long, and appeared very negligent of himself, which conduc'd in no small measure to the impairing of his Health.

He stated further that Thomas was a "man of very great Integrity and Honor" and that his collection of

books both for number and value [was] hardly to be equalled by any one Study in England, which was what really run [sic] him aground and brought him at last into so much trouble. For he was not a lewd, vicious Man, but on the contrary very virtuous, temperate, and sober.

He also, as Hearne had ample reason to know, had been extremely generous with the treasures of his library.

Hearne, fifty miles distant in Oxford and removed in distance also from the family ties that Richard was heir to, could speak dispassionately and analytically of the Rawlinson troubles. But no such easy acquiescence was possible for Richard, who found that, first of all, he had to face the fact of his brother's marriage and the reversals it represented to him. Of Amy Frewin, he wrote to a friend,

...she came to [him] from an adjoyning Coffea House service, and after trial, and pretense of pregnancy was admitted to his bed, afterwards by the force of gin, broke his heart, drunk so much herself, that no child was got before, or after his death, tho' endeavors, if fame lyes not, were not wanting. The marriage was clandestine...and the Preist [sic] and witnesses both ran their Country when the next heir came from abroad.

Richard realized that if he did not take action he would lose all claims to his rights; in bitter fact, he would be penniless. He considered challenging his brother's will; but, fearing a long court case and legal entanglements (which were not unfamiliar to him), he decided to come to terms with the widow, who remarried shortly after the death of Thomas. According to Thomas Hearne, in return for her interest in the Rawlinson estates Richard agreed to pay her a lifetime annuity of £120, to pay all of Thomas's debts, and to honor two large legacies left by Thomas. Further, in return for the sum of £300 paid to the widow, she agreed to turn over the administration of her husband's will to Richard, who agreed to organize and execute the auction sales of the remainder of Thomas Rawlinson's library, the proceeds of which were to pay Thomas's debts. Only after the collections had been sold could Richard sell or mortgage the real estate.

The situation was totally galling to Richard, who, while remembering his brother with sincere fondness even though he was angered by the terms of the will, soon found that in order to return the Rawlinson fortune to any semblance of its former status (or indeed even to repair it enough so it would provide an income) he, who was "never bred an oeconomist or accomptant," would have to study leases, rents, grain prices, fertilizer, and agronomy in general—all this a far cry from the classical education in which he had delighted. He spent arduous hours each day in the new discipline demanded of him, insisting on rigid economy and agreeing only to "absolutely necessary repairs so as to be wind and water tight." Hearne wrote in his diary soon after Richard's arrival in London:

> Last night I had a letter from a Friend, Dr. Richard Rawlinson...[who] hath been several years beyond the Sea, for the most part at Rome. He tells me his deceased Brother's embroiled affairs...take up more hours than he could wish, so that he hath not time to detail on his travels, but he flatters himself this summer to see me.

It is a bit of irony that the former carefree traveller who had ranged Europe freely was unable to travel to nearby Oxford to visit his friend, except as a side trip after the supervision of the ailing Rawlinson lands in Warwickshire, "where he hath been to view his estate" wrote Hearne. On this occasion they passed several hours of good company at the Mitre, but such respites were rare.

It was a bitter experience for Richard to be forced to organize and to supervise the sale of his brother's library. Probably only a person who is a true collector and bibliophile can participate in the indignity of his position, as of course he was forced not only to witness but also to direct the sale of volumes which he, himself, hungered to own. While the thirteenth sale, comprising four thousand books and lasting twenty-six nights, was taking place in 1729, Rawlinson wrote:

> Our last Matthew Parker takes its fate. I am told there is a latent commission of £50 for it from France, but I hope England will not lose such a treasure, tho' I can't...afford to be the master of it.

This was only one of the thousands of treasures Richard had reasonably supposed would be his by hereditary right, left him by the brother who knew of and applauded his younger brother's appreciation and careful custody.

The library sales were all the more cruel to Richard because he was forced to act almost as a day laborer in order to prepare for the sales. A hired agent, not knowing the true value of the books and manuscripts, would have bungled the sales, to the loss of the estate. Further, Richard was placed in the humiliating position of having to report all details of the auctions to

Sir Thomas Rawlinson in his Robes as Lord Mayor of London. Engraved by George Vertue from a portrait by Sir Godfrey Kneller. Rawlinson copperplate b. 9. Reproduced by permission of the Bodleian Library.

the husband of his brother's widow, especially humiliating since he considered that she had contributed to the economic disaster and also, as some thought, was actually involved in his brother's death: there was an ugly rumor of poison. It was necessary for Richard, according to the agreement with John Tabor (Amy's husband), to list all details of the sales, and these were to be presented for his inspection. These records still exist. John Matthews in 1727 was paid 9s. for porterage and marking books; Mr. Porteus received 1s. for a bundle of pens and Mr. Minshull 1s. for a pint of ink. Sweeping the chimneys cost 1s. A dozen pounds of candles was 5s. 6d. and a sack of "coles" was 3s. 3d. Today we can be grateful for his listings as a comment on typical eighteenth century book sales; but, at the time when Richard was enduring this heavy duty, this harsh discipline, and the long hours of lacklustre drudgery, he must have let his mind wander back to less difficult, less painful days.

Early Childhood

Richard's parents were married in 1680 in the nineteenth year of the reign of Charles II. They were both from prosperous middle-class families who lived in the old section of London—the Old Bailey, as it was then called. The modern visitor will know this location better by the mention of its proximity to St. Paul's Cathedral (which at that time was being rebuilt by Sir Christopher Wren), the Guildhall, the Tower, Tower Bridge, and Billingsgate. Mary Taylor, who married Thomas Rawlinson, came with a settlement of £3000. The marriage document, which is at St. John's College, Oxford, lists the groom's large properties which he was to bring to the marriage: the Manor of Heathcote in Warwickshire, the Manor of Saddlebow in Norfolk, and the rents from six properties in Lancashire. Since Thomas was in line to inherit additional properties from his father, Daniel Rawlinson, a wealthy tea merchant, vintner, and Keeper of the Mitre Tavern in London, the bride and groom had unusually firm economic security. (Daniel is often referred to in Pepys's diary; the two men were neighbors and close friends.) In the first year of their marriage the young couple made arrangements with the New River Water Company to supply water to their home. Water piped into the house was no doubt a great luxury as the alternative was to carry water from the neighborhood well or to purchase it from a water vendor. Thomas Rawlinson's contract with the New River Water Company, now Bodleian MS. Rawlinson D. 1212, guaranteed the delivery of water from Chadwell and Amwell (to the north, not far from Sadler's Wells) at least three days of the week. It described the supply pipe as being of lead and accommodating one half inch of water and controlled by a brass cock in the kitchen and one in the yard, "the said branch to be laid from the main pipe that lieth in Old Bailey" and was for the "proper use and service for said lessee's family." As for payment, there was an initial installation fee of 24s. with the yearly charge to be paid quarterly: at the Feast of the Nativity of St. John the Baptist, the Feast of St. Michael the Archangel, at the Birth of our Lord, and at the Annunciation of St. Mary the Virgin. The patron was enjoined to guard against waste; in time of frost, however, the water was to be allowed to run. Apparently the company had a supply problem, as one item in the contract stated that if the company failed to deliver water for a period of fourteen days, the lessee upon notifying the office at Puddledock, was entitled to retain that quarter's rent which the lessor "doth promise and covenant and grant."

In 1686 Thomas was knighted by James II at Windsor Castle. This honor lent an added aura of well-being to the family, as well as substantiating and reinforcing the already existing loyalty of the family to the Stuarts, a factor which was to exert a powerful influence throughout Richard's life, extending well into the time of the Hanovers. It began also a long career of public service for Sir Thomas, which culminated in his term as Lord Mayor of London in 1705-06. He died in 1708 at the age of sixty.

At St. Paul's School, where Richard had his early education, there were three tiers of benches on the two long sides of a large rectangular room which accommodated approximately 150 boys. With two teachers and a chaplain, these boys (beginning at the age of seven) went through the different forms until they were ready for the university. In Richard's case, however, there was a shift to Eton in 1702, when he was twelve. His school days at St. Paul's were, in all probability, very similar to the well-recorded days of John Milton, who attended the same school in the previous century. Since it was a day school and since it began at seven with Latin prayers and a chapter from the Bible, the boys probably arose at 5:30 or 6:00 in the morning to walk to school. The scholars took with them their quill pens, pen knives, ink, paper, and books; there were no desks, no lockers, and no closets. At eleven they went home for the mid-day meal and resumed class work at one; the afternoon session lasted until five. The school week was six days. There is no evidence that the regimen was relaxed for even the very young boys. The original articles of admission to St. Paul's were specific. "If your chylde can rede and wryte latyn and english sufficiently, soo that he be able to rede an wryte his owne lesons, then he shall be admytted into the schole for a scholar." The boys had their pre-grammar school training from tutors at home or from some other source, such as the then-popular "petty" school.

The boys studied Latin, Greek, and Hebrew, with grammar, translation, oratory, and other literary exercises, the greatest emphasis being on Latin. There was religious as well as literary instruction. A difference between Milton's experience and Richard's was that the Great Fire of 1666 had destroyed the original building; consequently, of course, Richard's school was a new building, but in all probability it retained the original curriculum and procedure. Since the school's location was adjacent to St. Paul's Cathedral, the young boy's attention could not always have been on Latin and Greek as he walked to and from school. The first stones of Christopher Wren's new cathedral were laid in 1675 and the last in 1710. During Richard's years there from age seven to twelve or from 1697 through 1702, he must have been fascinated by all the activity: the carpenters, the glaziers, the lead-cutters, the masons, the dray-men with their wagons, and the huge scaffolding rising into the sky. It is reported by J. E. Zetzner, who saw the re-building in progress, that a thousand men were employed daily. (Years later Richard was to purchase many of Sir Christopher Wren's papers, drawings, and other documents; they are in the Rawlinson collections now in the Bodleian.) William Lilly, the astrologer, whose lifetime approximated Milton's and who attended a similar school, said of himself: "For the last two years of my being at school, I was of the highest form in the school. . . . I could then speak Latin as well as English; could make Extempore Verses upon any Theme. . . ." Richard Evelyn, also of St. Paul's, was a virtuoso in Latin, Greek, and Hebrew. It is with no surprise, then, that we today look at Richard's exercise books from his Eton days and find extended Latin and Greek passages. But, however intensive the study of the classics was, the curriculum was well balanced, as we may judge from the fact that Edmund Halley, while a student at St. Paul's, excelled equally at the classics and mathematics.

Eton College

In 1702 Eton College was already more than 250 years old. It had been founded by Henry VI and positioned near Windsor for the purpose of royal supervision. In the eighteenth century it had the reputation of offering the finest in classical education as preparation for the universities. Richard's headmaster was already known to his parents since the elder brother Thomas had attended Eton some years earlier.

What was probably an exercise assigned to all the boys in his class has survived in Richard's handwriting:

> The School is situated at the West end of the first Quadrangle, built by Rich'd Allestree and cost 1500£. It is almost all of brick supported by free stone pillars, and underneath it a spacious Open walk, handsomely wainscoted within, having three Noble brass branches for candles, and att the North End a handsome Library, well replenished with Classick Authours…and containing near 150 manuscripts among which is the noble Chrysostom done by Sir Henry Saville.

Under the Headmastership of John Newborough, whom Richard described as having a "Presence fit to awe the numerous Tribe over whom he presided," and under the Housemastership of Stephen Weston, whom Thomas Hearne described as being "a good Scholar and a good natured man," Richard's education continued.

Since in later years Richard's family members were to exert unusual and decidedly difficult pressures on him, it is reassuring to glance at the substantial picture which the family presented in 1702, when Richard first attended Eton. (It is notable that *DNB* is in error in regard to Richard's Eton years, quoting 1707 as his year of entry there. Existing correspondence between Sir Thomas Rawlinson and Eton College regarding the payment of accounts for Richard is dated January, 1703.) His father, as Keeper of the Mitre Tavern, was not only involved with the successful family business but also occupied with his civic responsibilities as sheriff and alderman in London. In addition he was an officer in the city police force and served as president of Bethlem and Bridewell Hospitals. Although an indulgent landlord, he often visited the family estates, which were in various parts of the country, the ancestral lands being in Lancashire. Along with the Sandys, Sawreys, and the Penningtons, the Rawlinsons were one of the major landholders of the county.

The family continued to live in their home in the Old Bailey; in addition they had a country home in Hammersmith. In 1702 the fifteenth and last child, Tempest, was born. In that year the first child, Thomas, after two years at St. John's College, was reading law at the Middle Temple, where his name had been entered as early as 7 January 1696. (Richard, in later years of family discord, was to spend his vacations with Thomas in his rooms in the Temple rather than at the family home.) There was a brother Daniel, three years older than Richard. Nothing is known of him except that he, having died in 1705 at the age of eighteen of dysentery on shipboard en route to the East Indies, was buried on the island of St. Helena. In a family which is known to have spared no effort or expense relative to the education of the sons in these years, it is singular that we find no record of his schooling. It is probable that he was learning the family tea trade. Even though the tea business was leased to a cousin at this time, it was still in the Rawlinson family. The business had been founded by Daniel Rawlinson (1614-79) who had made a fortune; it might easily follow that this grandson Daniel had been encouraged to carry on the grandfather's trade. A poignant note is that an earlier child named Daniel had died in infancy. In the years prior to 1702, deaths among the children in the family were not infrequent; there had been five funerals. The loss which must have affected Richard the most keenly was that of his sister Susannah, two years older than he; she died in 1700 at the age of twelve. Since it is known that Richard had smallpox in 1700 (while a student at St. Paul's School), it is likely that she died in the epidemic of that period. Of the younger children in 1702 there were three sisters and four brothers: Mary, Anne, and Honor, William, John, Constantine, and Tempest, all of whom lived well into adulthood. By way of summary, then, Richard at that time had two older brothers, three younger sisters, and four younger brothers, the youngest being an infant of only a few months.

With all the pride of a fond son and with the zeal of a true archivist Richard collected and preserved his father's personal and business papers. It is from these that we get glimpses of a generous, hearty, flexible, and loving

The Wasperton Parish Church, Adjacent to Richard Rawlinson's Favorite Estate in Warwickshire, Wasperton Hill Farm. Photo by David R. Tashjian.

parent, who said, in 1702, 'I thank God I allwayes beleaved there was a Providence, who if we take care to sarve…will take care of us." He was anxious for his children to be prudent in the use of their "best Cloathes" and to "be chid" unless they came to table with "cleane hands and face." Sir Thomas, himself without much formal education, was eager for his sons to have the advantages of Eton and Oxford. It was during Richard's Eton years that his father became Lord Mayor of London (1705-06). His portrait by Sir Godfrey Kneller in the Lord Mayor's full regalia is now at the Goldsmith's Hall in London. One can readily imagine the pleasure of a fifteen-year-old schoolboy on the occasion of the colorful ceremonies in London—the carriages, the processions, the crowds of people, the fireworks. During his term of office Marlborough's victory at Ramillies took place, and it was at the petition of Sir Thomas that Queen Anne presented to the City of London the trophies of that battle.

The older Rawlinson sons, Thomas and Richard, saw before them in their early years a family reverence for books and libraries. The paternal grandfather had founded the school library in his native Lancashire town of Hawkshead, presenting books himself and obtaining others from seventy-five different donors. In addition he gave £100, the interest of which was to be used for the purchase of books for the Hawkshead School, for a writing master there, and for sending a poor boy to the university. Before his death in 1679 he had rebuilt the school, had refurnished a chapel, and had endowed the Hawkshead parish church. This school at Hawkshead was the one in the following century attended by William Wordsworth, whose initials can be found carved into one of the desks. Richard's maternal grandfather, also a vintner, settled an annuity of £14 on the first grandchild; it was to be spent solely on books. Although Thomas was the recipient, Richard shared in the benefit indirectly. In these circumstances the appearance of two scholars from families of vintners is not to be wondered at—nor is Richard's later driving desire to collect and to make handsome benefactions to institutions of learning.

The Years at Oxford: 1708-16

Richard's college at Oxford was St. John's. His days there began with his matriculation on March 9, 1708; it was the beginning of a lifelong influence, one which inclined Richard in later years to speak time and again of "my dearest Oxford" and of the place where he had the "happiness to be educated." His father, in 1707, had written for advice regarding Richard's tutor.

The letter was answered by Samuel Smith, who had been the elder brother's tutor (since retired) and who also, at the request of Sir Thomas, had been chaplain to him during his Lord Mayoralty. Perhaps this particular relationship, closer than most, prompted the following over-generous advice given to young Richard (even as young Laertes was abundantly advised):

> The Respect I have for you cannot be better Expressed than by offering some few directions for Your Conduct when at Oxford: Let me desire you to bee familiar with None but those that are sober. Ingenuity Cannot atone for Intemperance. A Dull Companion is better than a Wicked one; And it is much safer to be acquainted with a Blocked than a Madman. I hope you have a right notion of honour and will not bee Ambitious of the Applause a Rattlepated Fellow can bestow. Labour for the Esteem of wise and good men and take as much pains to preserve a good name as to get it. Whos[o]ever talks against the Exercise of the house and in particular against Filosophy is Ignorant and Conceited; And pray lett him be as much a fool in your eyes as he [is] wise in his own. Hear what the Factors for idleness say but Resolve at the same tyme to thwart 'em by your Practice. One Tutor is sufficient for you and I beg you to have no more. Whenever you want information Consult him; and despise all directions from your Equalls, which are contrary to his; Encourage him to give you instructions by your Readiness to Receive it. Look upon your Tutor as a kind of Father, And think it your duty to doe every thing [that] will please, and to avoid every thing you presume will offend him. If you have a mind to be Valued pay Ready money, Especially Let those have it in due time who Deserve more than what is Commonly allowed 'em. Make your Allowance exceed your expenses but keep no stock to lend to them whose Custome 'tis to borrow: If ever you Yield to the importunity of such reckon your loan no other than a gift. When you talk of others, if they have given you an occasion say something that will please 'em or be silent. Be sure to Respect your superiors, even though it should happen to be Unfashionable; Miss neither Exercise nor prayers wilfully. Read one chapter at least every day in the Bible. Be civil to every body Familiar with few. Consider dayly the end of your going to the University. Religiously observe the Sabbath. Stay not from Church. Endeavor to please your Parents, and to engage God's blessing by Deserving theirs. This is the sure way for you to bee happy. And that you may be so shall be the Constant prayer of...Sam: Smith.

The "way to bee happy" with its many injunctions could not have had the opportunity to happen in a finer setting. The *Gentleman and Lady's Companion for Oxford*, published in 1747, states that St. John's College was distinguished from its neighbors by handsome piazzas "in the Grecian taste" in the inner quadrangle; that it had a spacious library, elegantly neat and well-furnished with the best-chosen books and manuscripts; that its hall was the most beautiful in the whole University; that its gardens were unequalled. Further, the Canterbury Quadrangle, where Richard as a gentleman commoner had his rooms, had been the magnificent gift of Archbishop Laud, and as such was, no doubt, a constant reminder of the influence of a man whom Richard revered and honored.

Canterbury Quadrangle, St. John's College, Oxford. Photo by David R. Tashjian.

Academically, however, Oxford in the eighteenth century is pictured as going through a period of malaise, with slackness on one hand and pedantry on the other. The discontent in particular seems directed toward the inability and vapidity of some of the tutors, the irregularity or absence of examinations, and low moral standards on the part of certain college officials. Thomas Hearne, whose carping judgement should be evaluated in terms of his own individual biases, remarked that in Oxford the "most illiterate and stupid persons are looked upon as best qualified for Heads of Houses." We can be reminded, however, that the eighteenth century was not a bad time for the serious student, that under its *laissez-faire* conditions the scholar was liberated from obligations that a more regimented system would have demanded of him. Leisure, well used in the company of scholars, can be profitable, especially when one has a good tutor. Certainly it is to the credit of the system that John Lemprière of Pembroke while still an undergraduate began the compilation of his Classical Dictionary. In the same manner,

Richard while still an undergraduate began to compile his collections for his later antiquarian publications. Fortunately for him (and for his beneficiaries), at Oxford he not only received an excellent education but also became motivated toward a lifetime of inquiry, investigation, and study.

His time was not all spent with his tutor and his books, however. For leisure time activities he chose riding out into the countryside and trips on the river. His carefully kept accounts reveal that he loved oranges, that he had a "tea boyler," and that the college smith provided him with extra keys. On St. John's Day he paid five shillings "for musick" and ten shillings for wine. He was generous with his offerings at Communion; by way of private charities he helped a poor man in prison and assisted a "singing man in debt." He had his wig dressed regularly and delighted in new pairs of gloves. Further attentions to his personal appearance are indicated by payments made to his tailor, his shoemaker, and his washerwoman. He spent hours in coffee houses, establishments which were deplored by some members of the older generation as places where hours were idled away. Anthony Wood described them as "parasites on the tree of knowledge," parasites responsible for the "decay of study and consequently of learning." He deprecated the fact that scholars frequented these places where they "spend much of the day in the hearing and speaking of news. . . ." For Richard, on the contrary, they were a valuable part of the Oxford experience, his frequent visits there denoting an intense interest in politics. Like his father and his grandfather before him, he was an ardent Tory; he was also a Jacobite and a Non-juror. During the years at Oxford he was affirming these positions.

Richard's interest in politics came into sharp focus during the trial of Dr. Henry Sacheverell, an Oxford don and a High Church divine, who with fiery passion delivered a sermon from the pulpit of St. Paul's on March 5, 1709. He railed against the treatment that had been dealt out to James II and also inveighed against the principles of the Revolution of 1688. He urged "passive obedience," not necessarily overt allegiance, to the Crown. The Lord Mayor, highly pleased, took him home to dinner and together they arranged to have the sermon printed. Accordingly forty thousand copies were made ready and all England took notice. Underlying this, of course, was a general unhappiness with the Whigs, who were in power, and a widespread dissatisfaction with the continental wars with their incessant drain on human life as well as on finances. The Whigs cried for impeachment, and the Sacheverell case, which began on February 10, 1710, and which lasted three weeks, was tried in London. Although the verdict was against him, it was by so small a margin that it constituted vindication for Sacheverell, whose sentence was light. He became the man of the hour; the enthusiasm of the populace was overwhelming, with the result that the Whig influence at court was greatly damaged. The Tories were triumphant. The situation according to Richard and Thomas Rawlinson and to Thomas Hearne was exactly as it should be. A playing card of 1710 at the British Museum shows a complacent Sacheverell nodding to an admiring crowd from his carriage; the caption reads:

> Others would swell with pride, while thus caressed,
> But he bears humble thoughts within his breast.

Richard had followed the trial closely, paying 1s. 6d. for a transcription of Dr. Sacheverell's answer to his impeachment before the House of Lords. At the end of March he acquired two portraits of the cleric and undoubtedly saw his hero as he progressed with his entourage through Oxford in June of the same year.

As the world of learning opened for Richard, the happy domestic life of his childhood closed. His father died in November of 1708, after which time Richard's allowance was sent regularly to him by his mother. Remembering his early letter of advice from Samuel Smith ("make your allowance exceed your expenses"), he was careful to record his expenditures—his records (battels) are in his papers at St. John's College; similarly he recorded the allowances received from "my Honored Mother, the Lady Rawlinson."

An immeasurable benefit to Richard during his Oxford years was his friendship with Thomas Hearne (1678-1735), to whom he had been introduced by his older brother Thomas. Although separated in age by more than a decade, they were drawn together by their intense political and cultural interests. At the time Richard first attended St. John's, Hearne, who had retained his rooms at his college (St. Edmund Hall), was Underkeeper at the Bodleian Library. Thomas Rawlinson at this time had gone on to read law at the Middle Temple in London, his book-filled rooms there becoming a second home to the younger brother. As early as 1709, when Richard was only a student of nineteen, Hearne recognized his unusual abilities and made frequent entries in his diary of their mutual interests. It was the beginning of a long friendship, one which was mutually supportive. In the early years it was a means of helping young Richard establish himself and his goals; in later years it was a source of great benefit to Hearne, as the Rawlinson brothers supplied the out-of-favor librarian with manuscripts which he needed for his work in editing and publishing.

During his years at Oxford, Richard's rooms became a small museum. Thomas Hearne records that among the many items assembled were civil and ecclesiastical charters; a rare breviary on vellum; his transcript of the diary of Anthony Wood from the "original held by Mr. Anstis in London;" a work printed in 1642, quarto, about the Nunnery at Little Gidding, with a picture of the Nunnery House; a copy of the grant of Gray's Inn; in manuscript a "true account of the Manner and Form . . . of the Funeral of the Right Honorable Earl of Essex in three sheets;" a work of Demosthenes in Greek printed in Venice in 1554, octavo; a transcript of the prayers of King James I made upon his death bed; a pamphlet entitled "Of the church in Ireland during the reign of Henry VIII, Edward VI, and Queen Mary;" coins from the time of Vespasian and Constantius; Saxon coins found in a cellar in nearby Abingdon; and, among yet more specimens, an inscribed stone from the Nunnery of Godstow.

During his undergraduate years, Richard developed a great admiration for Anthony Wood, especially because of Wood's interest in antiquarian studies, in particular his work on the biographical histories of alumni of Oxford (*Athenae Oxonienses*) which remained uncompleted and which Richard, as one of his personal objectives, wished in time to be able to complete. With this goal in mind, he became a regular reader and transcriber at the Bodleian as well as at the library of the Ashmolean Museum. Not only was he an insatiable reader of biography, he also became extremely fond of topographical works which he was to pursue in the years to come. Since no biography of Wood had been attempted, Richard decided to compile one from his own transcript of Wood's diary as well as from other papers found in the libraries. Also he secured from Wood's sister the loan of a copperplate portrait. In due course, in 1711, he had an unsigned monograph printed. Thomas Hearne had only the severest criticism of this writing, recording in his diary that it was an inferior piece of work. Instead of encouraging Richard, he chastised him as though he were an errant schoolboy, of course, much to the young man's discomfort. Rawlinson's own copy, one of the few to survive, is annotated as follows: "Collected and Composed from M.S.S. by Richard Rawlinson."

As an accomplished writer and editor, Hearne worked on an entirely different level from that of the young student. The former's pattern of work was to take an anciently significant chronicle (or other work) in manuscript, edit it in his punctiliously exact manner, and then publish it for his subscribers. Thus he preserved many manuscripts for future scholars so that even today his works have not been superseded for excellence. Many scholars of his time were regular patrons, some of them expressing a wish for all of his future works; some persons of wealth purchased as many as twelve copies, as did Thomas Rawlinson on occasion.

A second publication from Richard's student days was the *Posthumous works of the Learned Sir Thomas Browne* (1712). The printing and binding were done in London, and Richard again said nothing to Hearne about it. Understandably, the fledgling editor-publisher was being self-protective. But Hearne writes "He hath given it to a bookseller [in the eighteenth century the bookseller was often also the printer] which I do not at all like in him, it being not a sign of friendship to me." But Richard did not want to defer to Hearne; he wanted to find his own way, and in so doing he came under the influence of the publisher Edmund Curll. Curll had the reputation of being a person without taste or scruple, but he was genuinely interested in antiquities and was useful to Richard at this time, although at a later date they would part company. With Thomas Hearne, however, he would not part company; their relationship was to be a lifelong friendship, and it is to the younger man's credit that he could overlook the older man's carping and censorious judgements.

While at Oxford, Richard had to manage difficult family problems. In 1711 his mother, three years widowed, married Stephen Hutchinson of whom we know very little; however, we do know that the marriage brought about the serious disapproval of Thomas and Richard. After this time Richard appears never to have considered himself comfortable or welcome in his mother's home, which was no longer in the Old Bailey but was instead in Fulham. The household must have gone through the necessarily difficult adjustments—not only because of the change of residence, but also because of the younger children involved. At the time of Lady Rawlinson's remarriage there were seven children at home who ranged in age from the twenty-year-old daughter Mary to the nine-year-old son Tempest. Richard was twenty-one; his older brother was thirty.

In the spring of 1712 Richard, who was completing his work toward his M.A., having earlier been awarded his B.A., took legal action; one of his papers (. 222) at St. John's College is summarized as follows: "Bill of Revivor of Richard Rawlinson and others against Lady Mary Rawlinson, late widow of Sir Thomas Rawlinson, and Stephen Hutchinson, concerning the estate of the said Sir Thomas Rawlinson and the trust under his will."

Hutchinson died in October of the same year, and seven months later his mother married again. The license is recorded as being issued to "Michael Lister, of St. Martin's-in-the-Fields, bachelor, 26, and Dame Mary Rawlinson, of Fulham, Middlesex, widow, 50." They were married in a Berwick Street chapel on 30 May 1713. It is recorded that on 16 June 1714, Richard (who now had completed his study at Oxford but who retained his rooms at St. John's College and still considered it his residence although some of his mail of the period is addressed to convenience addresses such as Child's Coffee House in London) made a deposition in

> Chancery on the part [of himself] and William, Constantine, and Tempest Rawlinson, and Mary, Anne, and Honor Rawlinson (all being...sons and daughters of Thomas Rawlinson, late of Lancs., Kt., deceased), Plaintiffs, against Michael Lister and Dame Mary his wife (late Rawlinson)... concerning the Will of Sir Thomas Rawlinson, deceased.

Lady Rawlinson's marriage with Lister ended in a separation the following year. In July of 1714, Lister agreed not to molest his wife provided he received a third of her income. Later he sold his interest in the estate for £1,000.

The Years at Oxford after Graduation: 1713-16

On 5 July 1713, Richard was awarded his M.A., but this event did not appear to change his life, which in numerous ways was to follow the pattern of his previous years. He would continue to live at St. John's College, maintaining his rooms there as his residence; he would continue with his publishing; he would continue to shoulder the responsibility of safeguarding the financial status of his younger brothers and sisters against the inroads made by his mother and her third husband; he would continue his involvement with his political position as a Tory; he would firmly establish his ecclesiastical position as a Non-juror; and, finally, he would continue to travel about the country, collecting items of antiquarian interest, especially memorial inscriptions. "Mr. Rawlinson of St. Johns hath an abundance of inscriptions of Staffordshire," wrote Hearne in his diary. These were burial inscriptions, and to Richard the gathering of such inscriptions was not an idle interest but almost a compulsion. He was well aware of the destruction to the monasteries that had accompanied the Dissolution, of the destruction caused by the Civil War, of the great loss of recorded history that had been on the land, the burial inscriptions being among the many losses. Only a true lover of the past and of his country could feel so overpowering a compulsion to preserve. On one occasion when Richard and his brother were recording epitaphs, moving about an ancient graveyard where the inscriptions had almost mouldered away, one of them recorded, "We rode above the dead in order to perpetuate the dead." It is not surprising that in later years Richard was to take as his ecclesiastical motto: "I collect and I preserve."

This aspect of his antiquarian interest came as an early preoccupation to Richard largely because of the example and influence of his brother who had often taken the younger brother, "tyrant Dick," on his expeditions into the countryside of the counties adjoining London. Once while making a journey into Kent for the purpose of copying inscriptions on grave markers, Thomas wrote, after detailing one of the inscriptions, "This Dick and I conjured for together." No doubt they had vied with each other for first rights to this very special inscription which was a memorial to Margaret (d. 29 June 1611), the daughter of William Lambarde de Westcomb, whom the brothers would have known to be the famous antiquary. In encouraging Rawlinson to compile inscriptions, Hearne pointed out that it was a "Task that requires Travell." Even though the roads in those days are reported to have been almost impassible and public conveyances sadly lacking in dependability, the challenge to travel was welcomed. Stage coaches were able to accomplish approximately twenty miles a day; a man could travel fifty or sixty miles a day on horseback. In the spring of 1712 the two Rawlinson brothers made the trip from London to Lancashire by way of St. Albans, Dunstable, Northampton, and Crick. From there they went on to Warwickshire, where they stayed at the Rawlinson property of Heathcote. They continued their journey to the old family property of Grisedale in Lancashire with frequent stops along the way to record inscriptions and to visit booksellers. In August they returned to London after a stop at Oxford where they visited Hearne. It was of such a trip that Hearne could write: "Mr. Thomas Rawlinson met with his perfect Hollingshede at Newark-upon-Trent and it bore the expense of his travels about England that time."

In March of 1713 Richard had another two-week excursion in the environs of Oxford, listing inscriptions and making notes for continued topographical work. In May he returned to Oxford, meeting there his younger brother John, who matriculated at Corpus Christi College on 21 May. Since this was the month of their mother's marriage to Michael Lister, the brothers were relieved to be removed from London. On July 5 of that year Richard received his degree and shortly afterward left for Hereford near the border of Wales to collect materials for a forthcoming book dealing with the antiquities of the Cathedral. Thence he went to London, where there were legal problems relative to his father's estate. During this time Thomas, with the objective of adding to his library, was making his second tour of Holland, where many choice Aldine and Elzevir volumes were available.

Looking Toward Residence in London

At the approximate time of his mother's marriage, which did not escape ribald attention in London, Richard felt reassured by being nominated a governor of Bridewell and Bethlem Hospitals, of which his father had been president and on whose boards his brother also was serving—a recognition which gave him much satisfaction. In July, 1714, he was elected to the Royal Society, which had been founded in the reign of Charles II for the advancement of science. During this period he frequently made the trip between London and Oxford. In this year Queen Anne died. It was during the early years of her reign that Sir Thomas had been Lord Mayor of London, and Richard recalled both the national triumphs of those years—with Marlborough in the field of battle and the happy times of his own family. In October Richard, a firm supporter of the Stuarts, wished to be absent from London during the time of the coronation of George I and returned to Oxford. In November he was noting and collecting inscriptions in Eton and Winchester. Back in London in January of 1715, he attended a meeting of the Royal Society, with Sir Isaac Newton as president. Other members of particular interest were the antiquaries Roger Gale, Ralph Thoresby, Peter Le Neve, and Humphrey Wanley, as well as the collectors Sir Hans Sloane and Dr. Richard Mead. Another member was an astronomer of note, whose fame lives to the present day and will continue into the future, Dr. Edmund Halley. Richard extended his time in London in order to assist his brother in the removal of his residence with his large library from his quarters in Gray's Inn to London House in Aldersgate Street, but in April he was back in Oxford.

In the late summer of 1715, when the Pretender landed in Scotland, there was a resurgence of Jacobite loyalty in Oxford, with many demonstrations in the streets. As everyone knows, the rebellion failed, but it served to unite the Stuart followers. Related to this loyalty was a strengthening of the non-juring movement. In January of 1716 Rawlinson went to London and while there attended the secret consecration of his non-juring friends Thomas Brett and Henry Gandy. He also visited the Reverend Hilkiah Bedford. (In years to come, Hearne would leave his manuscripts to the son of Hilkiah; Richard Rawlinson would purchase them from the son's widow and eventually would leave them to the Bodleian.) He wrote from London to Hearne:

> I waited on that worthy Confessour, Mr. [Hilkiah] B[edford], and delivering your books had much discourse with him, much to my satisfaction as well as my delight; I could not but adore a Man, surrounded by so many

cogent arguments of a family to relinquish his principles, yet firm and steady amidst such a variety of temptations, enough to stagger a Man less resolved than himself: I found his family at their devotions, and [he] behaving himself like a true Son of a distressed Church.

In March of 1716 Richard was again back at St. John's College, spending hours in the Bodleian working on manuscripts for future publications and assisting Hearne with his subscriptions. As the autumn of 1716 approached, Rawlinson, again in London, was ordained priest and later deacon of the Non-jurors in a secret ceremony on Tower Hill. Wishing to be inconspicuous and not desiring public life, he strove to keep his clerical activities secret, but nevertheless he lent quiet strength to the movement. He joined others in ministering to deprived Non-jurors and in conducting services at a private chapel set up in Gray's Inn. It was in this year that Richard gave up his rooms at St. John's College and took up his residence at Gray's Inn, only two or three miles from his brother at London House.

At this time the political rigors of the non-juring position were seriously affecting the lives of its adherents, and it may be useful to go more fully into its beginnings. In 1688 James II left the throne of England and, without giving up the crown, departed for France, his Queen and infant son having preceded him. In the minds of many Englishmen he was still their King (whose absence was temporary) and as such was head not only of the state but also of the Established Church of England, notwithstanding the Catholic preference which (as some felt) he had sought to impose upon his subjects. James, although attempting to do so, did not return to the throne; instead, an invitation was extended to the Protestant William of Orange and his wife Princess Mary, daughter of James II. Upon his accession to the throne, William insisted upon an oath of loyalty to him as head of state and recognition of him as head of the church. It was required that this oath be sworn by all who held any kind of state or ecclesiastical position, however minor, and this dictum went down through the ranks. The man who did not so swear lost all opportunity of church or state connection; those who were already in high positions lost their places and their livelihoods. The only alternate means of providing for an income was private business, private scholarship, collecting, and so on. Those who still claimed James as the true King and refused to swear loyalty to William and Mary were the Non-jurors. Samuel Pepys was one of the early ones back in 1688-89, as was John Dryden, who lost his position as Poet Laureate and was replaced by Thomas Shadwell. James II died in France in 1701 after several abortive attempts to reclaim the throne. In the minds of the Non-jurors, his son, James III, who had been born in 1688 to

Mary of Modena, became their King in exile or the King over the seas. In time, he became known as the Old Pretender, and his son, Charles Edward, became known later as the Young Pretender. Although James Francis Edward Stuart, as James III, had a large and influential following in England, his three attempts to reclaim the throne all ended in failure. In 1718, at the age of thirty, he married a Polish Princess, Maria Clementina Sobieski. They were invited to reside in Rome at the special invitation of Pope Clement XI, who openly acknowledged them as King and Queen of England. The Palazzo Muti, where they lived, became the continental center of Jacobite intrigue; here, where they lived with a guard of troops and with a liberal allowance from the Pope, their two sons were born. Richard later was to cross the Alps, carefully timing his travel in order to be present at the birth of Charles Edward in 1720. To the Non-jurors, steadfast in their loyalty to this family, the dispossessed Stuart king was the Chevalier of St. George. The oath to the Hanovers was a "vile oath," and only unprincipled men would adhere to it. The language of Thomas Hearne is particularly articulate on this subject. One such person, according to Hearne, was a "most silly, rash, hott-headed fellow;" another was "illiterate, mean, silly, trifling, and impertinent."

In regard to the clergy during this period, a definite rift occurred, separating as it did the Non-jurors from the Established Church of England. They were deprived of their positions and had their churches closed against them. Even the bishops who had spent all their years in the church were ejected from their pulpits and were superseded by those who did not object to taking the oath. A well-known case was that of Bishop George Hickes, the famous Anglo-Saxon scholar and writer. The clergymen, being deprived of their churches and their communion of worship, in consequence began to set up their own episcopacy with their own chapels and their own services. The Non-jurors thus carried much conscience, learning, and piety out of the church, and many of them suffered great economic hardship because of their principles. Among the thousands of these staunch, immovable Non-jurors were Richard Rawlinson, Thomas Rawlinson, and Thomas Hearne. At approximately this point in time the latter was beginning to feel a definite threat to his editing and publishing career which had depended mainly on the Bodleian Library for manuscripts; the situation would become more serious as time wore on.

The fraternal feeling shared by the Rawlinsons and Hearne made them supportive of each other; the assistance Hearne received at this time was the loan of their manuscripts from which to work and their help in getting subscribers for his publications. In February of 1713 Hearne wrote to Richard:

I thank you for continuing to promote the *Collectanea*. . . . If you owe me anything I can stay till Shrove Tuesday. . . . Is there no news yet of Mr. Strype's new ed. of Stowe's Survey going to the Press? I hope he will not alter the language. Nor should anything be left out.

And, again in February, he wrote to Richard:

Last night I rec'd your Letter of the 16 Instant, for which I thank you. I have sent you six more blank receipts [for subscriptions to the *Collectanea*]. Pray give my most humble service to your kind Brother, and thank him for the Trouble he hath given, and continues to give himself upon my account. I am glad he returned safe and that he finds it worth his while to make a second Voyage [to Holland]. I long to have some account of his purchases. . . .

In March of 1713 Thomas Rawlinson in London wrote to Richard in Oxford:

Dear Brother,—Your's received. I hope our friend [Hearne] will never recant whatever Fate attends his resolution. Is this the Day for that? When the Corne is almost yellow in the Field is the Sickle flung away? If the Place prove too hot, ours may support him. For my part if he pleases to resign, and to come up to me, I will repay him his Charges, fit him up a Room near me, and give him all the Support my Circumstances can afford; at least my Quota, besides private Friendship, shall be 10 Guineas per Annum. My heap may serve him to publish. . . . I hope this comes not too late. . . . I am in hast.

> Your loving Brother
> Tho: Rawlinson

In answer, Hearne wrote that he could not consider leaving the University which had given him his education, that he would not want it to appear to the world that he bore malice, even though the offer from Thomas was to his advantage since his salary at the Bodleian was only £10 a year. Thomas continued to urge him: "I wish your leisure would permit you to do for [organize] my study, especially my MSS. and rarer printed books which I mentioned to you at Oxon. You shall choose your own conditions." Hearne's reply explained the necessity of his scheduled work:

I should otherwise be very glad . . . of drawing up a Catalog of those very Curious Books with which your study is enriched. That ought to be done very nicely, and Critical and Curious Remarks should be made in the Progress of it, such as I am very sensible I could sometimes make. A Word of the Nature could be very entertaining, and at the same time no less useful, and I wish not only your Study but some other Studies were described in such a manner.

At about this time, Thomas Rawlinson, not only seeing that Hearne was in peril in Oxford but also feeling (rightly) that there was a time of greater stress ahead, was trying to get for him the position of librarian to the Royal Society in London, but Hearne was "fixed to Oxon, immoveable." In October there was once again an unheeded request to Hearne to come to the Rawlinson library.

While Richard was still at St. John's, he found that it fell to him to be the protector of the Rawlinson estate and the financial custodian of his younger brothers and sisters, duties which usually fell to the eldest son. During these years Thomas was devoting much of his energy and attention to the building up of his collections and was making frequent trips to the continent. Richard, by contrast, seems to have been developing into a serious and introspective young man, one who had a deep feeling of responsibility.

On July 19, 1715, he wrote on a sheet of paper that is today MS. Rawl. D. 863, fol. 127:

> My brother William was married to one...Anne Johnson of Rotterdam; an unfortunate match I fear, and productive of children and poverty. This I fear much but God's providence make me a false Prophet. If matters happen ill, he has nobody but himself to thank, having never wanted advice from...friends, as well as the rock of an ill-matched and indiscrete Mother before his eye; this ought to have been a rational motive to [any] one of us.

This ungenerous and judgmental criticism of his twenty-year-old brother is in contrast to his father's relaxed statement that he always believed that Providence would help those who helped others. It is also in sad contrast to the ample marriage arrangements settled on Richard's father and mother. Further, it is an unspoken comment on items among Richard's papers, now at St. John's College, which list Lady Rawlinson's and Mr. Lister's bills (1714-17, ten documents). Another series of documents describes sums payable to William, Mary, Richard, Anne, John, Honour, Constantine, and Tempest Rawlinson, children of Sir Thomas Rawlinson, deceased (eleven documents). Clearly the picture has changed—in one short generation—and where is the lavish plenty of yesteryear, the security of one's youthful days? *Ubi sunt?*

In contrast to the supposed bleakness and threat of poverty, there are contradictions. In February of 1715 Thomas Rawlinson moved from his cramped quarters at Gray's Inn (where his splendid collections worth thousands of pounds allowed him no bedroom, forcing him to sleep in a passageway) to the grandeur of London House, former home of the bishops of London. Richard took time to assist him in the move "which has so much disordered him that he cannot yet bring his Study into any method." And in September of 1716 Thomas Hearne wrote to Thomas Rawlinson "Your collection of books is admirable. I hope they will be kept together...." Surely these details deny the poverty which Richard feared.

During these years Rawlinson continued with his publications, none of which was expected to turn a profit. No doubt each publication found him with a loss, yet he continued. In rapid succession came ten or twelve books, most of which dealt with antiquities of England, such as historical accounts and descriptions of English cathedrals, their monuments, and their lands. Some few dealt with the political treatment of current subjects, such as the one dealing with the Oxford Riots or the one on the *Conduct of the Rev. Dr. White Kennett,* who to the Jacobites was an unprincipled turncoat. One of Richard's books did not fit the mould of the others: the story written in Latin of Héloïse and Abélard. (Hearne, always ready to give unsolicited advice, advised Richard not to identify his authorship because it was an "amorous subject.")

Most of the works were topographical studies such as *The Natural History and Antiquities of the County of Surrey* by John Aubrey, edited by Rawlinson. To some readers today topography more than likely may indicate an investigation of mountains and valleys, heights and depths, the contours of steep precipices, the courses of rivers, and other physical features; to Rawlinson and his contemporaries a topographical study included the civil, military, and ecclesiastical marks of man upon the land. Schools, churches, parishes, populations were included, as well as natural resources such as coal fields, tin mines, and other deposits. Of permanent interest, as we would expect, were the fortifications, shrines, and antiquities from former ages such as Maiden Castle, Stonehenge, Avebury, and the Cerne Giant. Topography, then, was a kind of worship of, and veneration for, the land. In the preface to his work on the Cathedral of Rochester Richard wrote his defense of antiquarian and topographical research:

> Tho' these studies are...made the jest of conversation, and charged with being dull, dry, and below the Care of a generous and free Mind, Yet I would apprise them, that England never [lacked for] Men of the most refined Tastes, that have thought these...Studies worthy [of] many hours of their time.

Again, and in the same introduction, as though to justify his own lengthy lists of burial inscriptions, Rawlinson discussed the damage suffered during the Civil War:

Many monuments were said to have been created here, [in Rochester]...
which might have given us some Light into History, had any Somner-like
Searchers into Antiquities been then living, to have preserved and to
have transmitted such Venerable Remains to Posterity. [Many such remains are] now wholly lost by the Injury of Time or the more injurious
and sacrilegious Hands of Triumphant Rebellion.

Thus, during his London years at Gray's Inn, having given up his rooms at St.
John's College late in 1716 and prior to his travels abroad, Richard was constantly involved with antiquities, with his publishing, with his family, and
with his church duties which were conducted in a more or less secret chapel
at Gray's Inn.

In his immediate family there were some changes. In August of 1716 his
mother's brother, Richard Taylor, died. Richard, his namesake, went from
Oxford to attend his uncle's funeral in Chiswick, which was very close to
the old Rawlinson country home in Hammersmith. There is no record of the
occasion other than the date and the place, but in view of the prevailing
legal problems within the family over the Rawlinson estates, there must have
been a climate of tension during this most sombre of family rituals. Richard,
prone to silence and a developing introspection, can be expected to have
felt hostile toward his mother because of the disrespect she had shown his
father and because of the financial drain his two step-fathers had imposed
upon the family.

Another family event was the 1718 birth in Holland of Thomas Rawlinson, son of William, son of Thomas, son of Daniel, and so on back to the battle of Agincourt, where two Rawlinson brothers were royally recognized for
their bravery and awarded extensive lands in Lancaster County and a coat of
arms. But Richard, who loved antiquities and the history of families and
who should have known that today's present becomes tomorrow's past, was
unable to welcome this first child of the new generation of Rawlinsons. To
him the child represented only responsibility and financial uncertainty—so
much so that he was totally unable to enter into the pleasure that a family
normally enjoys in its experience of growth, regeneration, and renewal.

We can wonder why this responsibility should be shouldered by
Richard. Again, why did it not fall to Thomas, who was the eldest and his
father's heir? The answer probably lies in the psychological constitution of
the two brothers. Thomas was a bon vivant, one given to indulgence who
turned away (until too late) from responsibility; Richard, by contrast, was a
realist who met responsibility with a hard clear gaze. However inconsistent
the situation may seem, Richard was soon to embark on an extended tour of
Europe, during which he would add to his collections, would use bank

notes freely, and would live with all the graces and appurtenances of a rich man travelling abroad. On this occasion he seemed to be able to turn aside from responsibility, as on June 12, 1720, he left London for Gravesend, where he set sail for the Continent, not to return for six long years. He was now Dr. Rawlinson, having been awarded the degree of Doctor of Civil Law at Oxford in June of 1719.

Motivations for Travel: 1720-26

In stating his reasons for travel, Dr. Rawlinson, while truthful, was less than all-inclusive when he said that his aim in going abroad was to become

> acquainted with the customs, manners, religions[,] etc[.,] different from my own, to learn languages and, as far as my weak capacity would permit, inform my judgment from the converses of wiser and better men than myself. This I take...to be the principal, if not [the] sole justifiable reasons for travelling, and spending some of our time, as also to discover that there are as great and good men on the Continent, as in our Island we are so strangely fond of.

Added to these reasons he had others: he wanted to enlarge his collections; he desired, since he was now a priest in the non-juring division of the Church of England, to have his consecration blessed by the head of his church, who, of course, was James Francis Stuart, then living in Rome as James III; he wanted to pay his respects to his court, his queen, and the child who would succeed. He desired also to gather burial inscriptions of Englishmen who had died while abroad, especially those who were in the non-juring denomination. He also wanted to attend foreign universities, having inquired at Oxford the procedure for obtaining diplomas on the Continent. He registered at the Universities of Leyden and Utrecht and later at the University of Padua, from which his friend and fellow bibliophile in London, Dr. Richard Mead, had taken a degree. An added incentive for travel at this time was that his brother Constantine, who shared Richard's religious and political views, wanted to join him.

In addition to these motivations toward the Continent, there also were factors that made Richard uneasy about his presence in England. He was uncomfortable with his family situation, especially with regard to his mother, against whom he had brought legal action. Also, Michael Lister (his mother's third husband) was in London, and, although a settlement had been made at the time of the separation six or seven years earlier, he was still making his presence known. One of Richard's correspondents referred to his "stepfather Michael Lister," an unwelcome relationship for Richard, as was the inevitable gossip in London. The following year, in 1721, Lister did indeed kidnap Lady Rawlinson, no doubt with a further monetary recompense in mind. Why not leave the London scene?

But beyond these family tensions there was in 1719 a strained relationship between Richard and Thomas Hearne. After many years of firm friendship, Richard's sense that he had been mistreated by Hearne must have been painful. From his lofty position, Hearne had been severely critical of Richard's publications. He accused Richard of lifting passages and illustrations from his work, derogated Richard's academic achievement in regard to his being awarded his doctoral degree, and, finally, was tactless in addressing mail to Richard, using his title as Reverend, even though Richard had requested all of his friends not to do so, preferring his clerical life to be non-public. This last was a matter of personal safety rather than mere personal preference. The use of his title on the mail advertised to the world his non-juring position at a time when it was politically dangerous to be so exposed. This mailing from Hearne was addressed to a coffee shop in London and posted there, completely public. True, these years were difficult for Thomas Hearne, but that fact hardly excuses injustice done to a friend of long standing.

A further reason for leaving England was a possible disagreement between Richard and his brother Thomas. The cautious Richard could not have failed to be aware of the manner in which Thomas was overspending in his mania for collecting. He must also have known that Thomas was a heavy speculator in the South Sea Company, using the family's resources for that purpose. It is recorded that Thomas in these years was £3000 in debt to Richard, and it is possible, if not probable, that Richard asked his brother for repayment of the loan and that it was this money that financed Richard's six years on the Continent. The South Sea Bubble burst in the fall of that year.

The South Sea Company

This "wicked Scheme in which so many thousands were utterly undone" began as a respectable trading company in 1711, resembling in organization the East India Company. At the time of the accession of George I, England had an affluent citizenry with money to invest. In 1719 the prosperous South Sea Company came forward with a scheme for taking over the National Debt and for paying it off in twenty-five years. The members of Parliament in charge of the Exchequer welcomed this opportunity to redeem their country's debts (and in some cases to enhance their own fortunes), and in 1720 the South Sea Bill was passed. Soon this company, which had caught the public fancy, probably because of the historical lure of the riches of the treasure-laden ships which had supposedly sailed into English harbors a hundred years earlier, was voting huge dividends. Rosamund Bayne-Powell describes the character of the time:

> "The King," Lady Ormond told Swift, "adopts the South Sea and calls it his beloved child...."
>
> Women of the higher classes, who would have protested only a few weeks before that they knew nothing about finance, crowded down to Change Alley to buy shares. Their coaches blocked the streets in the neighbourhood. They had to walk, pushing their way through seething crowds of rich and poor. There were fine gentlemen in cut velvet coats and lace ruffles, and the London slum dweller in his rags and tatters. There was the merchant in broadcloth and the stockbroker's clerk rubbing elbows with the poor jew from Monmouth Street and the pickpocket from Seven Dials....
>
> The jewelers' shops were full of persons who had made money and were coming to buy, while others, who wanted cash, rushed to sell, and were hardly restrained from raising money on their jointures or selling heirlooms.
>
> And then, suddenly, South Sea shares, which had been £1000 or more the day before fell to £135. All the bubbles in London burst in sympathy; ruin and bankruptcy were everywhere. The Duke of Chandos lost £300,000. Gay, who had refused to sell when his £1000 of South Sea stock reached £20,000, might have qualified for a character in his opera. Gibbon's grandfather, who was a director, had to relinquish £50,000 out of an estate worth £60,000.
>
> The fury of the people against the directors may be imagined. Lord Molesworth declared in the House of Lords that they ought all to be tied in sacks and thrown into the sea. Two members of Parliament, who were also directors, were lodged in the Tower. They were partners and their firm had to find a quarter million to satisfy their ravening creditors.
>
> Lord Sunderland, First Commissioner of the Treasury, resigned his office when charged with receiving £50,000 worth of stock. Nothing seems to have been done to him, but two Ministers, Craggs and Aislabie, who were convicted of taking bribes, were imprisoned. Craggs took the smallpox and died. It is probable that the majority of the directors were more fools than knaves. They had certainly hastened the downfall of their business by urging the prosecution of other unsound companies. The great bubble of confidence was pricked, and the South Sea scheme went down with the rest.

And Thomas Rawlinson, living in London House, which he had leased five years earlier, was among the ruined investors.

Six Years On The Continent

In the meantime, as recorded on the first page of his diary, Rawlinson went down to Gravesend and set sail for Rotterdam on Sunday, June 12, 1720. Holland and northern France were not new to him, inasmuch as he had made a short exploratory visit during the previous year. Keeping in mind that he wanted to arrive in Rome before the onset of winter, he planned a route through Antwerp, Brussels, Paris, Strasbourg, Augsburg, and on through the Brenner Pass and so to Rome through Bologna. Along the way there were visits to churches, cathedrals, synagogues, libraries, hospitals, and, among other attractions, local sporting events. Burial inscriptions, especially those of Englishmen who had died abroad, absorbed his interest, and there was the excitement that went with the purchasing of books and manuscripts as well as the details of dispatching the purchases. Although Rawlinson was more interested in these activities than in describing modes of travel, he does not neglect to relate that in Brussels he hired a "Berlin chariot" for the six-day trip to Paris.

While in Paris Rawlinson made a pilgrimage to Chaillot, the place where the hearts of James II and his Queen (Mary of Modena) were buried. At an English Benedictine convent in Paris he was greeted and very civilly entertained by the priest who showed him the "face of King James taken in plaster of Paris from his face, and afterwards in wax, in which are preserved the features of the dead prince very exactly." Again in accord with his zeal to honor the Stuart family, he visited a convent where there was an inscription honoring James II in the Nun's Choir. It was too far removed by the grate for him to read, and, denied access, he was obliged to "one of the fair Nuns who read it verbatim" to him. During this period of his travel he bought no fewer than five pictures of the Pretender and three of the Princess Sobieski, his wife. These, with his other purchases of books and manuscripts, were shipped to England from Paris before he went eastward to Strasbourg. On arriving by horse in Augsburg, he bargained for a coach for the journey on to Rome. Frontier formalities were often a nuisance, the inns indifferent, and the beds poor, but these were only minor complaints. He took pleasure in seeing the new and unfamiliar, often comparing the sights with equivalents in England, always to England's advantage. Travelling with him was his brother Constantine, eight years his junior. Along the route, as expected, they continued to make frequent stops for purchases and to satisfy Richard's passion for collecting burial inscriptions. He recorded visits to libraries, convents, monasteries, and churches, which often had relics for sale. (Earlier, at Antwerp, Rawlinson, with expected skepticism, had purchased "an inestimable relique of twenty saints' bones for about two shillings.")

Once in Rome, Rawlinson was relieved of the rigors of travel, remaining there for six months. The focus of attention for him was the Chevalier de St. George, as James III was affectionately known to the Jacobites, and of primary importance was the birth of the royal child. The exiled family was constantly in Rawlinson's thoughts, and any day that brought them together was noted with great pride and satisfaction. At about this time Pope Clement XI, who had actively supported the Stuart cause, died. The Vatican was walled up, and the election of the new pope (Innocent XIII) was a subject which commanded Rawlinson's interest. Other attractions were the theatre, catacombs, libraries, almost endless churches, executions, and the purchase of rich stores for shipment to England.

In June of 1721 Richard, accompanied by his brother, left Rome for Naples where they remained for several months. Here, aside from the usual searches, two events took place: Richard ascended to the top of Vesuvius, which was quietly active at the time; and an English naval officer died from a duel wound and Richard as a clergyman was asked to administer the last rites. This act was more daring than it would appear; inasmuch as Richard represented a church which was not recognized by the Church of England, it was tantamount to treason. The end of 1721 saw the brothers back in Rome where, in addition to the usual occupations, Richard took on the disciplined study of Italian with a tutor. He was beginning to be sought out by visiting Englishmen who enjoyed his company and his admirable skill as a guide. In November Rawlinson wrote: "I met the C[hevalier] and his Spouse walking…going to St. John Lateran." He paid a visit to the young Prince of Wales, who was in the care of Mrs. Hay, and described the infant as lovely, with fine eyes and fine features. On November 29 Rawlinson was delighted to report that he had been received by the Chevalier and his Lady, attended by Col. John and Mrs. Hay.

From Rome Rawlinson went to Siena, Florence, Bologna, and Venice. He made his headquarters in the latter and spent the year 1722 exploring the cities of northern Italy. Never tiring of churches and church music, of cathedrals, libraries, and universities with their lists of Englishmen, he would have been content even if there had been no cemeteries, but indeed the latter existed in abundance. In Pisa he began his translation of du Fresnoy's

New Method of Studying History, and his loyal pulse quickened on learning that the Chevalier and his Lady were in Pisa on their way to nearby Lucca. He went to Lucca for a few days, then returned to his work of translating, always spending time with his searches for additions to his collections, and adding Leghorn as a rich source for burial inscriptions. He spent some time in Florence and later in Siena. There, the purity of the Italian language induced him to devote several months to its study and to making contact with renowned Italian scholars. Thus the year 1722 drew to a close. Constantine rejoined him in Siena after an absence of several months. Since his brother did not seem to share all of Richard's activities and enthusiasms, the time spent separately was probably welcome to both.

33

In January of 1723 Richard returned to Rome and recorded the attendance of the Chevalier and his Lady at the theatre. He spent much more time in churches than in theatres, however; he continued to indulge his insatiable appetite for church services and sermons. He also continued with his translation and to guide his compatriots about the city which he had come to know so well.

In the meantime, back in Oxford, Thomas Hearne wrote to Thomas Rawlinson in London. No doubt as a safety precaution, he addressed his letter to Amy Frewin at Mr. Frewin's, a cooper in Bull and Mouth Street, near Aldersgate. Thomas was publicly known to be in debt and was keeping his whereabouts secret; in addition, he was ill:

> I most heartily wish you freed from your Confinement & am sorry that your Catalogues do not raise larger Summs. But 'twas the wrong time. I did, indeed, say something about *lib. rar.,* purely out of Affection to you, being sensible that now & then such an Expression [too frequently used] (especially when the Book appear'd not to be so) would rather prejudice than enhance the Value of your Catalogue. Nor do I think you ought to be at the Trouble and Expense of printing some Titles at full, when short ones may do as well.... Glastonbury [Hearne's work] hath been so well rec'd that I had much ado to keep a single Copy for myself. I never printed any Book that hath had a quicker Vend....

However slowly and uncertainly news travelled in those days, it is difficult to believe that Richard could have been unaware of Thomas's desperate condition, unless the brothers had quarreled and there was no attempt at communication.

Whatever the situation, Richard continued to travel. Next was Naples, from where he decided to visit Sicily. At this time Constantine travelled east, going as far as Constantinople. When he received a letter of introduction to an antiquary in Malta, Richard took passage. He arrived there to admire the broad beautiful streets of Valletta and the excellent hospital and to enjoy the attention of the governor. His greatest satisfaction, however, as the reader has come to expect, was afforded by a proliferation of inscriptions in the cemeteries. He returned to Sicily to enjoy the lavish works of nature there, and he especially appreciated—given his classical training—the geographical points treated by Homer and Virgil. In Sicily he ended the year 1723.

In February, 1724, the energetic traveller returned to Naples, where he again ascended to the rim of the crater. While in Naples, he learned of the death of the pope and returned to Rome in time for the election of Pope Benedictine XIV, whom he saw as a reformer, an ascetic pope, one who "would be treated as a Fryer." From Rome he wrote to Thomas Hearne in faraway Oxford: "...a few books, and fewer friends occupy all my hours; sometimes I retire to some shady ruin and frame ideas of its antient grandeur. ..." However removed from the bustle he thought he was, he was still intent on his acquisitions, his tastes now running to landscapes and papal medals as well as books and curiosities of all kinds. At this time, midsummer and fall of 1724, despite doing his utmost to get an audience with the pope, he was disappointed, but inasmuch as a great papal jubilee was taking place Rawlinson was fortunate in being able to attend a ceremony in the Sistine Chapel, receiving, as he reported, from the pope's hand a small packet wrapped in paper and cotton. He continued what had now become a marked pleasure: escorting his fellow countrymen around Rome. It was noted that his use of Italian was so good that he was able to plead in court for the release of an accused man. With these occupations, he ended the year of 1724.

His pleasure at the birth of a second son to the Chevalier on February 23, 1725, was tempered (as stated earlied) by the alarm he felt on receiving a letter from his younger brother Tempest telling of the death of the family banker who was not only a close and trusted friend but also the person who held the mortgages on the Rawlinson family estates. A short time later he received word of the death of his mother. Deciding to return to England (Constantine remaining in Italy), he left Rome on June 9, 1725 with the intention, as expressed to a friend, of visiting and revisiting northern cities along the way. His pattern of interest did not change; the earlier occupations engaged his attention, as he performed what we might think of as the exercise of putting the final touches onto any pursuits which he had not earlier accomplished to his satisfaction. It was in Genoa that he learned of the death of his brother Thomas at London House.

London House and Thomas Rawlinson's Library

Upon his return to London in 1726, one of Richard's first duties was to call at London House, where his brother Thomas's widow was residing. With the sense of history that was an ingrained part of Richard, it was probably impossible for him to enter the house without thinking about its past days. In the sixteenth century it became the town house of Lord Petre, who was secretary to Henry VIII, Edward VI, Mary Tudor, and Queen Elizabeth. In size it was substantial. An inventory of 1562 listed the main hall, dining chamber, outer and inner great chambers, great and little parlours, chapel, the master's bed chamber, the chamber over the parlour, the cook's and Kyme's chamber [Kyme was personal steward to William Petre], the wardrobe chamber, and the servants' lodgings. Also there was a gallery and "my master's study at the end of the gallery." Other rooms were the nursery, the chambers in which "the gentlewomen lieth," the schoolhouse, the winter chamber, the porter's lodge, housekeeper's chamber, and at least six smaller rooms. In addition to kitchen and stable there were numerous other accommodations: buttery, wet and dry larders, bakehouse, fishhouse, washinghouse, and woodyard. Since Lord Petre's main residence was at the more commodious Ingatestone Hall in Essex, his town house was never truly regarded as his home although it was kept open by his housekeeper for his use whenever he, his family, and his entourage should need their London accommodations.

After Lord Petre's death in 1572, the property became his son's and on his death the property reverted to the Crown. During the Civil War of the next century certain apartments of this mansion were used as a prison. As such it was the place of confinement in 1648 of one who was, as Anthony Wood described him, "the most amiable person that ever eye beheld, a person also of inate modesty, virtue, and courtly deportment, which made him …much admired and adored by the female sex." His name was Richard Lovelace, the author of the Lucasta and Althea poems. During his six months in prison, he spent his time preparing his poems for the press. As A. E. Waite says "forced to lay aside his sword…[he] sought in the creations of a poetic mind relief from the monotony of prison life, from sorrows for his king's misfortune, and doubtless, too, from many dark thoughts about his own future." When released from his stone walls and iron bars, he, as a Royalist, had to make himself inconspicuous. Thus at thirty-one, Lovelace disappeared from view; almost nothing is known of the remaining decade of his life. In the seventeenth century the house became the palace of the bishops

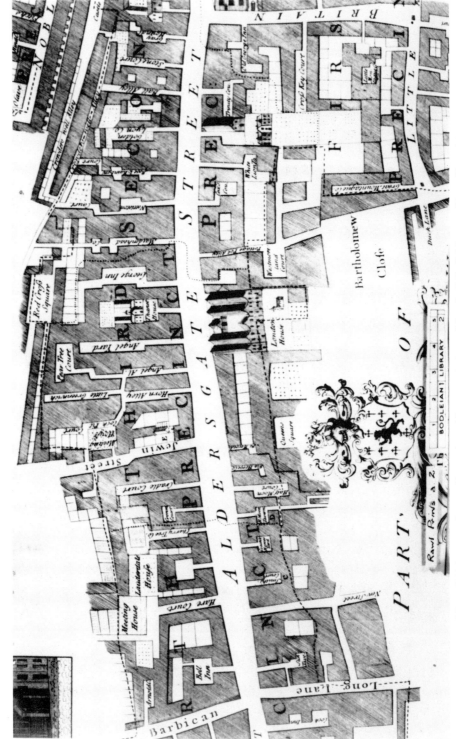

Map of Aldersgate Street. Reproduced by permission of the Guildhall Library, City of London.

of London, and the name was changed from Petre House (sometimes Peterhouse) to London House.

In November of 1688, when James left the throne, Princess Anne, fearing coercion toward Catholicism, deserted her father and in her midnight flight with Sarah Churchill was conducted to London House, the home of Bishop Compton, who had been Princess Anne's advisor, instructor of religion, and chaplain since her girlhood. By order of Charles II both daughters of James II were brought up in the Protestant faith. Just after Queen Anne's reign, the property again reverted to private ownership, and it was in those years that Thomas Rawlinson was searching for the proper house for his extensive collections.

Façade of London House. Reproduced by permission of the Guildhall Library, City of London.

38

A PLAN of LONDON-HOUSE.

DECEMB. 18. 1747.

THIS Houſe is now in the Poſſeſſion of Mr. JACOB ILIVE.

It is ſituate on the Weſt-ſide of *Alderſgate-ſtreet*, in the Pariſh of St. *Botolph*. (It was formerly belonging to Lord *Petre*; but revolving to the Crown, K. *Charles* II gave it to the Biſhops of *London*.) This Houſe and Garden was bounded by the Priory Wall of *St. Bartholomew's the Great*, which Wall encompaſſed the Garden and Houſe, as appears by the Plan. When the Priory was diſſolv'd in *Henry* VIII's Time, Ld *Petre* built *A* then call'd the *Infirmary*, now the *Garden-Houſe*, on the Ruins and Foundation of the Priory-wall, and therefore belongs to the Pariſh of St. *B*—'s the *Great*. This is likewiſe the Caſe of *B* the *Audit-Houſe*, which is alſo built on the Priory-Wall.

In the Ward of ALDERSGATE, Pariſh of St. BOTOLPH's.

C. The Court-yard and Lamp.
D. The CHAPEL.
F. The Coach-yard.
G. The Garden, and lofty Elm.
H. The Piazza, and Library.
I. The Scale twenty Feet to one fourth of an Inch.
K. The Paſſage into *Bartholomew-Cloſe*.
L. The Great Gate and Porch to *Alderſgate-ſtreet*.

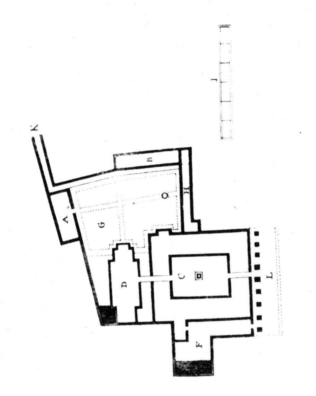

Printed, in Order to determine what Part of this Houſe is in the Ward of *Alderſgate*, Pariſh of *St. Botolph*, and what Part is in the Ward of *Faringdon Without*, Pariſh of *St. Bartholomew's the Great*. It ſtands on near two Acres, or 14256 Feet Square.

A Plan of London House. Reproduced by permission of the Guildhall Library, City of London.

When Richard returned from Europe in April, 1726, he resumed his residence at Gray's Inn. During his absence not only his brother Thomas but also his mother had died. It was necessary for him to make an immediate call upon his brother's widow, her lawyer, his lawyer, and the Rawlinson family lawyer. Further, the death of his family's banker and trust officer of many years' standing while Richard was in Rome compounded the difficulty of the business affairs. At the time of Thomas's death (August 6, 1725), Hearne wrote several long pages in his journal:

> Mr. [Thomas] Rawlinson was a Man of very great Integrity and Honour, and so loyal that he would have done any thing for the Interest of K. James, that now lives in exile beyond the Sea. He died in Communion of the Non-juring Church of England, being a perfect Hater of all new fangled Doctrines. And 'twas the Happiness of his Father (to whom he was eldest son), Sir Thomas Rawlinson, Kt., who was Sheriff and Lord Mayor of London, to be also very honest & loyal.... Mr Rawlinson's father spent in two Years' space thousands of Pounds to keep King James II on the throne. Mr. Rawlinson had seen his Father's Expence under his own hand, and it amounted to 4600 libs....

> Mr. Mattaire [sic] then told me that Mr. Rawlinson made his Will in June last, that one Mr. Ford is his Executor, that he hath ordered all his books to be sold, in order to pay his Debts, that hath left 120 (I had before been told 150) libs. per an. to his Wife during her Life, that he hath left only two Legacies, viz 150 libs. to Mr. John Griffin, of Saresden in Oxfordshire (the person that married them) and 100 libs. to Mr. Clavell, (I suppose, Mr. Walter Clavell, of the Inner Temple, Esq.), and that he hath died (the Interest and principal...to be reckon'd together) ten thousand libs. in debt. Mr. Maittaire said Mr. Rawlinson was apprehensive, and spoke of it (at least) a year before that he should live but a little while. He said he was perfectly raving and in a strange delirium for many hours before he died. Neither Mr. Anstis nor Mr. Maittaire seems to have any good opinion of Mr. Rawlinson's Widow. Mr. Rawlinson, however, spoke well of her, and I see no reason (as yet, at least) to think any thing ill of her, tho' Mr. Anstis let drop a word, that...she had...poysoned Mr. Rawlinson. Mr. Rawlinson owed Mr. Anstis something more than 30 libs. Mr. Anstis does not seem to think he shall ever be paid....

> Mr. Wm. Oldisworth told me that Mr. Rawlinson...had put his Money into the South Sea Stock, and was one of those who had lost all by that wicked Scheme, in which so many thousands were utterly undone, whilst others were as great Gainers. He said this was certainly true...and was what ruined his Fortune, and forced him to run so much in debt, and was the principal occasion of all his Miseries.

Further praise of Thomas Rawlinson came indirectly from Joseph Addison. On April 13, 1710, the *Tatler* included an essay entitled "Tom Folio."

Thomas Rawlinson was only twenty-nine years old at the time and as yet was not so experienced a collector as was Dr. Richard Mead (or others such as Sir Hans Sloane or Dr. Radcliffe). Nevertheless, Thomas Rawlinson, no doubt because of his given name, is generally supposed to be the Tom Folio of Mr. Bickerstaff's nimble and agile imagination in the essay which follows in part:

> ...not a sale of books begins till Tom Folio is seen at the door. There is not an auction where his name is not heard, and that too in the very nick of time, in the critical moment, before the last decisive stroke of the hammer. There is not a subscription [sic] goes forward, in which Tom is not privy to the first rough draught of the proposals; not a catalog printed, that does not come to him wet from the press.

Although Addison is derisive of Tom Folio in this essay—assuring us that Tom knows more about the printing, the format, and the binding than about the content of his books—he admired even as he mocked. Thomas Hearne with his usual candor had his response to Addison:

> Some gave out, and published it too, in printed Papers, that Mr. Rawlinson understood the Editions and Title-Pages only, without any other Skill in them, whereupon they stiled him *Tom Folio*. But these were only Buffoons, and persons of very shallow learning. 'Tis certain that Mr. Rawlinson understood the Editions and Titles of Books better than any Man I ever knew (for he had a very great Memory), but then, besides this, he was a great Reader, and had read abundance of the best writers ancient and modern throughout, and was interely master of the learning contained in them. He had digested the Classicks so well as to be able readily upon all occasions (what I have often admired) to make use of passages from them pertinently, what I never knew on so great perfection in any other person whatsoever.

The Years of Trial

In 1898, in his history of St. John's College, W. H. Hutton wrote: "The life of Richard Rawlinson is soon told." Such is hardly the case. The life of Rawlinson, particularly the first fifteen years after his return from Italy, was made up of too many delays, hindrances, and disappointments to be "soon told." For many years the establishing of his own private collections had been a driving force in his life, beginning with his early days at Oxford and continuing through his pre-Continent years in London, when he had been able to become acquainted with the many fine private libraries there. On February 20, 1715, Hearne wrote in his diary: "Glad R.R. finds such diversion in the Cotton and other libraries. I heartily wish I had the same happiness." (This was sixteen years prior to the Cotton Library fire.) These pleasures, added to his admiration of his own brother's massive collections which Hearne described as being second to none, reinforced Rawlinson's passionate desire to have his own finely chosen collections. These years of Rawlinson's servitude to family duty were years that stood between him and the attainment of his expected fulfillment, and these years were characterized by his constant disappointment that his brother's collections had not come into his hands, as he could normally have expected.

Before he died, Thomas had already held six auction sales. Even while ill, he had compiled his catalogs with full descriptions and had them expensively printed and bound. In April of 1723, Hearne in his usual critical manner wrote to Thomas:

> . . . I do not see any Necessity for you to throw away Money, if short Titles
> to many of the Books would do as well in the way of Sale. However, if
> you have regard rather to the interest of Posterity than your own Profit,
> . . . I say no more.

But Thomas Rawlinson had probably known that he would not survive the sales and that his catalogs would be his monument.

However disappointed Richard was on finding that neither the estate nor the library automatically devolved upon him, he knew that he had to proceed in a practical and rational manner. Consequently, in January of 1727, an agreement was reached between Richard and John Tabor, the man whom Amy Rawlinson had married in her early widowhood. In the curiously arranged will (according to Hearne, made only two days before Thomas died, when he was sinking fast) all of the estate of Thomas Rawlinson was deeded to William Ford, a lawyer, to be held in trust for the widow and heirs of his marriage. Small wonder that Richard termed it a "barbarously framed" will. But William Ford, the holder of the properties, died intestate, "choked with beans and bacon." His sons became the heirs; one died of consumption shortly after, and the other broke his neck in a hunting match. "All these removed, the widow comes in next" wrote Richard to a friend. Richard knew that if he elected a legal contest, there could be a great expense and delay and that the estate would be sadly diminished during a probable prolonged period of litigation, during which time the debts and interest on them could not be paid. He, therefore, was forced to begin his long years toward redemption of the Rawlinson fortune working under the terms described earlier.

All told, there were sixteen sales, the last ten organized by Richard, with each sale requiring months of preparation. In addition to the distressing loss to the younger brother, there were trials, vexations, and irritations beyond number: working with an incapable auctioneer, competing with numerous concurrent book sales, being required to report each detail to Mr. Tabor, preparing catalogs, being unable to purchase except as the final bidder, and other indignities, such as having London House locked against him. Further, it was understood that creditors might cancel indebtedness by an exchange of books or MSS, an arrangement which led to confusion. An added problem was that by the terms of the agreement no lands could be mortgaged or sold until the total library was disposed of. Thus, for seven years, he was necessarily forced to stay in or near London and therefore hindered in his attempts to supervise estates which had fallen into neglect and disrepair. In 1734 the final sale was completed. It was sometime during the last years of the sales that Richard moved from Gray's Inn to London House with his own collections, which he augmented with as many items from Thomas's library as he could afford. During the sales he had developed a bookkeeping system which indicated the selling price and the purchaser, a private system which enabled him later to buy back many rare and unusual items which are now in the Bodleian as part of his benefactions. During the sales, bitter as he was, Rawlinson had no choice but to continue if the debts were to be paid and the widow's influence terminated.

Managing the estates was an occupation that had to be learned, one for which Richard, the academic, had no training. It appears that in some cases he did not have the services of an agent or steward and that he took care of all details himself. Since the Grisedale lands in Lancashire and the large estate at Wasperton in Warwickshire were already mortgaged, only a small income could be realized from them, but they had to be kept in repair. The widow's income came from the estate of Heathcote in Warwickshire. Only the London properties and the extensive estate of Saddlebow in Norfolk could be counted on for a yield on which the Rawlinson family could be supported, and from which the debts could be paid. Richard's time was taken up with leases, rents, the price of grain, woodcutting, tilemaking, and other such details. Also, hours were spent in keeping records of expenses and income. His work was indeed a far cry from the pleasures of the academic life of Oxford which he loved—the familiar streets there, the shelves of the Bodleian, the conversations with Thomas Hearne, the ringing from the bell towers, its medievalism, the total order of the place. Troubles with tenants who had become used to Richard's indulgent father and brother were constant; rentals in arrears, which were common, brought angry letters from the owner who threatened: "I write to you once more by myself; the next will come from my Lawyer." Again he wrote to a tenant: "I am no stranger to your using my Muck on the Glebe land, which be pleased to know I resent, and will have satisfaction for." Another tenant received word in fine balanced rhetoric: "I am as unwilling to be thought litigious as I am uneasy in being so grossly insulted." This last letter was written in 1732, two years before the end of the wearisome auction sales.

There was never enough income to satisfy the creditors. One legatee, a fellow Non-juror, was persuaded not to press for full payment, but another (Mr. Griffin, who had performed the marriage of Amy to Thomas) insisted on his entire rights. In 1733 Rawlinson's hopes rose on hearing that his wealthy distant cousin, Christopher Rawlinson, the Saxonist from Queen's College, had died and had named him the heir. The following is Thomas Hearne's notation of 27 January 1733:

> On Monday the 8th inst. the Prints tell us, died of dropsy, Christopher Rawlinson of Chark [Cark] Hall in the Parish of Cartmell in Lancashire, Esq., after two days of extreme illness, and taking a purge, at his Lodgings in Holburn Row, Lincolns-Inn Fields. A foul draught of a will, all wrote by his own hand and signed by himself, was found, in which he left Dr. Richard Rawlinson all his real and great part of his personal estate, to a considerable value; but the original is not yet found.

Again on 12 February, Hearne writes of the will:

> Had Christopher Rawlinson Esq. left my friend Dr. Rawlinson his personal estate by a Draught under his own hand, it would have been enough; but his real Estate could not be legally conveyed, without being attested by Witnesses, which being wanting in the Draught, written by his own hand (of which I have a copy, given me by Dr. Rawlinson) I fear 'twill miscarry and be looked upon as wholly invalid, unless an attested one (which I much doubt of) can be found, and yet no doubt can be made that Mr. Rawlinson designed and willed, that the Doctor should have every thing. It was a pity he had not got witnesses, a thing he must needs know to be necessary in the case....

On 18 February Hearne again states his concern:

> Mr. Rawlinson having given me a copy of Christopher Rawlinson Esq.'s will, I thereby fully understand that he designed all his estate, real and personal to the Dr., but being not witnessed, I fear 'twill miscarry, unless another attested should be found, which I much doubt. His personal estate limited to the Dr. is...in Lancashire, where the said Christopher Rawlinson had not been for 25 years before he died, so that, except there

may be some family library, which the Dr. knows not of, 'tis suspected
that nothing but old goods will appear. The Dr. knows not the tenure of
the Estates, which are several, that are particularly mentioned in the will.
Perhaps Leaseholds for terms of years, not lives, are personal.

On 4 September of the same year the issue is losing ground:

> Dr. Rawlinson finds great Difficulties with respect to what was left him
> by Christopher Rawlinson Esq. so that the Legacy is not likely to be so
> beneficial, as I hoped it would, occasioned by the wickedness & base-
> ness of some people who are willing to frustrate what was designed for
> the Dr.

And so the whole year passed, with its glimpses of deliverance, with its high
hopes that rose, then fell, only to be revived and again to fall. It is recorded
that in this year Richard became ill—small wonder after enduring this
Tantalus-like experience. In the end he gained very little—two houses in
London on Devonshire Street and £200—which was the merest fraction of
what he needed. He even borrowed small amounts from his sisters. Finally,
when the library sales were over, Richard sold the estate in Norfolk for
£3,200, but still he could not meet all the obligations.

Suppose, (he thought) he were obliged to sell his own treasured collections? It was a chilling thought which he could not easily dispel. In 1738 he
lamented: "My affairs are in so distracted a condition and mony [sic] so
scarce, so much owing and so little coming, that I know not where, or how
to turn myself." In 1739 he melted down plate and mortgaged the estate in
Essex. Even so, he feared he would have to give up the struggle "soon now
after selling what most distracts me to think of, my books." But there was a
way out: Richard could have married and have redeemed the family estates
with a wife's fortune. His antiquarian friend James West had married well, as
had his friend Browne Willis, and Richard was a personable young man
from a good family, well educated, and well travelled. Surely his hand would
not have been refused. But "Who can find a vertuous [sic] woman?" said he.

Family Responsibilities

Of the once large family there were now, besides Richard, only four
brothers and three sisters. Their father's will had left £1000 to each son on
reaching the age of twenty-one and to the daughters the same amount with
the clause that if they married before the age of twenty-one (with the approval of their mother), they were to have the legacy upon marriage. Al-

though this was not a great fortune, it was enough, if safeguarded, to provide a comfortable living. The oldest brother was heir to the total property with the exception of Richard's estate of Waltham in Essex. The younger brothers were not given lands; nor were they given the fine expensive educations that Thomas and Richard had had, although John had two years at Oxford.

His sisters were Mary, Anne, and Honor. Anne married in 1731 at the age of thirty-seven. She had three children, of whom only one reached maturity. Richard borrowed money from Anne and often begged her "to have a little more patience." Honor married in 1734 at the age of thirty-nine. She had no surviving issue. Richard borrowed from her and considered the interest she charged on her loan to him excessive. Mary, the eldest of the sisters, did not marry. She lived in Chelsea and was often visited by Richard who took care of her life insurance and other details. He borrowed small amounts of money from her.

Of the brothers the eldest was William, who married, as stated earlier, in Rotterdam, where he had established himself in the trading business. He, like Thomas, lost heavily in the South Sea speculation and, in order to escape his creditors, fled into Flanders. He died in 1732, during the late years of the library sale in London, leaving his wife and son Thomas (b. 1718) as Richard's responsibility. "My presumptive Heir is my Nephew about fourteen years of age" wrote his uncle Richard, who cast about in his mind as to the best way to deal with the situation. Feeling that the boy was being given inflated hopes regarding future riches by his mother, also feeling that London life with its temptations was not a good environment, and also being irritated by his presence, Richard considered the choice between sending him to Virginia and apprenticing him to a shipbuilder in Liverpool. When the mother's influence increased, Richard wrote to his agent in the north:

> If by any means he can be kept from corresponding with that wicked woman that bore him I have no objection to Liverpole...tho' I think being at board so long may be of ill consequence, promote idleness and encourage him to be too much the Master, whereas once in the chains of a seven year's servitude, a knott as indissoluble as that of marriage, he'll be obliged for his own sake to make it easy.

But the expenses of the apprenticeship proved greater than Richard had planned, and again he wrote to his agent:

> [They are]...beyond my expectations. London itself would not have been dearer...if nothing but superfine Cloth clutterlings to his hands will do, I must tell you it pleases me not. My affairs are not to be gov

erned by his growing pride... He probably does not know the state of
my embarass, that my death would only let him into a world he would
not easily turn in.... These are motives for thoughts and saving, and he
ought to be undeceived as to his vast expectations.... I think boys
should not haunt Alehouses or Merry Meetings.... An article of boots
will, I suppose be succeeded by a Horse; the necessity of them, except
for pleasure, I can't understand, and I should be sorry he was not better
employed than in learning to ride. My shoes I blush not to mend, my lin-
nen and Cloathes also; should a dependent do less?

When the nephew came of age in 1739, Richard had hopes that he would
contribute to the family's welfare, but his expectations were again dashed:

To my great surprise, I find my nephew in despite of gratitude, contempt
of me, and contrary to his own interest, by marriage has engaged himself
to one of his Master's Nieces, and tho' it is strongly denied, I doubt not,
but by his encouragement.... I will no longer be answerable for his ex-
pences.... He is yet an apprentice and to his Master, his wife and his
wretched fate I resign him. The more unpardonable, as he had a Grand-
mother, an Uncle, and Father before his Eyes, but he has followed his
own dictates, and proved so unnatural to his best benefactor one much
more so, than his father, if ever you see him, or his Master, shew [him]
this, and let him know that I will endeavor to forget, that there ever was
such a relation.

When Richard heard about the birth of a son, the disaster seemed complete.
He had hoped to obtain Parliamentary authority to sell part of the estate, in
order to pay off debts, mortgages, and interest:

Nor now an infant's concerned [he wrote to a friend in Oxford] can I
hope relief from Parliament, the usual dernier resort, and I almost fear I
must part with what has been the pleasure, I may almost say, the only
pleasure of my life [his library], but my only comfort is, that all my suffer-
ings will be owing to my endeavors to [do] justice to other people.

But the child died. Then a second child was born and died. In 1742 Rawlinson announced: "My nephew having had two children and both dead, and
so both of us *sui juris*, I have reason to think he will join with me to make all
easy." Later in the same year the nephew agreed, for the consideration of a
thousand guineas, to renounce all claims for himself and his heirs, his plan
being to purchase and to fit out a ship for the Liverpool to Virginia route. It
was a slave ship. In 1749 in a mutiny the slaves on his ship killed him and
while in harbor destroyed the ship. A full account of the disaster appeared in
the *London Evening Post* in December, 1749.

The next son after William was John, who was born in 1697. After two years at Oxford, he became a Captain in the First Regiment of Foot Guards. In 1731 Richard wrote of him:

> There is above 1000 pounds absolutely bad from my brother John, who if seized may dye in Gaol, which pays no debts...but as I have neither seen, nor heard from him, I presume he is far enough from danger.

Further, Richard accused him of selling his commission in unsuitable if not cowardly circumstances. After a short time John reappeared, and it was considered necessary to get him out of London. Richard wrote to a contact in Cheshire in December 1732:

> Capt. John whom your self may have some memory of, and who has not only wasted all his substance, but contracted debts, which threaten him with a Goal, [sic] My request therefore is to you as to your terms of his retirement boarding, lodging, washing, diet &c. My affairs at present will not permit much, nor can his circumstances require great things, as those past he must endeavor to forget, and conform to what his indiscretions have brought on him. I think you mentioned ten pounds per annum. Be pleased to give me as expeditious an answer as possible, as also the nearest and most reasonable conveyance that comes your way.

When John complained of the accommodations, Richard wrote again to his agent:

> Your homely fare, as you are pleased to call it, is what would well content me, and must him, he may thank god he is not entirely destitute.... He is sent, as the Hermits are to a cell to retire, to consider an ill spent youth, a dissipated fortune, not to cultivate expensive acquaintance with Gentry, but to mortify [himself] for his former ill conduct, and to forget, if possible, his antient grandeur.... He is not to be known or treated as a Knight's or Citizen's son, nor must I injure my own or [my] Brother's creditors by more than absolutely necessary support.

John had been smuggled out of London by Rawlinson's friend and apothecary John Markham in January of 1733. In September of the next year, John wrote to Richard expressing the desire to leave the imposed life of indolence which did not suit his active nature. He proposed emigration to a "foreign land whereby I may honestly earn the bread I eat," but Richard in London, working on the library sales, warned his brother that "words are wind," that his debts could be made public, that imprisonment could follow if he were believed in England, and that he must stay hidden in Cheshire, away from the anger of his creditors. A strange twist was that John's major indebtedness was to a deceased family friend for whose estate Richard was now executor. Richard was thus forced either to raise the money, or to publicize the debt of his brother, an action which could have resulted in John's imprisonment. On ten pounds a year John's existence was at poverty level, and when he wrote to his brother that "my shirts with frequent mending each other are reduced to two old rags," Richard sent him some old cast-offs of his own. John reproved him, "feeling sure, had you looked over the things you sent with innumerable moth holes[,] you would not have sent them as they cannot be of any duration." When Richard told him to remember his sins and be grateful for the generosity shown him, John replied that he would prefer to work his way through "the cruel paths of want and misery than thus to be continuously lashed with false accusations." Richard moaned about the sacrifice demanded of him (£10 a year): "Does consanguinity or any other tye oblige it?" In 1738 Richard was concerned when he was "threatened with a summons before a Judge in order to a discovery where the Captn is. I cannot perjure, so that I must act the honest part, if it comes to that issue, nor can he blame me."

In December 1737, their mother's sister Susanne Taylor, whose husband had been Lord Mayor of London in 1718, died and left a legacy to John, but he saw nothing of it. He immediately paid his brother, which act brought about a reconciliation; yet he remained in Cheshire until his death in 1752 when the agent there wrote: "he did not keep his bed till the day he dyed.... He was buried in as decent a manner according to the Country Custom as we could, and with as little expence as possible." In his last letter to Richard, written three months before he died, John showed remarkable charity:

> Days of sale are frequent here and old books sold for little, but as I do not know the best Editions or Printers [I] desire your instructions...not that I flatter myself to find anything more curious than which you have, but perhaps may meet with what may please you.... As to inscriptions on monuments I shall writ them over fair in a book exactly line for line as engraven and keep it carefully by me, till you please to have it sent you.

The brother next younger in age was Constantine, who had gone abroad with Richard in 1720 and who had settled in Venice, never to return to England. Between these two brothers there appears to have been a spirit of camaraderie which was unusual in the family. This fraternal feeling was reinforced by their mutual antiquarian interests and loyalty to the nonjuring position. Constantine never married and he outlived Richard by twenty-four years. The generous provision that Richard made for him in his will is an indication that he had agreed to give up his hereditary right and not to contest Richard's sole ownership of the Rawlinson estates.

Tempest Rawlinson, the youngest of the brothers, named after his god-mother, Maria Tempest, was born in 1702 (the year Richard went to Eton). Since the family fortune did not provide fine educations for the younger sons, Tempest had borrowed £1500 for the purpose of establishing a dry-salting business while Richard was in Italy, a debt which he had not paid. As in his brother John's case, Tempest borrowed from the lenient family banker, John Hannam; on his death Richard was made trustee for Hannam's widow. This was another large debt which Richard had to repay in order to redeem the family honor. Tempest died in 1737. Richard's recorded comment was: "The loss of my brother Tempt...will be truly such to me as the beginning of a great deal of trouble, which had he lived might have been avoided." Tempest had worked cooperatively with Richard throughout the eight years of the Thomas Rawlinson library sales. His name can be found as a constant assistant and factotum in the accounts kept by Richard for Mr. Tabor. He appears not only to have been genuinely helpful but also to have taken an interest in the social life of his sisters. The following notation from Hearne's diary, while focussing on Richard's great passion, includes a reassuring reference in regard to Tempest's fraternal regard and attention to the family:

> Dr. Rawlinson tells me by Letter from London House, 7th inst., that his last Mat. Parker brought 46 libs., that large Commissions were sent from beyond sea, that it is gone into Hertfordshire, and, as he fancies, to Sr. Thomas Sebright, but this is only conjecture. He says, Lord Oxford, he is assured, regrets the loss of it; that it had more merit than the news discovered, and that indeed its value was then too much unknown. He says, had his circumstances permitted and himself uncensured for vanity, he could joyfully have kept such a Treasure but that was forbid.... The Doctor's Letter was brought to Oxford by his brother Tempest Rawlinson, with whom were two young ladies, sisters to them; but I saw neither of them, all three coming in late & going out of Town very early this morn.

And again Hearne writes on 2 August 1734:

> Last night called upon [by] Mr. Tempest Rawlinson, brother of my late friend Thomas Rawlinson Esq., and of my friend Dr. Richard Rawlinson. He said, he came to Oxford to shew the town to two sisters of his and their husbands, his Brothers in law. They lodged at the Blewboar in Fish Street.

The Rawlinson sisters are shadowy figures. Adolescent when Sir Thomas died, they must have severely felt the loss of their genial, easy-going father. Their mother's two subsequent marriages occurred during the most impressionable years in the lives of young girls. Lady Rawlinson's third husband, easily young enough to be her son, could have been more suitably paying court to one of the daughters. As earlier stated, one sister did not marry; the other two took husbands when they were almost forty. Their husbands did not have any particular wealth or social position. As to reasons for their delayed marriages, one may only wonder. Were they emotionally influenced to their detriment by their mother's marital relationships? Were their ideas of romantic love affected? Were their sensitivities trampled upon, their perceptions warped? Or did the mother as executrix withhold their dowries? At St. John's College in the Rawlinson papers there is a rough draft of the will of the unmarried sister, Mary Rawlinson, who outlived her brother Richard by ten years. In contrast to the munificence of Richard's will, it gives to the "person who shall be my companion at the time of my death 300 pounds and all my furniture."

Rawlinson's Non-juring and Jacobite Connections

In spite of Rawlinson's preoccupation with family affairs after his return from Italy, he took an active role in the work of the Non-jurors. Although a person who preferred a "non-publick" life, he was prevailed upon to serve as a bishop. As such he conducted services, assisted in the financial care of the "distressed" clergy, and became a moderator between two factions—those who wished to keep unchanged the ritual and form of the Anglican Church and those who wished to introduce additional "usages" into the worship service. It was a rift which threatened to destroy an already endangered denomination. He was instrumental in bringing harmony to the two groups with the resulting Reunion Settlement of 1732 by which the opponents agreed to relinquish the added forms to the ritual. In 1742 Rawlinson again was a leader in persuading the bishops to approach the Pretender (as head of the Church) for confirmation of their consecrations. Also during these years, especially after 1740, he was engaged in compiling a history of the movement, complete with biographical studies of the members of the clergy, realizing as he did that in future years such information would be valued as an important part of the ecclesiastical history of England.

Rawlinson's strong attachment to the Stuarts was one of the enduring enthusiasms of his life. In this he was influenced by his father, just as that father had been influenced by his father, Daniel Rawlinson. Daniel had been a close friend of Samuel Pepys, who had held a high position in the Admiralty under James II, and both men were completely loyal. They resented William of Orange and lived for the day when James would return to the throne. After William's reign, Anne was next in succession. Even though she was a Stuart, the daughter of James II, she was not considered by the Jacobites to be the true monarch while the son of James II lived, though in exile.

Macaulay in his biography of Samuel Johnson made a rather individual reference to the succession of the crown and to the extent to which it pervaded individual lives:

> He [Johnson] had inherited from his ancestors a scrofulus taint, which it was beyond the power of medicine to remove. His parents were weak enough to believe that the royal touch was a specific for this malady. In his third year [1712] he was taken up to London, inspected by the court surgeons, prayed over by the court chaplains, and stroked and presented with a piece of gold by Queen Anne. One of his earliest recollections was that of a stately lady in a diamond stomacher and a long black hood. Her hand was applied in vain.

Johnson's father accounted for the failure, as would any Jacobite, by the reflection that William, Mary, and Anne were usurpers and as such could not be expected to have inherited a power which came only with "divine right."

In her book *Travellers in Eighteenth-Century England* Rosamond Bayne-Powell writes of an incident which sounds curiously modern.

> ...there were special occasions and of these perhaps the chief was the Lord Mayor's procession on the 9th of November. Zetzner [a visitor to London] tells us how he went to this, and saw three men, entirely naked ...running through the streets. They had vowed that they would never wear coat or shirt till James II had been restored to the throne.

It is recorded that in these years of loyalty to the Stuarts the use of fingerbowls was suspended at court and in other high circles because of the ease with which those at table could drink to the king "over the water."

But these incidents, in large part, are in the area of sentiment and do not deal with matters of genuine political import. The Jacobite loyalty from time to time would reflect an ebb and flow. James II made real attempts to regain the throne, but they, of course, were unsuccessful. These attempts, however, fanned the hopes of the true supporters. There was a possibility of Queen Anne's tipping the scale in favor of her young half-brother, James Francis, shortly before her death in 1714. (James II had died in 1701.) Again, the strong opposition to the Hanover election in 1715 provided a politically fortuitous time for a Stuart invasion, and such an expedition landed in Scotland in that year. In this encounter the English prevailed over the Stuart forces who had expected French support (an expression of Roman Catholic sympathy) which did not materialize because of the death of Louis XIV. The victor was the Duke of Argyll, who, merciful to the prisoners, executed only about thirty of the invaders. Others were transported to the colonies. A second attempt to 1719 was planned with the promise of Swedish assistance; it also came to nothing. These attempts to gain the throne caused constant rumors and disquiet in England. In Rome the hopes of the King of England in exile were fanned by expatriates who gathered at his court, reassuring him of (and often exaggerating) the high pitch of Stuart enthusiasm in England. The last real attempt came in 1745-46 when the son of the Chevalier, Prince Charles Edward Stuart, landed in Scotland and after victories in minor military skirmishes, settled into Holyrood Palace. In January of 1746 the Prince won a second victory; it was his last. In April English forces under the Duke of Cumberland destroyed the Jacobite army at Culloden Moor. The reprisals were so severe that they earned for the victor the name of "Butcher." After this battle the Highlanders were forbidden to bear arms, to wear Scottish dress, and to play the bagpipes; the prohibition against the kilt was maintained until 1782. Any clergyman who did not pray in express words for King George was liable for transportation to the colonies, and any laymen who attended services of suspected clergymen were fined and imprisoned.

There were among the Jacobites certain extremists who were willing to go to any lengths to put the Stuart king back on the throne of England. One such man was Christopher Layer, whose story in relationship to Richard Rawlinson can be found in Nichol's *Literary Anecdotes.* Layer was a London lawyer, only a few years older than Richard, who hoped and expected to be made Lord Chancellor upon the restoration of the Stuarts. He went to Rome in the summer of 1721, had an audience with James III, and disclosed his plot which was to use his already-enlisted soldiers to seize the Tower, the Mint, the Bank, and other public buildings. His plans included securing the royal family and assassinating the commander-in-chief and ministers. Full instructions for the insurrection were drawn up. It is known that the Chevalier and Layer had conferences and also that James and his Queen agreed to stand (by proxy) as godparents to Layer's infant daughter, a ceremony which took place later in Chelsea. Layer left a copy of his incriminating papers with two women whom he had charmed; they betrayed him. The case was tried in October of 1722, and Layer was condemned to be hanged, drawn, and quartered, with the execution set for May of 1723. According to Nichols, who loved to dress up a story, the head of Christopher Layer, having been placed on a pike atop Temple Bar, was blown down and purchased by a non-juring attorney named Pearce, who years later resold it to Richard Rawlinson. The lurid story related that Rawlinson kept the skull in his study and left instructions that at the time of his burial it was to be placed in his right hand. This is not a proven fact; it is no doubt fiction and included here only because it is almost always brought up in any discussion of extreme Jacobitism or of Richard Rawlinson. All the same, one cannot but wonder, since Rawlinson and Layer were both in Rome in the summer of 1722, whether or not they saw each other. Indeed it would have given Rawlinson great satisfaction to see a Stuart on the throne but "without that evil should attend it." He was ready to recognize the destruction that it could cause, and this was one of his reasons for working furiously to preserve the past—to keep it safe from possible annihilation. However, he showed his loyalty in his own quiet and unostentatious way. When he went to Rome in 1720, he chose not to take the easy route even though it was winter; instead, he went to the east as far as Innsbruck, carefully choosing that route because it had been the one taken by the entourage of Princess Maria Clementina Sobieski as she was conducted to Italy to marry James III in 1719. Again, while in Rome, he awaited the birth of the royal infant in an anteroom, having planned his arrival in the city in time for the event. His love for the Stuarts was a kind of respect and veneration; throughout all his years, he was true to this loyalty. Even his burial arrangement was an expression of his Jacobitism; the heart inurnment was in the Stuart tradition.

Publications after 1726

After his return from Italy, Rawlinson, as an unbending High Tory, resented the political power wielded by the Whig Prime Minister Robert Walpole, who had served under George I and who continued into the reign of George II, who came to the throne in 1727. Seldom had one man held this office for so prolonged a period. This was the political climate that brought about Rawlinson's first publication in his post-Italy years: *The History of Sir John Perrott,* which was a thinly-veiled attack on Walpole. This work, probably transcribed from a copy at the Ashmolean years earlier, in the preface boldly informed the "learned world, that they stand indebted for this valuable piece to Richard Rawlinson." In part the introduction read: "The unparalleled Efforts of the Great Man's Enemies are a sufficient *Memento* for all *Prime Ministers.*" Although the book was well received by his contemporaries as a piece filled with "stirring anecdotes and sturdy prose," it is unlikely that the intended political parallel went unnoticed.

Rawlinson's next publication was his translation of *A New Method of Studying History: Recommending more Easy and Compleat Instructions for Improvements in that Science* by Nicholas Lenglet du Fresnoy. Rawlinson introduces the work thus:

> The Version, with the Corrections and Improvements of both French and German Editions, was the agreeable Entertainment and Amusement of a Summer's Recess in Italy, an Opportunity given me of making many material Additions, as to the History of those Celebrated Scenes of Action, and of forming an exacter Judgement of the Characters these Historians bore in their Native Countries. As to the Reflections, I may boldly say, That our Author will be generally found judicious and impartial.... I shall make no Apology for annexing the small Treatise, wrote by Count Scipio Maffei, the living Ornament of Italy, whose Character in the various parts of Literature is too well known to need any Commendations and whose entertaining Dissertation on Medals and Inscriptions is wrote in a Method entirely new, and as it has attracted the Eyes and Applause of the Lovers of History and Antiquity amongst the Italians, I am the less doubtful of its pleasing in an English Dress.... [And I have] endeavored to perserve [sic] the Turn and Spirit of the Author, as far as the Nature of Translation, and the different Idioms of Language will bear, and having industriously avoided Castrations and Reforms, or putting Sentiments of My own, which were never in the Author's Thought's; a practice no less common than inexcusable amongst modern Translations.... The other Improvements, if the Reader will think them such, are some Notes, Corrections, and Additions interspersed throughout the whole Work: And as I have been biased by no narrow, mercenary Views in this Undertaking, it would gratify me much if the Reader can take half the Pleasure in the Perusal, which I have done in the Translation.

Thomas Hearne wrote that he was eager for a copy of the book. Another close friend and antiquary thanked him graciously for "the noble present of your Translation of du Fresnoy...as soon as received I fell a reading it: and found the performance not only to answer but exceed my expectations." In spite of praise from his contemporaries, Rawlinson, with his usual shyness where his publications were concerned, decided to discontinue publishing except for very small private printings for friends only. One such was a single sheet entitled "The Dimensions of St. Peter's Church at Rome and St. Paul's Cathedral in London as taken in the year 1725," which one of Rawlinson's friends thought so highly of that he reprinted it in 1734. Another was the printing of a copy taken from the Thomas Rawlinson library of Archbishop Laud's *Speech Delivered in the Starr Chamber.* Hearne considered it as unworthy and spoke of it as "the trifling notes...you have published." To this Rawlinson courteously replied: "The difference between printing a few for friends and dispersing or making them public is very wide, and as to the reason upon which they have been printed, the sentiments of people here may innocently differ from yours." Rawlinson's further explanation was to the effect that he, in preserving the notes, vindicated Archbishop Laud, who had always been one of the public figures he most admired, not only for his Erastian views and his courage as a martyr but also for his devotion to St. John's College. Several other small efforts came from Rawlinson, but he was hindered by lack of funds; also, he had to accept the fact that during these years there was a falling off of interest in historical documents. A few years later even Thomas Hearne, with his superlatively fine attention to scholarship and with his loyal subscribers, wrote of the study of antiquities: "There is a continual decay and I cannot see that it [shall] be otherwise... for which reason I must lessen the number of copies I print."

Civic Duties and Societies

During the difficult years of the reorganization of the Rawlinson properties, the library sales, and family problems, Rawlinson found some respite in other activities which included his work on three hospital boards: Bethlem, Bridewell, and St. Bartholomew's. Since his father had served on these boards, Rawlinson took satisfaction in continuing the family tradition of discharging his civic duty. In his will he left a sum of money for the "coffee" of the hospitals, implying appreciation for the coffee served him over the years at meetings.

Another diversion was the regular meetings of the societies of which he was a member. In January of 1715 he had written:

> I was admitted fellow of the Royal Society and signed a bond to pay 52s per annum forever, which was witnessed by Dr. Pound and Dr. Halley. After this I signed an obligation to promote naturall knowledge.... At this admission I paid to Mr. Thomas the Under Keeper of the Societies [sic] Musaeum [sic] 2–3s–0.

At the meetings under the presidency of Sir Isaac Newton, Rawlinson was able to meet antiquaries such as Humphrey Wanley, Ralph Thoresby, Roger Gale, and Peter Le Neve, as well as such outstanding collectors as Dr. Richard Mead and Sir Hans Sloane. In May of 1727 he was admitted to the Society of Antiquaries, and in June of the same year he became a member of the Freemasons, a society which attracted him because of its interest in antiquity as well as its supposedly arcane secrecy and mystery. Additionally, he must have been attracted by the Lodge's provision for a "safe and pleasant Relaxation from Intense Study or the Hurry of Business." During these years the majority of the Fellows of the Royal Society and those of the Society of Antiquaries were also Freemasons, and there is indication that in the Freemason meetings he was able to meet freely with fellow Jacobites, to express devotion to the Stuarts, and to damn the Hanoverians, a climate not easily found elsewhere. In 1732 he was Master of one Lodge, Warden of another, and a member of two more. He continued his interest in Freemasonry until 1753, two years before his death. With his predilection for preserving records for posterity, he assured that the records of meetings, minutes, and membership rosters were among his papers, now in the Bodleian. In 1734 he served as a Grand Steward, an office that demanded both goodwill and good fellowship for it meant personal trouble and expense. It can be assumed that he enjoyed this sociability and camaraderie; there is a report of his "wonderful brags of being Fifth Order." Since these overlapping memberships assured that the members were well acquainted, Rawlinson could find release from the social timidity which he confessed to, as "not feeling at ease where I am not known."

Rawlinson's connection with the Society of Antiquaries began the year after his return from the Continent, and this relationship was to be a major factor throughout the remainder of his life. The group began as a "tavern society" in 1707 under the leadership of the greatly gifted Humphrey Wanley, librarian to Lord Harley. For various reasons it disbanded for a time, but was revived in 1717 by Dr. William Stukeley, a medical man but one who acknowledged antiquities to be his first area of interest. These early years were years of struggle. A visit to the Society's present-day grand and splendid rooms at Burlington House in London does little to prepare one for an understanding of what the members faced in 1727, when Rawlinson joined the Society. In the previous year arrangements had been made for the rental of a single room at Gray's Inn for £20 a year, including "fire and candle." Though it was poor in contrast to the Crane Court home of the Royal Society, it was an improvement over earlier quarters at the Mitre Tavern as described by Roger Gale in April, 1726, in a letter to a friend in Scotland:

> As for the Antiquarian Society, I cannot but look upon it in its infancy and scarcely formed into such a body as it should be, tho' of five or six years standing. It was first begun by a few gentlemen, well-wishers to Antiquities, that used to meet once a week and drink a pint of wine at a tavern for conversation, from which we have not yet been able to rescue ourselves, thro' difficulties we have always had to encounter in providing ourselves with a private room to hold our assemblies in.... I think it will be of more advantage to us than in the general view, for by this

means it shall not only be honoured with the accession of some persons of the first quality, who object with a good deal of reason to our present place of meeting, but I am sure it will cut off a great many useless members, that give us their company more for the convenience of spending two or three hours over a glass of wine, than for any love or value they have for the study of antiquities.

During his early years of membership, Rawlinson was less active than one would expect, in light of his long-time interest in antiquities and his unique collections, particularly in the area of early English manuscripts. But he had his reasons. These years made up the long winter of his discontent. He was outraged at having his hereditary rights undermined and was struggling to repay the debts of his four improvident brothers. He had to sell his brother's glittering library and endure the humiliation of having to deal with a barmaid as his brother's wife and heir. His position as a Non-juror presented difficulties, and he was insecure as a Jacobite among Hanoverians. Finally, he was hindered by a shyness and near-illness which had plagued him since his return from the Continent.

The antiquarians faced a fading of interest in these years. Dame Joan Evans, in her *History of the Society of Antiquaries,* writes of the changing times:

> Medieval studies in the years after 1730 were at a low ebb. The generation of the Saxonists was dead. A new relation between Church and State discouraged ecclesiastical polemics and with them the study of ecclesiastical history. Men were interested less in research than in criticism, less in history than in political theory. The study of national history offered no hope of preferment or patronage, since it could hardly be turned to the glory of a German dynasty. It was an age of reprints and of belated publications rather than of original work.

But even so, this low ebb acted as a spur to Rawlinson; he was used to working under difficulties and with opposition. In the middle and late thirties, with his usual tenacity of purpose and overcoming his earlier lack of self-confidence, he became one of the most active of the members and earned for himself a respected place among the Fellows as one who was undeniably a capable leader. In 1737 an annual feast was decided upon—to be held at the Mitre Tavern on St. George's Day and "that the Ordinary for dining be four shillings pr. head and one shilling more for a pint of Port wine." The members dined and the custom became established. In January of that year there were exactly one hundred members, which by agreement was the maximum membership. In 1740 a motion to increase the membership to one hundred and forty was passed; these were years of expansion for the Society, which was again meeting at the Mitre Tavern, having some years earlier moved back into the inner city from the Gray's Inn location which was considered too remote for convenient attendance. In these years much attention was focused on the objectives of owning its own property, establishing its own home, and obtaining its charter.

The latter subject came to a head when a member left his valued collection of drawings and prints to the Society. His bequest elicited the following comment:

> By the advice of the learned in the law, they cannot receive that donation; their Society being nominal only. Dr. Rawlinson spoke, that it was high time to think of obtaining a charter, and of removing from a tavern, to a place, where they could be secure of what they already had. He was pleased to add, that then he could assure them, they never would [lack for] Dr. Stukeley's company, who was the founder and ornament of the society.

In 1749 the matter of the charter was all important to Rawlinson. It was in this year that he was finally out of debt and the Rawlinson properties free of entail. The dreaded financial ruin had been averted; the estates were under his control; and he needed no longer to be fearful of indebtedness or of interference from family members. His vast collections, which he had carefully assembled, were now securely in his hands, and he would be careful as to their disposition after his death. As stated above, his great fear had been that his library would be dispersed, a fate he had seen happen repeatedly to other private libraries. His great wish (almost an obsession) was that his library should be preserved for posterity, for "a less ungrateful age." His many years of association placed the Society of Antiquaries at the head of his list as recipient of his enormously large benefactions. The Society's drafting of the petition to the "King's Most Excellent Majesty" began in early 1751 and was granted in November of that year. The Letters Patent under the Great Seal were read, the members standing. Dr. Rawlinson presented "a neat Mohogony [sic] Box with three locks to Deposite [sic] the Charter Seal, and other Valuable Papers of the Society."

Rawlinson's Collections and Their Disposition

In 1742 one of Rawlinson's friends from Warwickshire called at London House and reported

> ... such a confusion of Books and MSS that there was no end in viewing of them. It would have took me up a twelve months time to have gone

through with them and in short I looked into very few of them [no] more than what he shewed me in a transient prospect for he has no conveniences to sitt down to see or write out any thing for he does not spend much time in his Chamber but only to take his Breakfast for I went 3 or 4 times before I could be admitted for he gets up into the uppermost Rooms and there is no making him hear at the Door you enter into.

And in 1749 there was still the same disorder. George Vertue, the engraver, coming to call on Rawlinson, commented on the clutter:

> I saw his great collections of manuscripts, many finely-illuminated writings, and innumerable printed books, pamphlets, &c., many in confused heaps on the floors, stools, tables, and shelves; and many marbles, pictures, bronzes, stones, prints, &c. All the great rooms in this house filled with them in presses, and also more [miscellaneous items] in the garrets.

But Rawlinson with his remarkable memory knew what he had purchased, and when, and the life's history of his books and manuscripts. His leviathan-like collections, one of the largest ever kept intact, included history in all its varied branches, early English literature, heraldry, genealogy, biography, and topography. His manuscripts, of which there were more than 4,800, included the Thurloe papers, Pepys's Admiralty papers, Thomas Hearne's diaries and letters, medieval music, log books, account books from the reigns of Henry VIII and Queen Elizabeth, monastic charters, the papers of Bishop Compton and his successor Bishop Robinson, historical law, and medical works. Further subjects included classical literature, travels, religious dissertations, foreign ambassadorial and conclave reports, Rawlinson's own correspondence, poetry, sermons, Hebrew, Greek, and Latin liturgical works, college and university statutes, papers of the Non-jurors, and collections which Rawlinson made for his proposed continuation of Anthony Wood's *Athenae Oxonienses*. In addition to the printed and written word, he left statuary, numerous engravings, portraits, and a collection of Persian, Roman, Italian, and English medals and coins; in fact, almost any object of artistic or antiquarian interest was included there.

As a collector, Rawlinson demonstrated his universality and what he called the "itch of curiosity." Between 1730 and 1750 hardly a book-sale took place that he failed to attend. At some of them he was able to repurchase items which had of necessity been sold in the Thomas Rawlinson library sales. It is particularly gratifying to note that the Matthew Parker the loss of which he had bemoaned when it was sold to the Earl of Oxford for £40 was safely back in his presses. In addition, he had been able to purchase a second copy (the one described by John Strype in his *Life of Parker*), which had been in the library of the Bishop of Ely. Almost all of the finest items from the forced Thomas Rawlinson sale in the 1720s and 1730s were, in similar fashion, gathered back into the fold of the Rawlinson collection.

The cost is a matter for weighing and for reflection. Richard's brother John was being kept in poverty on £10 per annum in Cheshire during this time. His sisters, whose total fortune had been their scant settlement on reaching the age of twenty-one, were approached for loans by Richard, who complained that they charged him interest. Percy Fitzgerald in his book, *The Book Fancier,* could almost have taken Rawlinson for his prototype:

> The [bibliophile] or book fancier is a favorite and almost dramatic figure, with his dim eyes, rusty clothing, and eccentric affection for his treasures. We have a sympathetic tenderness for his lone, solitary ways, his self-denial and privations, his hungry ardour and prowlings.... If the truth were known, this sympathy would be thrown away; for his greed, akin to that of the miser, would make him sacrifice all that is human to all that is of *paper.* He is likely enough to be morose, snarling, grasping, and would find the most exquisite pleasure in getting from some poor and ignorant dealer for a shilling what was worth guineas. This is the triumph of the *chasse à livres.* The prospect of parting with his old friends adds a new pang to death. Friends, relatives, he can leave behind with indifference, but his dear books "cannot bear him company." Here was the departure of a late book lover thus quaintly portrayed:—"He had a quite human fondness for his books; nothing annoyed him so much *as to hear one of them fall;* and dusting them, which he reduced to a science, seemed to give him real pleasure."

Rawlinson, like Fitzgerald's bibliophile, savored to the full the pleasures of ownership, but he also felt the social satisfaction and civic responsibility of sharing his abundance. His father and grandfather had given lavishly to the old family school in Hawkshead in Lancaster. In similar fashion Richard added to the shelves at Eton College and was a constant donor to the Bodleian, sending yearly shipments during his last two decades. But in a more individual and personal manner, he had been entering into the lives of his friends and contemporary scholars by making his resources available to them. "All the abilities . . . we have were given to us to that end that we might advantage others by communicating our gifts unto them." These are words from one of his sermons. Hardly a day passed without such a loan to a friend. In this way many rare items were lost; many others returned to him richer for the marginal notes from scholars who were his acquaintances. Socially retiring by nature, he preferred to communicate by letter, and his friends, in following his example, have left fine words of appreciation, more to be desired than any epitaph. Bishop Tanner, the scholarly editor of historical chronicles, spoke of him as one who obliged "all lovers of…Antiquities." To Thomas Baker of Cambridge he was so liberal with loans that he desired Rawlinson to "hold your hand, and not plunder your Study, by filling mine." Michael Maittaire, the classical scholar, recommended Rawlinson as "this honest industrious gentleman, who already obliged the learned…." William Brome, the Saxonist, classed Rawlinson with Dr. Mead and Lord Oxford as one of the "great Patrons" of the age. George Ballard, another Saxonist, protested a "passionate affection" for Rawlinson's work and assured him that without "these Learned Correspondents that Honour me with their acquaintance, my life would drag heavily on, and the World would become burthensome to me." A Regius Professor of Hebrew at Oxford received so many gifts and loans from Rawlinson that he could not specify in asking for further loans; he could say merely: "Everything in the oriental way is acceptable to me." The biographer John Lewis congratulated Rawlinson on possessing the "true spirit of an Antiquarian…. I shall always gratefully remember your generosity to me." Another correspondent remarked: "After so long Silence your last letter refreshed me as like a dry day after a run of wet weather." Thus in these years after 1730, although Rawlinson sent nothing to the press, he was able to encourage others who continued to publish.

In 1750 Rawlinson set up an endowment for the Chair of Anglo-Saxon Study at Oxford. He was sixty years old and had not yet made his will—nor would he until 1752. Where should he leave his collections? Where would they be best preserved, and where would the greatest use be made of them? There were two logical choices: The Society of Antiquaries and the Bodleian Library; each had a claim to his loyalty and to his favor.

Rawlinson, as stated earlier, had a long connection with the Society of Antiquaries in London, where he met once a week with congenial friends and scholars. He had been serving on the Council, and in the absence of the President (who had a long final illness), he, from time to time, presided at meetings. No member had done more to further the course of antiquarian study. Now that the Society's Charter was obtained and its own house in Chancery Lane provided for, he could feel reassurance as to the wisdom of leaving his treasures there. However, the Bodleian beckoned. The librarian, Humphrey Owen, had shown great appreciation for the donations already received, and Oxford had always been the place where Rawlinson was happiest. It was his "beloved Oxford." He had been making annual visits for the last ten or fifteen years, during which visits he had frequently used the Bodleian and the Ashmolean.

In 1752 he made his will. Besides the legacies to the remaining members of his family, he had three main provisions: to St. John's College he left the bulk of his estates; to the Bodleian Library he left his manuscripts, his rare books, and especially his annotated printed books (which he classified as manuscripts); to the Society of Antiquaries he left his collections of antiquarian interest and also the Rawlinson family estate of Fulham in Middlesex. He specifically mentioned the possibility of future codicils, should there be such a need.

During the last five years of his life Rawlinson made repeated and often lengthy visits to Oxford. He went for the pleasure of going back to his College and the congenial atmosphere of the libraries where he was welcomed and to see his medical doctor, whom he needed. In addition, he wished to be on hand to supervise his shipments which were already arriving. Remembering the disaster to Bishop Tanner's books which had been sent by water and sank in a lock and which, though recovered, still show ravages of water damage, Rawlinson was supervising his own shipments. Some were sent directly to the Bodleian with instructions that they remain unopened. Others were shipped to St. John's College. In 1752 in a letter to his friend John Markham in London he wrote: "I have hird [sic] my own old Chambers at St. John's for a Ware house at £8 per annum where they [the collections] will be safer than in private hands, and all are in cases." During these visits to the Bodleian, Rawlinson often requested the Junius *Caedmon* and became particularly eager to have engravings made from the manuscript, an enthusiasm he shared with the Saxon scholar Edward Rowe Mores. Inasmuch as in these years there was a diminishing interest in the study of Anglo-Saxon, and inasmuch as Rawlinson for many years, while deploring his own lack of skill in the language, had been interested in a revival of the study, this relationship with Mores was an extremely gratifying one. Rawlinson's health improved during this year, and during the Christmas time visit to Oxford he enjoyed "sosedges," "coecoe," and "bambery chese" at his lodgings.

Back in London in January of 1753, Rawlinson was annoyed to find that his interest in making engravings from the Caedmon manuscript was not shared at the Society of Antiquaries. For a number of years one of his wishes had been to persuade the Society to commission engravings of the complete work, but he found a lack of enthusiasm in this regard. He was out of step in his long-lasting admiration of Saxon manuscripts. Rawlinson found also that he was out of step in another way which was more damaging by far to his popularity—and that was his political position. A man by the name of Blacow had become prominent because of his efforts to secure the convic-

An Illumination from MS. Junius 11, fol. 68, the Cædmon *Genesis* (c. 1000). Note the hinged door on the ark, a detail of Saxon life. Reproduced by permission of the Bodleian Library.

tion of the Jacobites who had demonstrated in Oxford in 1747. Although it was now almost seven years later, the controversy was still very much alive. Since 1754 was a parliamentary election year, the issue which at any other time would have lost fire flamed up again. Thus Rawlinson's well-known Jacobite position made him an unpopular choice for re-election to the Council. William Cole wrote to a fellow Society member:

> I hear Dr. Rawlinson is designed to be left out in the next Council: surely a man so indefatigable in the search of antiquity, and so deserving of the Society, very well deserves all the distinctions of it! I am sorry to hear they are so little united.

Rawlinson wrote to George Ballard, his Saxonist friend in Oxford:

> If... I am sacrificed to morrow, and tho' every way the best benefactor the Society of Antiquities has, be dropt from the list of the Council, and if they use me so ingratefully I have done with them. Instead of an agreeable, it has become, a Society of Faction, and you may depend on it, sooner or later, it must perish. Tomorrow, St. George's day, is the annual Election, when, if I am used, as I expect, I shall by a deed ready prepared cancell all my generous intentions towards them, and indeed I shall exclude them or their successors from receiving any benefit by what I design for Alma Mater, so that the being a member of the Royal or Anti-

quarys Societys shall be a disqualification to enjoy any benefit from me. Such ingratitude, if it happens, deserves punishment, to more than the third generation.

Rawlinson was indeed removed from the Council, and he again wrote to his friend Ballard of the injustice done him:

> ...tho' in fact the first promoter of the Charter to which I contributed more than a double share of Tax, made the Society before and since presents to a very great value; had in my will made above two years since, left them an Estate, and effects worth near 2000 pounds; had laid by for them a large Collection of English history; and been in fact their founder, and at last sacrificed to [factions]. Unfashionable principles, were sett against my donations; and intentions.... They begin to repent but as I meet with them and their dissembled Courtesy I tell them they mistake me for one Mr. Spaniel, for such they must take a creature to be without resentment.... My revocation is as irrevocable as the Laws of the Medes and Persians.

At this time the President of the Society, Martin Folkes, died. His demise left a vacancy on the Council. Here was the opportunity for the Society to make amends to Dr. Rawlinson. When he was ignored, he signed a codicil to his will, angrily revoking all bequests to the Society. With an unaccustomed dramatic touch, he requested four Fellows to witness it; this was done in the Society's chambers on 25 July 1754.

On 18 June 1754, Rawlinson had written to Ballard: "The discharge the Antiquaries have given me will hasten me to Oxford." The "hastening" to Oxford was not without a rehearsal. Ten years earlier, during the period of his desperate efforts to establish his ownership to his estates and while still in debt, he had written to a friend in Warwickshire that he feared being ejected from London House, where he had "eleven rooms above and below" (for which he paid £40 per annum). The thought of leaving London House "chills my blood," he had written to Ballard. This worry regarding his quarters was the result of a possible change of ownership of the house with the usual related uncertainties but magnified in Rawlinson's case by the task of moving the mountains of books, manuscripts, and other collections. During these years Rawlinson was searching about in Oxford for a suitable house to rent as the repository of his vast (and still growing) collections. He went so far as to make requests of the Keeper of the Bodleian to attempt to locate suitable housing for him there, but nothing was available. One may reflect that Rawlinson, much as he enjoyed and admired Oxford, would have missed the excitement of the London book sales, the stimulation of his acquaintances in the city, and the growing satisfaction that he was finding in those particular years (prior to his quarrel) at the then appreciative Society of Antiquaries. The loss of the lease of London House became less and less of a threat to Rawlinson as time passed, and in 1749 he reported in his correspondence that his books were safe there, at least temporarily. In 1750

Rawlinson made a new rental agreement in which he agreed to pay £10 for additional rooms which gave him "possession of the other part of the staircase." At no time did Rawlinson rent the entire mansion. People of fashion in those years were leaving the inner city for more desirable housing in the West End, and this old mansion with all its history was rented out in sections as separate apartments. For Rawlinson, as for his brother Thomas earlier, it was completely suitable since it was near the book shops, printers, sales rooms, and all the other areas that attract book lovers.

Rawlinson needed to see to it that all his collections, formerly intended for the Society of Antiquaries, would be properly taken care of at the Bodleian. At one time he had confided to Hearne:

> It would be a torment in another state to know the ill usage posthumous papers meet with; by nothing has mankind more suffered, than by the vanity or avarice of those who have come after them. Was it not an injustice this procedure would induce a Man to burn all his papers and deprive an ungrateful world of any benefit they might receive from them.

An additional codicil followed soon after which more specifically detailed further revoking of his bequests to the Society of Antiquaries, which in his angry haste, he had neglected to specify. Of particular importance was the valuable Fulham estate in Middlesex, which years earlier had been the home of Lady Rawlinson; the codicil stated that it was to go instead to Hertford College in Oxford. The document was printed and sent to each member of the Society; this was in August of 1754.

Rawlinson's health was failing although it was a subject seldom mentioned in his correspondence. In 1733, which was the year before the last Thomas Rawlinson library sale, he had complained of a "severe indisposition" brought on by family problems. And in 1736 he wrote in a letter to Ballard about being troubled with "great colds." In 1750 his London doctor advised the waters of Bath and Bristol. Knowing that he could have the pleasure of stopping at Oxford before and after the cure, he did not resist the prescribed course. Before going to Bath, he lingered at Oxford, meeting with his old friends, finding new inscriptions to copy, transcribing in the Bodleian, and purchasing manuscripts. Going on to Bath and Bristol, he continued his active interests there, to such an extent that a friend could write to him that he was "heartily glad that your indisposition is removed."

Richard Rawlinson's Heart Burial Urn (Bayley Chapel, St. John's College, Oxford). MS. Don. a. 7, fol. 21. The inscription begins *Ubi Thesaurus, ibi Cor.* Reproduced by permission of the Bodleian Library.

On returning to Oxford with recovered energy, he again copied inscriptions and made extracts from church registers, extending his searches into the neighboring towns and villages. In May of 1751, he again became ill and went to Islington, which was a short distance to the north of the old city of London—a country village well-known as a spa. Here the water was particularly good; it was from this approximate area that the water had been piped to his parents' home in 1680. The country air and exercise were beneficial, and his health improved. Again, becoming ill in February of 1755, he returned, staying at "Mrs. Westbrooke's, next door to the Coach and Horses beyond the Church." His housekeeper, Mrs. Debroche, went to Islington with him. One day in March he wrote to his apothecary and good friend John Markham that "I was abroad yesterday above two hours and returned not fatigued nor did I nap the whole day...." He sympathized with the condition of "Poor Ballard ... an invalide retired to Campden" but did not think his own condition to be serious. One of his last recorded actions was the purchase (on March 15, 1755) of a view of Oxford. On Saturday, April 12, 1755, an Oxford journal reported:

> Last Sunday Night died, at Islington, in the Sixty-fifth Year of his Age, the ingenious and learned Richard Rawlinson, Esq; Doctor of Laws, Fellow of the Royal Society of London, and one of the first Promoters of the Antiquarian Society.

A week later another report appeared:

> Last Monday night the Remains of Richard Rawlinson L.L.D. arrived here from London; when his Body was interred in a new Vault lately made by the Doctor's own Directions in the North Isle of St. Giles's Church; and his Heart, inclosed in a Silver Vase, was deposited according to the Directions of his Will, in the Chapel of St. John's College in this University.

Richard Rawlinson and the Non-juring Movement

Division within the Church of England

As recently as November, 1988, the non-juring movement was in the news—no doubt a matter of surprise and one that sent thoughtful readers to their history books. J. Enoch Powell, writing of the Non-jurors on the occasion of the third centenary of their appearance, stated that the Glorious Revolution—glorious only because it was bloodless—could never have effected its smooth, almost eventless transition without their position which was that of individual and unbending dedication to principle; thus, he argued, they can be thought of as the element that made the acceptance of William III respectable, a kind of surrogate national conscience. Their members represented an organized church which began in 1688 and which maintained itself until the last congregation disappeared in the early years of the nineteenth century.

Richard Rawlinson was one of these Non-jurors. In his day, along with the thousands of others who suffered because they would not violate allegiance or condone usurpation, he would have been heartened if by some kind of science-fiction projection he could have read Powell's words in the London *Times* of November 14, 1988. "It was one of those occasions when public faith needed the witness of men of the non-juring mentality. There have to be those who say 'No, that can't be right' and who say it at their own cost." This article is an attempt to describe some aspects of the movement and the costs involved.

Richard Rawlinson's non-juring position was one expression of his Jacobitism, affirming as it did his loyalty to James II and his descendants. Frank McLynn, in his book *The Jacobites,* states: "The most striking thing about the Jacobites was that they considered kingship to be indefeasible, a God-given right that could not be taken away by man, whatever the monarch did." This is the position that had been staunchly supported by the Rawlinson family for at least three generations. It was from Daniel (1614-79) that this branch of the Rawlinson family derived its intense loyalty to the

Crown. It is reported that Richard's grandfather's tavern had been confiscated because he dared to hang his

> ...signe in Mourning [on the day of the execution of Charles I]. The Honour of the Mitre was much eclipsed thro' the loss of so good a Parent of the Church of England. [They] say this endeared him so much to the Ch. men that he soon throve amain and got a good Estate.

Daniel Rawlinson did indeed thrive again, returning as keeper of the Mitre, which was the favorite tavern of Samuel Pepys; also he established a flourishing tea trade and became prosperous enough thereby to purchase valuable lands in the counties of Essex, Norfolk, and Warwickshire, as well as properties in London.

Among several events in the history of the Church of England, the period of the non-juring movement is perhaps the least understood and certainly the most ignored by historians. Yet the movement had great impact on the then existing Anglican Church inasmuch as the members of the group on leaving the Established Church removed with them much learning, piety, and conscience.

The Non-jurors as a group had a unique interest in the study of the Old English period: they found in the study of the early Saxon Church a justification for their ecclesiastical position. George Hickes, who figured prominently in the movement, wrote in 1714: "I know not any work an antiquary can do more serviceable to the Church than this, which will show the... chief doctrines of the English-Saxon Church to be the same as ours...."
D. C. Douglas in *English Scholars, 1660-1730* makes the following statement:

> But it is equally certain that the great positive achievements of the age in medieval scholarship would never have been attained had the scholars not been urged to their work by motives derived from religious convictions. Nowhere, for instance, could this stimulus be better observed than in the work of those who, for religious reasons, suffered for refusing to take the oaths of William III and George I. The Non-jurors had a special interest in patristic literature.... They were keenly concerned with English ecclesiastical tradition. Moreover the circumstances of their lives, and the controversies in which they engaged, turned their attention particularly towards the early history of their country.... [T]he distinction of the Non-jurors in all fields of medieval investigation was one of the most striking phenomena of the time. To name such as Hickes and Hearne, William Lloyd and Jeremy Collier, is alone sufficient to indicate the work which was zealously undertaken by many of this company. This small minority of disinherited, and often penurious, men doubtless

in many respects invited the criticism which they have received, but in their learned works they compelled a respectful attention even from their ecclesiastical opponents. They remained a scholarly leaven in English society, and their contributions to historical studies were out of all proportion to their numbers. Isolated by their opinions, and scattered over the land, they yet maintained an intellectual unity among themselves. They achieved a fertile collaboration, and sent out to each other, across a hostile world, their learned missives like balloons from beleaguered cities.

We can see this force at work in Rawlinson's life. In order to understand the early church, he reasoned, one must be able to read the writings of the people of that earlier time, to comprehend their laws, and to understand their charters. This was undoubtedly one of his reasons for establishing the Anglo-Saxon Professorship at Oxford.

The Non-jurors were a relatively small group of men who refused to swear allegiance to William of Orange in 1689 and to the rulers who followed him. They believed that James II, who had fled from England in 1688 under threatening circumstances but who had not abdicated and who expected to return to England as monarch, was still their King; as such, he was the head of the Anglican Church, and their allegiance still belonged to him, although they did not accept his Catholicism.

The three most definitive works about the period of the Non-jurors are Thomas Lathbury's *History of the Non-Jurors* (1845), J. H. Overton's *The Non-Jurors* (1902), and Henry Broxap's *The Later NonJurors* (1924). The first of these deals at length with the many tracts, letters, and pamphlets written by both the Non-jurors and those in the Established Church who opposed them and thus gives substance to the arguments of the time without dwelling on the personalities of those involved. Overton stated in his preface that his book drew extensively on Lathbury and sought to update the information in the earlier work while frankly defending the position of the Non-jurors. Broxap based his writing largely on the collections of Thomas Brett, a man who joined the movement somewhat late and who sought to bring about a change in the liturgy to an earlier form than that used in the Established Church. Brett's effort split the Non-jurors in the 1720s and weakened their stand.

While still the Duke of York, James II had become Catholic in 1671. When he assumed the throne in 1685, he agreed to uphold the Protestant Church of England; however, before long he began to celebrate mass publicly, and, when he thought he perceived a serious division within the Established Church, he privately felt that he might displace it with Catholicism by the use of a vigorous policy which would exploit the divided loyalties of high churchmen. Hence, in addition to the public avowal of his faith, he prohibited preaching against Catholicism and published the Declaration of Indulgence, which allowed Catholics and dissenters to hold government and church positions. Further, he placed Catholics and dissenters from the Established Church in high political positions. In April, 1688, he made what proved to be a serious error in judgement: he issued a proclamation which required the bishops and other clergy to read the Declaration of Indulgence from their pulpits. When seven Anglican bishops petitioned the king to reconsider his edict, James had them arrested. They were acquitted in June. There was a great rejoicing in the streets of London when the news of the release of the bishops reached the people. Even James's army celebrated. In his *Short History of the English People*, J. R. Green reports: "The peerage, the gentry, the Bishops, the clergy, the Universities, every lawyer, every trader, every farmer, stood aloof from him, and now his very soldiers forsook him." But James was adamant in his refusal to retract the Declaration of Indulgence, and from this point on his days as monarch in England were numbered.

Richard P. Thompson in *The Atlantic Archipelago* has described the action which followed:

> ...When the bishops' trial was about to begin, the royal court announced that the Queen, Mary of Modena, had given birth to a son (June 10, 1688). The king's age (56) gave rise to nasty rumors about the baby's origin, but the cold fact was that now there would be a Roman Catholic successor. Before this, James's daughters, Mary and Anne, both raised as Protestants, were in line to succeed. Seven leading English politicians (Whigs and Tories) wrote secretly to William of Orange (Mary's husband) and offered to support him if he would invade England to "preserve their liberties." By September, William had decided to go ahead with the invasion.

William came to England with his army in November. In December, James fled, and a convention was assembled to discuss the future of the government. Some wished to set up a regency, or caretaker government, but William refused to act merely as a regent. There were some who wished to recall James, but under certain restricted conditions. At length, the Commons declared the throne vacant. William, however, would not accept the throne in the right of his wife and much debate ensued before William and Mary were declared king and queen, with the administrative power residing in William's hands.

The national church existed by act of the King: all members of the clergy were appointed by him. Therefore, William's first act to stabilize the government was to demand an Oath of Allegiance whereby all agents of the government and all the clergy were required to swear allegiance to him as king. This action was not at all unusual; such an oath had been required at the time of James's accession. The two houses of Parliament took the Oath in 1689, as did the Archbishop of York and the bishops of Bristol, London, Rochester, Llandaff, Winchester, Carlisle, and St. David's. Others, however, refused to do so. To them, James was still their king, and, since they had previously sworn allegiance to him, they could not, in good faith, swear allegiance to William. Those refusing included William Sancroft, Archbishop of Canterbury; Thomas Ken, Bishop of Wells and Bath; John Lake, Bishop of Chichester; Thomas White, Bishop of Peterborough; Francis Turner, Bishop of Ely; and Robert Frampton, Bishop of Gloucester, as well as the Bishops of Norwich and Worcester. They were joined by a band of over four hundred vicars of local parishes and many distinguished persons—some ecclesiastical, some scholars, and some non-clerics. Among them were Jeremy Collier, the ecclesiastical historian; George Hickes, Dean of Worcester; John Fitzwilliam, Canon of Windsor; Henry Dodwell, the Camden Professor of History at Oxford; Henry Hyde, the second Earl of Clarendon; and Roger North, a distinguished lawyer. Many scholars of the community at Oxford joined them. Eventually all of the clergymen of the Episcopal Church of Scotland were counted among their numbers. Such men formed the nucleus of the non-juring movement, and their refusal to take the Oath of Allegiance to William led inevitably to persecution. Some were tried and executed; nearly all endured hardship and deprivation.

A number of the non-juring bishops had served for many years and were elderly. Archbishop Sancroft and his followers, who maintained that they represented the true Church of England, recognized that if it were to continue over the years the Church would require new and younger men. At the time Sancroft was in failing health. He stepped aside from the immediate action and delegated his powers to William Lloyd, the Bishop of Worcester. The bishops discussed the matter at length, and Lord Clarendon was asked to write a letter to the court of King James, then at St. Germain in France, asking for royal approval of the new church and new ordinations. A letter to Lord Melfort, the king's secretary, elicited "a most gracious answer," stating that His Majesty was "well pleased with the design and concurred in it." His Majesty later requested a discourse on the subject, and George Hickes visited the king in St. Germain, carrying a list of non-juring clergy from whom successor bishops might be chosen. James sent Hickes back to England with instructions that two new bishops should be consecrated, one to be chosen by Archbishop Sancroft, the other by the remaining deprived bishops.

Hickes's return to England was delayed by his own protracted illness in Holland, by war on the high seas, and by the necessity that he avoid detection by the authorities upon his re-entry into the country. Sancroft had died in his absence; therefore it was Lloyd who selected Hickes, and the bishops nominated Thomas Wagstaffe. Hickes and Wagstaffe were consecrated in 1694. The details of this series of events are preserved for us in Hickes's *Record of the New Consecrations.* A copy of this invaluable historical paper is among the documents left to the Bodleian Library by Richard Rawlinson.

With the consecration of Hickes and Wagstaffe, the schism was affirmed; there was no retreat. Without these new leaders, the continuity of the Non-jurors would have been irreparably weakened after the demise of the originally displaced bishops. Their replacements represented the final, irrevocable declaration that the Non-jurors were indeed a separate church. Following the death of Lloyd in 1703, George Hickes became the leader of the non-juring movement.

William's reaction to the refusal of Sancroft and the other bishops to take the Oath of Allegiance was predictable. He quickly caused an Act of Divestiture to be passed, which forced all the ecclesiastical Non-jurors from their sees, took away their state-given rights to their pulpits, and left them homeless, destitute, and hunted. He appointed John Tillotson to be Archbishop of Canterbury and ordained other bishops to fill the places of those who had been expelled. By so doing, William erected a barrier which prevented the Non-jurors from returning to their former places. From positions of affluence, they were reduced to the greatest extremities, forced to live on the bounty of others. They incurred the animosity of many who were loyal to the government because of their adherence to the principle that James was their lawful, rightful ruler and the leader of their church. They might have preferred to live quietly under the government, but they were not permitted to do so. One of the many disruptions in their lives related to their places of worship. Because of the divestiture of the non-juring clerics from their churches, one may wonder whether these men and their followers attended services in their local parishes as formerly. Many of the laity did so, but the non-juring bishops held secret services and offered Communion to sympathizers at various meeting halls and in their now humble, hired homes. Richard Rawlinson was one of those holding such services; it is recorded that he officiated in "Mr. Blackbourne's Chapel" at Gray's Inn.

The members of the lesser non-juring clergy also were subject to much hardship, as was the laity. Oaths were tendered again and again to all suspected persons. Those who refused were often imprisoned; magistrates were often dismissed for what was deemed to be undue leniency in administering the Oath. In many cases great severity was exercised. The wearing of a white rose was considered a badge of the Pretender. Those found with a rose were punished; in one instance, two soldiers were whipped almost to the point of death in Hyde Park on this account. Such measures deterred the Non-jurors from defending their position in the public press. A few did step forward, although they were generally subjected to punishment. Such a person was the learned Lawrence Howell, a non-juring cleric. Howell was publicly outspoken in his support of the movement, and, when a pamphlet of his entitled "The Schism in the English Church, Truly Told" was discovered at a printer's, he was arrested, brought to trial, fined £500, and imprisoned for three years. He died during his prison term.

George Hickes and Thomas Hearne as Non-jurors

Two particular instances of persecution are of note, not because they were unusual but because they were typical and involved men who are remembered today as outstanding scholars. George Hickes, mentioned earlier, was one of these. He was probably the most remarkable figure among English historical scholars of his time, or perhaps of all time. It was not merely that his knowledge and scholarship were outstanding, but also that he endured great deprivation while remaining thorough in his scholarship and steadfast in his beliefs.

Hickes attended St. John's College, Oxford, and his brilliance as a student soon showed itself in his rapid rise from Fellow of Lincoln College to Lauderdale's Chaplain in Scotland and later to the position of Dean of Worcester Cathedral. He was a man of strong beliefs who, while wishing for passive resistance, felt he could not violate allegiances. On the morning of May 2, 1690, he nailed a notice to the door of the cathedral:

> Whereas the Office, Place, and Dignity of Dean of this Cathedral Church of Worcester was given and granted unto me for a Freehold during my Natural Life by Letters Patent under the Broad Seal of King Charles II of happy memory who had an undoubted Right to confer the same...
>
> And whereas I George Hickes...have for several Years peaceably enjoyed the same...

And whereas I am given to understand that my Right to the said Office and Dignity has of late been called in question, and that one Mr. Talbot M.A. pretends a title to the same...

Now know ye therefore, and every one of you,

That I the said George Hickes...do hereby publickly PROTEST and declare, that I do claim Legal Right and Title to the said Office and Dignity of Dean—and that I am not conscious of any Act or Misdemeanor the conviction whereof, if any such were, should or can determine my said Right; but do conceive that I was, and still do continue, the only Rightful and Legal Dean of this Cathedral Church of Worcester; and that I do not in any way relinquish my said Title, but shall, God willing, use all just Means which the Laws of this realm allow for the Preservation and Recovery thereof....

This was a challenge that could not be ignored by William's government. Hickes immediately became a fugitive, an exile, his next years spent in semi-seclusion.

White Kennett, who was later to become Bishop of Peterborough, had taken the Oath of Allegiance to William. In *The Life of Kennett*, it is recorded that Hickes found friendship with this member of his opposition:

Having contracted an intimate Acquaintance with Dr. Hicks [Kennett] received him freely into his Vicarage-House, and finding that by his condition of Suffering for the cause of King James his Head and Thoughts were too much determined to Politicks..., Mr. Kennett to divert him from that Mischief (as well for other reasons) desired his Instruction in the *Saxon* and *Septentrional* Tongues. While Dr. Hicks was thus pleased by the Country Vicar, it gave the latter an Opportunity to intreat the Doctor to look more upon those Studies, to review his *Saxon* and *Islandic* Grammar. It was upon the frequent Discourse and Importunity of Mr. Kennett that Dr. Hicks then and there laid the Foundation of that noble Work [Hickes's *Linguarum Veterum Septentrionalium Thesaurus*] which he brought to Perfection about seven Years after.

When the completed work appeared, George Hickes paid tribute to his hospitable opponent:

...to that reverend and most learned man who seven years ago often urged me to gird myself to this work....In his house I began without delay books in which, now that they are at length brought to a close—if I have in any way helped the republic of letters—to him as the begetter of all that I have done it is to be attributed.

Hickes was forced to leave the shelter of Kennett's home when his presence became known to his enemies, and he then went to the Hereford home of

William Brome. But again his retreat was detected and he was forced to flee. A third and fourth repetition of these periods of shelter and escape followed, including an interval in the home of Francis Cherry, of Shottesbrooke, the non-juring patron of Thomas Hearne. Yet throughout these turbulent times Hickes continued his studies and writing, as well as his quiet direction of those who shared his non-juring views.

Hickes was pardoned by the Lord Chancellor in 1699, but he refused to rejoin the national church. In contrast, in 1710 Henry Dodwell (1641-1711) made the decision to leave the Non-jurors, feeling it the wisest course for the sake of a unified church, and sought to bring the displaced members back to the Church of England. Dodwell's tracts pressing his position are remarkable pieces of writing, quoted extensively by Lathbury, and for students of ecclesiastical history, they are exceedingly informative reading. Hickes, however, remained constant to his position and through his force the movement went on. He died in 1715, leaving a legacy of scholarship, encouragement, leadership, and faith.

The case of Thomas Hearne is of interest because it also typified the hardships forced upon the Non-jurors. As a young boy of poor parents, Hearne was taken into the household of Francis Cherry, who recognized the boy's unusual talents. After his early education at Bray School he was sent to Oxford, to St. Edmund Hall, where he was to live throughout his life. Following his graduation he was employed at the Bodleian Library where he was occupied in the cataloguing of books and manuscripts. David C. Douglas, in *English Scholars, 1660-1730,* describes Hearne:

> His natural home was the Bodleian, and he was fortunate to become...
> Under-Keeper in that Library. But in 1715 he refused to take the oaths,
> and was in consequence deprived of all his academic offices. In view of
> his own poverty the act commands admiration, and henceforth he was
> dependent upon what he could privately earn. He never lacked forti-
> tude, and though he was mocked by his enemies, he faced them consis-
> tently without ever making the easy sacrifice of his convictions. "By
> means of this Industry and of a good Disposition he raised himself from
> the lowest state of Dependence to a Station of Ease and Honour. When
> his worth was in some sort acknowledged by the offer of the best Offices
> the University had to bestow, he manifested uncommon Integrity in
> declining those Offers because the Acceptance of them appeared to him
> inconsistent with the Principles which he had adopted."

For many years, both before and after his expulsion from the Bodleian, Hearne was faithful in keeping a daily journal. This meticulous record of his life and the contacts which he maintained with other scholars constitutes an unusual record of the life and times of the early eighteenth century. We are indebted to Richard Rawlinson for its preservation. When Hearne died, he left his papers to the family of the Reverend Hilkiah Bedford, who had been his close friend. Hilkiah's heir, his son William, died in 1747. Soon after, George Smith, who had married Hilkiah's sister, wrote to Dr. Rawlinson:

> I am very much concerned, that Bro' B[edford] did not take care...to put Mr. Hearne's Books and Papers in proper hands,...and were never designed to be sold to a bookseller....The Bookseller has bid 100 guineas...; I suppose you should offer the same.

Rawlinson agreed to pay the sum, and was congratulated by Smith: "I... heartily wish you joy of your new purchase, and doubt not that you will take proper care, that after your decease they shall never run the hazard again of being dispersed." Thus, with Rawlinson's bequest, the diary found its way to the Bodleian Library with the other Rawlinson manuscripts. In this manner Hearne returned after death to the library which he had been forced to leave during his lifetime. Hearne's most important work, the editing of historical and ecclesiastical English chronicles, typifies his careful and accurate preparation; students of history today find them an invaluable resource.

Besides the diary, Hearne's letters to Richard and his brother Thomas are among the Rawlinson papers. In them there are many direct references to the pressures brought on Hearne—his constant fear of arrest—as shown in his letter of 6 January 1716, to Thomas Rawlinson:

> Much pleased to have your letter after long silence, but T.R. has said nothing in answer to H's except about the oaths. Wants particularly to know if he can safely act as sub-librarian. I fear the Malice and Roguery of three or four persons....But before I resolve I want to be advised. And the best advice in this case would come from some Whig Lawyer provided it could be obtained without acquainting him with ye Name of the Person that wants Advice. Colleges and Halls at present are the safest places for Retirement, and I shall not think of Removing into Town till forced to it. But I take it for granted that if all Members of Colleges and Halls are forced to swear, there will be the same Imposition upon the Town,...if so, the best way will be to retire to some village near Oxford.

His fear of arrest was equalled by his frustration at not being able to carry on an open contact with the world of books and scholars, which was his true source of satisfaction. He had been offered the Camden Chair of History, but refused since it would have meant the taking of the Oath. Hearne is buried at St. Edmund Hall, where a plaque has been erected to his memory. Behind glass doors in the library are preserved a few of his personal books. The room where he is believed to have lived out his life is now a museum and is used for small college meetings.

There were many others whose stories of deprivation paralleled that of Hearne. Also forced from his position at Oxford was Henry Harte, a non-juring clergyman who was a Fellow of Pembroke College, Prebendary of Wells, and Vicar of St. Mary Magdalen, Taunton. All of these he lost for refusing the Oath of Allegiance, as did Theophilus Downes, who sacrificed a Balliol Fellowship.

Throughout the reigns of William (1688-1702) and Anne (1702-14) pamphlets, tracts, and books were published and letters exchanged which sought to persuade the Non-jurors to rejoin the national church. A few among these were letters by White Kennett and Edward Stillingfleet. Defense of the non-juring position was made by many who wrote anonymously, as well as in tracts written by well-known leaders such as Hickes, John Kettlewell, and Samuel Grascome. Towards the end of the reign of Anne the movement had weakened, as all of the originally unseated bishops except Thomas Ken of Bath and Wells had died, as had Archbishop Sancroft. Ken, as the sole successor, was elderly and sought to retire. His personal feeling was that all would be best served by the return of the Non-jurors to the national church. He was strongly opposed by Jeremy Collier, who continued to visualize a non-juring church stronger and larger than the Church of England. Through Collier's forcefulness he had become the new leader of the movement in the days of Hickes's final illness and death.

When Queen Anne died in 1714, Parliament passed the Act of Succession, guaranteeing for all time that there would be a Protestant ruler of England, and establishing the House of Hanover as the rightful heirs to the throne. Thus, George I became king, bringing with his accession the customary requirement for new Oaths of Allegiance. This strengthened Collier's position by giving the faltering and divided Non-jurors a new determination and a new reason for the solidarity of the movement and for their continued political and ecclesiastical separation, although by this time there were few remaining who had sworn allegiance to James II.

Richard Rawlinson as a Non-juror

The brotherhood and the loyalty of the Non-jurors was demonstrated by the establishment of a fund to assist members who were without employment or income. Together with Nathaniel Spinckes, divine and Anglo-Saxon scholar, Rawlinson was made responsible for the administration of this fund. By coincidence, in 1676 Spinckes had been ordained deacon of the Church of England in the chapel of London House, at that time the residence of Bishop Compton and later the residence of Dr. Rawlinson.

Through the years two factions developed among the Non-jurors. A number of the non-juring clergy led by Collier and Brett wished to adopt a form of the liturgy which differed from that of the established Church. This faction became known as the "Usagers" and those opposed to such a change were identified as "Non-usagers." When Rawlinson was ordained a bishop in 1728 he joined with his consecrators, Blackbourne, Doughty, and Gandy, in supporting the position of the Non-usagers. They wrote:

> We...utterly dislike and remonstrate against any alterations at all, the usages contended for having been regularly rejected; and we do forbid so far as in us lyes any adding to or diminishing of the liturgy of the Church of England.

The healing of this breach and the restoration of harmony between the two factions was largely the work of Rawlinson, one of his several important contributions to the movement.

Rawlinson also became the chief historian for the Non-jurors. This was a natural consequence of his abiding interest in history, archives, and antiquarianism. Here he could pursue two interests at once: the research into old records which he so loved, as well as his support of the Non-jurors. He worked long and carefully at this task, using as his sources records in the libraries of Westminster Abbey and Lambeth, as well as replies from "Quaeries" which he had printed and circulated to all known non-juring clergy and academics. Replies to these questionnaires are today among the Rawlinson papers at the Bodleian; they provide both a valuable and unique record of this aspect of English Church history and biographical information about men whose lives would otherwise have gone mostly unrecorded. It is said that Dr. Rawlinson, who during those years was extremely involved with family estate responsibility and his brother's library sales, became indifferent to many minor issues of ritual such as whether or not an altar should be set eastward. But, a born archivist, he was never indifferent to the gathering of information relating to the history of the Non-jurors. In a divided denomination there was much correspondence; Rawlinson was constantly aware of such collections and eager to acquire them. A clergyman put him on the track of Bishop Turner's papers. He succeeded in acquiring the Sancroft papers and the manuscripts of Gandy and Blackbourne. One of Rawlinson's fellow churchmen commented wryly that the Doctor could hardly wait for a colleague to die before he pounced upon his papers.

Throughout the years a number of new bishops were ordained by the Non-jurors. In 1742 Richard persuaded the church to approach the Young Pretender (Charles Edward, grandson of James II, in Rome) for confirmation of their consecrations. Although the Non-jurors were definitely non-Popish, they still held that the hereditary line of James II was the titular head of their Church and as such his approval was a desired formality.

A result of Rawlinson's efforts in the cause of the Non-jurors, and one of the instances in which his participation set him uncomfortably apart, was the unpopularity he experienced in the Society of Antiquaries. The early membership had included a number of Non-jurors, but the group of loyal friends and supporters diminished with the years; there was a corresponding rise in the number of members who were opposed to the Non-jurors. One active opponent was Richard Blacow, who labelled Rawlinson as a dangerous man to have on the Council of the Society even though he had served in this capacity for a number of years. Thus he fell into disfavor in 1754 and was not re-elected. Feeling angry and unappreciated, he wrote a Codicil to his will revoking his intended bequest of his collections to the Society, and he transferred them to Oxford, where they now are.

In 1755 Dr. Rawlinson died in a suburb of London to which he had gone for the country air and the restorative waters. He had been a staunch Non-juror for most of his life and an important factor in the movement. Although the group continued quietly for another fifty years, its force was spent with the passing of all who had been its original members and active supporters. Without strong personal leadership the movement was doomed. It passed from view, one of the last of the divisive chapters which have punctuated the ecclesiastical history of England.

Richard Rawlinson and the Anglo-Saxon Professorship at Oxford

The Endowment and Its Supervision

The will of Dr. Richard Rawlinson specified a deed of trust in which are enumerated certain of his lands and other properties in the county of Lancaster not far distant from Grasmere and Lake Windermere—the Lake District of the Wordsworths—where the Rawlinson family had lived for generations, going as far back as Walter and Henry Rawlynson, who fought with Henry V at Agincourt, from whom they received the favors of extensive lands and the right to a coat of arms. The rents were payable twice a year, usually at the Feast of St. Michael the Archangel (Michaelmas) and again on Annunciation Day of the Blessed Virgin Mary (Lady Day); they amounted to approximately £85 per annum, and they were to be used to endow an Anglo-Saxon professorship at Oxford.

Dr. Rawlinson's will was in two parts: the first, drawn in 1750, arranged for the professorship; the second, executed in 1752, contained his other benefactions, both to family members and to public causes. Later, four codicils would be added. After his death in 1755, the will was printed, bound, and sold in St. Paul's Churchyard in accordance with his request. Having had almost endless problems with the wills of his father and his brother Thomas (in addition to that of his distant cousin Christopher), he was careful to insure that his will was clear to all, and that his wishes as detailed below would be observed.

> ...IN TRUST TO CONVEY and assure the said annual or fee-farm rents hereby granted and released, with their and every of their rights members and appurtenances, and all their right title trust interest and estate therein and thereto, unto the chancellor masters and scholars of the university of Oxford and their successors for ever; to the end intent and purpose by and out of the said annual or fee-farm rents, to found constitute and establish and from time to time to support uphold and maintain one Anglo-Saxon, lecture or professorship in the said university to have

Dear Sr.

I beg your pardon for having usd to much importunity in my last about the Specimens, which came in good time and give a great deal of satisfaction to all that have seen them; Mr Archdeacon Clements speaks with a great deal of earnestnesse towards the advancing of contributions, and I shall endeavour by all means I can, the furtherance of so good a work. I must desire your excuse if in return for your discovery about the ormulum, I trouble you with a conjecture of mine about the abbreviations. Ð ð Þ þ in which I am inclin'd to favour the reverse of Sr H. Spelmans opinion, namely that Ð ð should be pronoun'ed like this, that, in wch we seem to hear something of the letter d, the stroke or dash in Ð ð being only for mollifying the sound of that letter, as it is still preserv'd in the German and Dutch. dis. bat. whereas the derivation of the other Þ þ Þ Þ manifestly declares that the Th should be heard, as in thing, θεòς. however Authors confound them.

I design Godwilling to be wth you in a fortnights time, making Glocester and Worcester in my way, as I said in my last. I am

Sr

Bath. Sept: 13th 1698.

Your very much obliged Humble servant.

Will. Elstob.

My service to Mr Dean, and to our Oxford friends.

Letter from the Anglo-Saxon Scholar William Elstob, probably to Edward Thwaites of Queen's College, Oxford. MS. Rawl. D. 377, fol. 78. That Rawlinson preserved such papers as this demonstrates his interest in the Anglo-Saxon scholars who preceded his years at Oxford. Reproduced by permission of the Bodleian Library.

continuance for ever, and to be ruled governed directed and regulated by and under such rules orders and constitutions as the said Richard Rawlinson shall at any time hereafter in writing direct limit and appoint....

This document was signed in Fleet Street, London, in 1750. The Anglo-Saxon Professorship at Oxford would not become a reality until forty years after Dr. Rawlinson's death. The delay was the result of instructions given in his will—not, as some accounts have indicated, because of lack of interest on the part of the University. In Dr. Rawlinson's wording of the first codicil, we read further: "I do appoint the Convocation of the University of Oxford, if they kindly accept my settlement made in August one thousand seven hundred and fifty, to be the electors of the professor therein named." Accordingly, in 1795 the Convocation of the University elected Charles Mayo, M.A., Fellow of St. John's College, as the first Rawlinsonian Professor of Anglo-Saxon at Oxford, a position he held for the designated period of five years.[1]

An account of the study of literature and language at Oxford by Sir Charles Firth discusses this early period:

> ...the ardour with which the study of Anglo-Saxon had been pursued at Oxford in the early part of the eighteenth century...declined toward its close. An Oxford bookseller wrote to Richard Gough in 1795 saying, "Since the death of Mr. Lye, Rowe-Mores, and two or three of Bishop Gibson's encouragers at Queen's, I cannot hear of a buyer of Saxon books." With the foundation of the Rawlinsonian Professorship, the study revived again. Two of the early professors, Ingram and Conybeare, made notable contributions to the literature of the subject, as did Joseph Bosworth, who became professor much later.[2]

As arranged by Rawlinson, the several Colleges of the University were to enjoy the professorship in succession according to their antiquity; and his own college, St. John's, was to have every fifth term.[3]

When considering the emolument received by the Professors, one may conclude that the honor was greater than the remuneration. An extant correspondence in the Bodleian regarding the payment of the rents by the agent in Lancashire indicates a discontent on the part of the University concerning the amount of moneys collected. In a paper of 1869, entitled "Report on Ulverston Rents," we read "The income of this trust has seriously diminished, the total amount of rents now being collected being only £72.13.6 as against £87.16.8, or in round numbers £13 per annum short after allowing property tax."[4] From this evaluation of the financial situation, one is prepared to read later on that funds from the University Chest were used to augment the salary of the professor; certainly this was the case when Dr. Bosworth was the

Lancaster Rents in Account for the Anglo-Saxon Professorship (1862). WPβ 7/13/14. Reproduced by permission of the Oxford University Archives.

Rawlinsonian Professor (1858-76). A notation from an account book of the University follows.[5]

To Anglo-Saxon Professor, 14 November, 1870
Cash received of Mr. Butler [Agent in Lancashire] . . . . . . £ 68.12.3
Balance from general fund for augmentation of
Professor's stipend to end of March, 1871 . . . . £152.12.3
. . . . £221.5.0

In view of Dr. Rawlinson's overall generosity to Oxford, attention may properly be called not to the meagerness of this bequest (which appears to be here presented as less than adequate) but to the fact that Dr. Rawlinson left to the Bodleian his library, the largest bequest of any benefactor to date;[6] to St. John's College he left his extensive lands; and to the Ashmolean he left his collection of rare medals, portraits, antiquities, statuary, and other art works, as well as a salary in perpetuity for a curator of that museum.[7]

In 1849 John Earle, M.A., Fellow of Oriel, was elected for his five-year period; his term expired in 1854 and from then until 1858 the Chair was vacant. Enough time had elapsed since the date of Dr. Rawlinson's original deed of trust to allow for statutory changes. The *Oxford Historical Register* of this period states that the professorship was then made tenable for life, that the range of the professor's lectures was no longer confined to the language of the Anglo-Saxons, that it might deal also with (a) the history of that people, (b) the Low-German dialects, and (c) the antiquities of northern Europe. The election of the Professor was vested in the Congregation of the University, and the stipend was augmented to £300 per annum from the University Chest. These changes were made by statute and approved by the Queen in Council.[8] At this time it had been 108 years since Dr. Rawlinson had set down his wishes in regard to the Chair. The term "the election was vested in the Congregation of the University" may be interpreted as an indication that Rawlinson's original limitations need no longer apply to the candidates.

In 1894 the University passed a statute to the effect that the Rawlinsonian Professorship should, as soon as it became vacant, be united to the Merton Professorship of English Language and Literature and that the stipend be raised to a figure of £700, which was to come from three sources: the original Rawlinson grant, the University Chest, and Merton College.[9] Dr. Arthur Sampson Napier had become the Merton Professor in 1885; and upon the concurrent Rawlinsonian Professor's death in 1903, the two professorships were joined, the name of the Chair continuing as the Rawlinsonian Professor of Anglo Saxon, Dr. Napier thus becoming holder of the Chair.

Dr. Bosworth, whose term as Anglo-Saxon Professor had been from 1858 to 1876, in the meantime had made his will, which would further alter the University's governing of the Chair. In summary of his will, Dr. Bosworth's heirs were immediate family members who were to enjoy his bequests during their lifetimes, and after the death of the last survivor of these relatives (which occurred in May, 1910), funds were to be transferred to the University. His deed of trust reads[10]

> 7. The University shall stand possessed of the Endowment Funds Upon trust out of the income thereof to pay so much to the Rawlinsonian Professor of Anglo Saxon in the University of Oxford for the time being as shall from time to time be sufficient to augment his Salary as such Professor as aforesaid to Five hundred pounds per annum. And subject thereto shall pay the Income of the Endowment Funds to the Bosworth Anglo Saxon Fellow to be elected as hereinafter mentioned. 8. After the transfer of the Endowment Funds as aforesaid the Vice Chancellor of the University of Oxford for the time being The Very Reverend The Dean of the Cathedral Church of Christ in Oxford for the time being and the Rawlinsonian Professor of Anglo Saxon in the University of Oxford for the time being shall form a Board who shall once in every year elect a person who shall have taken the Degree of Bachelor of Arts in the University of Oxford and whom the Board in their absolute discretion shall deem to be the best Anglo Saxon Scholar of the time and the person so elected as aforesaid shall be called and be the Bosworth Anglo Saxon Fellow.

It is apparent that with the Bosworth funds available for augmentation of the original Rawlinson grant[11] there was no longer a need for financial bolstering from the University Chest and/or funds from the Merton Professorship. It was to the interest of the University to revoke the action of 1894, thus freeing the University and Merton augmentation for other purposes. Although there were dissenting voices (because the action did not follow Dr. Bosworth's instruction in item 8 of the foregoing deed), the new system came into being as recorded in the *Oxford Hebdomadal Report* of January 15, 1913:

> 1. As from the date of approval of this Statute by His Majesty in Council the Rawlinsonian Professorship of Anglo-Saxon shall be separated from the Merton Professorship of English Language and Literature, and the present holder of the united Professorships shall cease to be Rawlinsonian Professor of Anglo-Saxon but shall continue to be Merton Professor of English Language and Literature.
>
> 2. In Statt. Tit. IV. Sect. II. F. § 5 (*a*) (ed. 1912, p. 105), in the title the word "Rawlinsonian" shall be struck out, and the words "Bosworth and Rawlinson" shall be substituted therefor.

3. In Statt. Tit. IV. Sect. II. F. § 5 (*a*) (ed. 1912, p. 105), in clause 1 the word "Rawlinsonian" shall be struck out, and the words "Bosworth and Rawlinson" shall be substituted therefor.

4. In Statt. Tit. IV. Sect. II. F. § 5 (*a*) (ed. 1912, p. 106), clause 2 shall be struck out and the following clause shall be substituted therefor:—

> "2. He shall be entitled to receive the annual sum of £500 per annum payable out of the University Chest, inclusive of the income of the Rawlinson Endowment and of the Bosworth Endowment."

In 1916 Dr. W. A. Craigie became the first to hold the new Chair. Although Item 2 directly above specifies that the name shall be the Bosworth and Rawlinson Professor, the *Yearbook of the Universities of the Empire* (1916 and 1917) lists Professor Craigie as the Rawlinson and Bosworth Professor. This title is correct, and has been consistently used since Dr. Craigie's term beginning in 1916.

The Codicils

Dr. Rawlinson's endowment stated the purpose, listed the lands, and gave instructions in regard to trustees; his codicils took care of additional items and clearly specified other conditions. In the first codicil, signed on 17 June 1752, he requested that the Convocation of the University of Oxford should be the electors of the holder of the Professorship,

> which place I direct to become vacant every ten years; and that the several colleges of the same university do enjoy it one after another upon every vacancy; and that my own college of St. John Baptist, in which I had the happiness to be educated, shall have the first and every fifth turn. And I do further direct that such professor or lecturer so from time to time to be elected, shall continue a bachelor and single man so long as he shall hold the said professorship and enjoy the profits of the said endowments.

The second codicil, signed on 25 July 1754, gave further instruction in regard to the professorship:

> And I do declare and it is my true intent and meaning that no native of Scotland or of Ireland or of any of the plantations abroad, or of any of their or either of their sons, or any present or future member of the royal or antiquary societies, shall have take receive or enjoy any profit benefit or advantage from by or out of any part of my estate, real or personal which I have heretofor given devised or bequeathed for the foundation of any lecture, or to any charitable or publick use, or be capable of being elected into any professorship of my foundation.

The third codicil dealt with other matters and omitted any mention of the professorship, but in the fourth, signed just a few months before his death, he again directed a change; it reduced the professor's term of office from ten to five years, St. John's continuing to have every fifth turn.

Much has been said about the restrictions and limitations on the benefactions in Rawlinson's will, but they are less of a hindrance than they seemed to be and to him they were not unreasonable. Codicil One, as stated above, insists that the holder of the Chair shall be a single man as long as he is in that office. This is not necessarily an eccentric or deep-seated objection to matrimony; instead it can mean merely that Rawlinson wanted the professor to be in residence at the college and thus more available to students. Married men were excluded from living in the colleges at that time.

In the second codicil (1754) Rawlinson was showing his reaction to extremely trying circumstances. According to his wish, no present or future member of the London Society of Antiquaries was to be admitted to election to the professorship, nor was any member of the Royal Society. In looking back at those years, we can see that Rawlinson, who had been one of the most loyal and generous of the membership and who was, in fact, in line for a post of honor in the Society of Antiquaries, was treated shabbily, probably because he was unable to relinquish certain unpopular political positions. Since the Royal Society had almost the same membership, he included it in his ire. Excluding natives of Scotland and Ireland (or their sons) can be better understood when one remembers that Rawlinson, always totally loyal to the Stuarts, felt that Scotland had been less supportive to the Old Pretender (James III) than it could have been in 1715 and also to the Young Pretender in 1745. But why the exclusion of the Irish? Perhaps because they had not been effective against William III, who ousted the Stuart kings. Also because the Irish were considered the "Celtic fringe" and hence in nature similar to the Scots. And why exclusion of those from the plantations abroad? The answer can probably be found in Rawlinson's bitter fate in being forced to extricate the family from debt. One of the contributing factors to the loss of the family fortune was Thomas Rawlinson's investment in the South Sea Company, which was involved in trade with the colonies, and Thomas was not the only loser in the family: William, in Holland, and Constantine, in Venice, also suffered severe losses. In addition, Richard abhorred the slave trade. He wanted no connection with it and, hence, excluded the sons of planters from his benefaction. Finally, Rawlinson was English to the core; he wanted only Englishmen to stand as professors of that Germanic stage of the English language, before Latin and then Norman-French changed it toward what we now speak.

Holders of the Chair

The London *Times* of 14 November 1794 carried the following item:

> On Thursday came on, in full Convocation, the Election of the First Anglo-Saxon Professor, pursuant to the will of the late Dr. Rawlinson. The candidates were the Rev. William Finch, LL.D and the Rev. Charles Mayo, M.A. Fellows of St. John's College. On calling up the Votes the numbers were for Dr. Finch 101, for Mr. Mayo 167.—Whereupon Mr. Mayo was declared elected.

He was the first to hold the Professorship, and he held it for the allotted five years. Dr. Samuel Parr states that his lectures were much applauded.[12]

The second professor was Thomas Hardcastle from Yorkshire, born 1751. In 1769 he matriculated at Queen's College, and in 1775 he became a Fellow of Merton. In 1800 he was elected to the Chair.[13] He was succeeded by James Ingram in 1803, a Fellow and afterwards President of Trinity College. As an Anglo-Saxon scholar, Ingram was no doubt the best of his generation. In 1807 he published his inaugural lecture on the utility of Anglo-Saxon literature to which is added the geography of Europe by King Alfred. In 1823 he published his *Saxon Chronicle,* which is considered superior to any earlier edition.[14]

In 1808 John Conybeare (1779-1824) of Christ Church was elected, leaving the chair in 1812 to become Professor of Poetry at Oxford. An extremely versatile scholar, Conybeare was not only a gifted linguist, but also a divine, a chemist, and a geologist.[15] In 1812 his successor was Charles Dyson (1788-1860) of Corpus Christi College, who held the Chair until 1817, in which year he was ordained and retired to the life of a clergyman in Yorkshire.[16] In 1817 Thomas Silver (1777-1853) of St. John's became the Rawlinsonian Professor. He held the Chair until 1822,[17] at which time John Charles Ridley (1792-1854), Fellow of University College, was elected. Ridley was also a librarian at his college and a divine who held a parish in Norfolk.[18]

Next in succession was Arthur Johnson of Wadham College; very little is known about him except that he was born in Shrewsbury, probably in 1798. He held the chair for only two years, 1827-29. His death occurred in 1853, and it is of interest that his memorial is in memory of A. Johnson Danyall, which name he assumed after his marriage to the daughter of John Danyall, Lord of the Manor of Rampisdam in Dorset.[19]

In 1829 Francis Pearson Walesby of Lincoln College took the Chair and served for his five years. According to a recent history of Lincoln College, he was a person of rather individual interest:

Walesby was extremely able, a witty conversationalist especially after a bottle of port, but somewhat indolent. He became professor of Anglo-saxon in 1829 (though without experience in the subject), and then went to London to practice as a lawyer. He had political ambitions, was Recorder of Woodstock and, in 1857, stood for Parliament against the Marlborough interest and was inevitably defeated. The expenses of the contest impoverished him; he gave up the bar, returned to Oxford as a private coach and died, well alcoholized, on 5 August, 1858.

The account continues with the following footnote:

Octavius Ogle recalled that when he was Subrector, an old member, the Rev. J.M. Jackson (1820) came to place his son Frederick (1858) at College. He mentioned that he would like his son to have a private tutor but objected to the possible choice of Walesby whose pupil he had himself been. "...He was a fellow; and I do not approve of his method of tuition. His method, Sir, was this; I read through with him the second decade of Livy in which, as you are well aware, Sir, the name of Hannibal not infrequently occurs. There was a bottle of port on the table, and whenever he came to the name of the Carthaginian general, Mr. Walesby would say:— "Here's that old cock again! Let's drink his health" never failing to suit the action to the word." Walesby's name often occurs in the College betting book.[20]

Robert Meadows White (1798-1865), who held the Chair from 1834-39, was vastly different from his predecessor. E. Irving Carlyle in writing of him says:

Anglo-Saxon professors at that time were sometimes defined as "persons willing to learn Anglo-Saxon." White, however, was known as a scholar before he was elected to the chair. He had already contemplated the publication of a Saxon and English vocabulary, and only abandoned the project because it appeared likely to clash with the "Anglo-Saxon Dictionary" then being prepared by Joseph Bosworth. On giving up this design, he turned his attention about 1832 to editing the "Ormulum," a harmonised narrative of the gospels in verse, preserved in a unique manuscript in the Bodleian Library. The task, owing to other demands on his time, occupied nearly twenty years.[21]

In 1839 Henry Bristow Wilson (1803-88) of St. John's College was elected, as the University followed Dr. Rawlinson's instruction that every fifth term should be held at St. John's College. As was the pattern with many of the professors in the nineteenth century, Wilson was in holy orders and was presented by St. John's College to a vicarage in Huntingdonshire which he retained until his death.[22] In 1844 William Edward Buckley of Brasenose, a divine, scholar, and antiquarian, became the next in line. His obituary in the *Peterborough Diocesan Magazine* stresses his fine qualities as a clergyman rather than his years of involvement in the study of the early English language, although his library is said to have included Thorkelin's works on *Beowulf* and numerous manuscript notations on papers written in Anglo-Saxon, as well as a copy of *Beowulf*.[23]

Another professor to make truly significant contributions to the field (and the only one to serve two tenures) was John Earle of Oriel, who occupied the chair from 1849 until 1854, after which it was vacant for four years. During this period legal changes resulting in life-time tenure were made.[24] The first to serve under the new arrangement was Joseph Bosworth, who served from 1858-76. On Bosworth's death, John Earle was reelected and served until he died in 1903. He was only twenty-five years of age when elected for his first five-year term; his second election allowed him twenty-seven more years. These were productive years for both scholars, each of whom had numerous studies and publications to his credit. It is fair to say that all of the Anglo-Saxon professors at Oxford after the middle of the nineteenth century were respected leaders in their field, excelling not only in their lectures but also in their publications many of which are still relied upon. Dr. Bosworth's talents were remarkable. One of the few Rawlinson professors to be educated at Cambridge (having first attended the University of Aberdeen), he was ordained deacon in 1814 and priest in 1815 and became a vicar in Buckinghamshire for the next twelve years—a life which left him time to pursue his literary interests. In 1823 he published *Elements of Anglo-Saxon Grammar,* and in 1826 he published a second grammar, incorporating philological theories of the Danish scholar Rask. In 1829 he went to Holland to serve as a chaplain in Amsterdam and in Rotterdam. While there he began the preparation of his principal work, the *Anglo-Saxon Dictionary,* published in 1838. Other works on the Germanic languages followed, and in 1857, after returning to the life of a clergyman in England, he was incorporated a member of Christ Church, Oxford. The following year he was appointed Rawlinsonian professor. According to his own statement, his works realized for him the sum of £18,000. He made two endowments: in 1867 he gave to the University of Cambridge the sum of £10,000 for the purpose of establishing an Anglo-Saxon professorship; and he left a bequest in his will to Oxford University to fund an Anglo-Saxon lectureship, which was later to be combined by the University with the Rawlinson bequest.[25]

As stated above, John Earle's second term as professor ended in 1903, after which Arthur Sampson Napier came to the Chair. His status as Anglo-Saxon professor was unique in that his chair was at first combined, as earlier stated, with that of the Merton Professorship of English Language and Literature, prior to the separation of the two chairs. Dr. Napier's early years of study were at Manchester College, at Exeter College, Oxford, and at the University of Berlin. During his productive life, which ended in 1916, his contributions to philological studies in both German and English were numerous.[26]

In 1916 William A. Craigie became the first Rawlinson and Bosworth Professor. A Scotsman (contrary to Rawlinson's stated wishes), he was born in Dundee in 1867 and studied at St. Andrews, where he took his M.A. with honors in 1889. Later at Copenhagen he studied the Scandinavian languages before becoming a lecturer at Oriel College in Oxford. For many years he was joint-editor of the *Oxford English Dictionary.* In addition to his English studies, his publications include Scandinavian language and literature, particularly the Icelandic sagas and ancient Norse religions.[27]

The London *Times* of Wednesday, 22 July 1925, announced:

> Mr. John R. R. Tolkien, M.A. (Exeter), Professor of the English Language at the University of Leeds, has been appointed to the Rawlinson and Bosworth Chair of Anglo-Saxon, in succession to Professor W. A. Craigie, to hold office from October 1 next.

(The adjoining column in the *Times* reported the news of ground breaking for the cathedral in Liverpool.) Born in 1892 in South Africa, Tolkien was educated at King Edward VI School in Birmingham and at Exeter College, Oxford, before becoming a fellow of Pembroke College. During World War I he served with the Lancashire Fusiliers after which his academic life took him to the University of Leeds as Professor of the English Language before going to Oxford to serve as the Anglo-Saxon Professor. After fifteen years in this capacity he moved to Merton College, and his later years were devoted to private teaching and writing. His critical essays are universally acclaimed, as is his editing of Anglo-Saxon works. *The Hobbit*, which appeared in 1937, was the first of a series of fantasy writings.[28]

The Chair was not filled in the period 1940-47, probably because the nation was at war or attempting to recover from it. In 1947 Professor C. L. Wrenn (b. 1895), Fellow of Pembroke but educated at Queen's College, was elected, and he held the Chair until his death in 1961. In 1920 he had gone to India to hold the position of Professor of English at the Universities of Madras and Dacca; in 1927 he returned to England and lectured at Leeds University. He held many positions with international language societies and was a visiting professor at a number of universities, several in the United States. He was a prolific writer of books and of scholarly articles for periodicals devoted to language studies.[29]

In 1964 Professor Alistair Campbell was elected after the Chair had been vacant for three years. Born in Birmingham, he attended the University there before going on to a lectureship at Balliol College in Oxford. A gifted linguist, he edited works not only in Old English but also in Latin and Old Frisian. His tenure ended in 1973 and the Chair was again vacant until the election in 1977 of Professor Eric Gerald Stanley, who has filled with distinction many positions in the United States and in England. A member of several different academic societies and the author of numerous Anglo-Saxon studies, he is also co-editor of *Notes and Queries*.[31]

These, then, were and are the scholars whose work was encouraged by their appointment to the Chair. They, in turn, have given added lustre to it by their talents, their enthusiasm, and their diligence. It was for the realization of his ecclesiastical motto, "I Collect and I Preserve" that Rawlinson made this endowment—so that the oldest English manuscripts would be appreciated by future generations and their language venerated in years to come. It was with such thoughts in mind that in 1750 in the lonely recesses of London House he drew up his document. One may imagine his candle guttering and his quill scratching across the pages as he enumerated his lands and their revenues: all that fee-farm rent issuing out of the rectory and parish church of Ulverstone; all that rent issuing out of twelve acres of glebe land of the said rectory of Ulverstone; all that lawful money issuing out of those two watermills called Crake-mills; all that rent payable out of the rectory of Pennington and its tithes of corn; all that rent payable out of the Vaccary called the Greenham; all that rent payable out of all those lands, tenements, houses, edifices, meadows, feedings, and pastures called Sandscale; all that annual rent from Rowse-mill and Little-mill and a third called Argrave-mill—and so the listing continued as he enumerated his Lancaster properties, his manors, lands, tenements, and hereditaments, which he was transferring to Oxford University.

The Rawlinsonian and Rawlinson-Bosworth Professors of Anglo-Saxon at Oxford University

1795-1800 Charles Mayo, Fellow of St. John's
1800-1803 Thomas Hardcastle, Fellow of Merton
1803-1808 James Ingram, Fellow of Trinity
1808-1812 John Conybeare, Student (Fellow) of Christ Church
1812-1817 Charles Dyson, Fellow of Corpus Christi

1817-1822 Thomas Silver, Fellow of St. John's

1822-1827 Charles Ridley, Fellow of University

1827-1829 Arthur Johnson, Fellow of Wadham

1829-1834 Francis Pearson Walesby, Fellow of Lincoln

1834-1839 Robert Meadows White, Fellow of Magdalen

1839-1844 Harry Bristow Wilson, Fellow of St. John's

1844-1849 William Edward Buckley, Fellow of Brasenose

1849-1854 John Earle, Fellow of Oriel

1854-1858 Vacant

[During this period legal changes were made which made it possible for the holder of the Professorship to have lifetime tenure in the Chair.]

1858-1876 Joseph Bosworth, Student (Fellow) of Christ Church

1876-1903 John Earle, Fellow of Oriel

[Second term.]

1903-1914 Arthur Sampson Napier, Fellow of Exeter College

[During this period the Anglo-Saxon Professorship was held in conjunction with the Merton Professorship.]

1914-1916 Arthur Sampson Napier, Fellow of Exeter College

[During this period the Anglo-Saxon Professorship was separated from the Merton Professorship.]

1916-1925 W. A. Craigie, Fellow of Oriel

[The first occupant of the new Chair now named the Rawlinson and Bosworth Professorship.]

1925-1940 J. R. R. Tolkien, Fellow of Pembroke

1940-1947 Vacant

1947-1961 C. L. Wrenn, Fellow of Pembroke

1961-1964 Vacant

1964-1973 Alistair Campbell, Fellow of Pembroke

1973-1977 Vacant

1977 Eric Gerald Stanley, Fellow of Pembroke

Notes

[1] *The Historical Register of the University of Oxford... With an alphabetical record of University Honours and Distinctions, 1220-1900* (Oxford, 1900), with Supplements.

[2] Charles H. Firth, *The School of English Language and Literature: A Contribution to the History of Oxford Studies* (Oxford, 1909), p. 18.

[3] Firth, *The School of English Language and Literature,* p. 10.

[4] Oxford University Archives, W.7.β.7.

[5] *University Account Book,* Oxford University Archives, Mc/A/3/22.

[6] W. D. Macray, *Annals of the Bodleian Library 1754-55* (Oxford, 1890), pp. 168-84; *The Deed of Trust and Will of Richard Rawlinson, of St. John's College, Oxford, Doctor of Laws. Containing his Endowment of an Anglo-Saxon Lecture, and other Benefactions to the College and University* (London, 1755).

[7] *The Deed of Trust and Will of Richard Rawlinson.*

[8] *The Historical Register of the University of Oxford,* p. 66.

[9] *Hebdomadal Council Papers* (Oxford, 1911), pp. 81-82 (21 January 1911).

[10] *Hebdomadal Council Papers* (Oxford, 1910), pp. 1-2 (October, 1910).

[11] Dr. Joseph Bosworth's Will, University Archives. See the *Hebdomadal Council Report* for 15 January 1913 (Oxford, 1913), p. 33 for the specifics of the bequest.

[12] *Dictionary of National Biography,* ed. Leslie Stephen and Sidney Lee, reissued in 22 vols. (London, 1909), 13.170.

[13] Joseph Foster, *Alumni Oxoniensis: The Members of the University of Oxford 1500-1714,* 4 vols. (Oxford, 1891-92), 2.609.

[14] S. Austin Allibone, *A Critical Dictionary of English Literature and British and American Authors,* 3 vols. (Philadelphia, 1902), 1.933.

[15] *Dictionary of National Biography,* 4.986.

[16] *Dictionary of National Biography,* 6.298-99.

[17] *Alumni Oxoniensis,* 4.1296.

[18] *Alumni Oxoniensis,* 3.1200.

[19] Personal correspondence with Mr. Clifford Davies, Keeper of the Archives, Wadham College, Oxford (26 March 1982).

[20] Personal correspondence with the Rev. V. H. H. Green, D. D., Librarian, Lincoln College, Oxford (29 July 1982).

[21] *Dictionary of National Biography,* 21.74-75; *Magdalen College Record* (Oxford, 1815), pp. 265-89; personal correspondence with Mr. Jasper Scovil, Librarian, Magdalen College, Oxford (15 April 1982).

[22] *Dictionary of National Biography,* 21.568; Allibone, *A Critical Dictionary of English Literature,* 3.2771-72.

[23] *Peterborough Diocesan* (March, 1892), n.p.

[24] John Foster Kirk, *A Supplement to Allibone's Critical Dictionary of English Literature and British and American Authors,* 2 vols. (Philadelphia, 1902), 1.531.

[25] *Dictionary of National Biography,* 2.902-04; J. A. Venn, *Alumni Cantabrigienses,* part 2, vol. 1 (Cambridge, 1940), p. 228; Allibone, *A Critical Dictionary of English Literature,* 1.223.

[26] *Who's Who, 1911* (London, 1911), p. 603; Neil Ker, "A. S. Napier, (1853-1916)," in *Philological Essays: Studies in Old and Middle English Language and Literature in Honour of Herbert Dean Merrit,* ed. James L. Rosier (The Hague, 1970), pp. 152-81; *Oxford Historical Register, Supplement 1901-1930* (Oxford, 1930), p. 5.

[27] *Who's Who, 1921* (London, 1921), p. 611.

[28] *Who's Who, 1941* (London, 1941), p. 3148; *Current Biography Yearbook, 1967,* ed. Charles Moritz, et al. (New York, 1967), pp. 415-18; *The Oxford Companion to English Literature,* 5th ed., ed. Margaret Drabble (Oxford, 1985), pp. 986-87; Humphrey Carpenter, *J. R. R. Tolkien, a Biography* (London, 1977).

[29] *Who's Who, 1960* (London, 1961), p. 3320.

[30] *Who's Who, 1973* (New York, 1973), p. 507.

[31] *Who's Who, 1977* (New York, 1977), p. 2285.

Publications on Anglo-Saxon Studies by Rawlinsonian and Rawlinson-Bosworth Professors

This bibliography does not include reviews. Much of the information on publications prior to 1973 is adapted from A Bibliography of Publications on Old English Literature, *ed. Stanley B. Greenfield and Fred C. Robinson (Toronto and Buffalo, 1980).*

James Ingram

Inaugural Lecture on the Utility of Anglo-Saxon Literature: to which is added The Geography of Europe, by King Alfred, including his Account of the Discovery of the North Cape in the Ninth Century (Oxford, 1807).

[The extract from Orosius is provided with the translation and notes from the edition of Daines Barrington, *The Anglo-Saxon Version, from the Historian Orosius—by Ælfred the Great. Together with an English Translation from the Anglo-Saxon* (London, 1773). Appendix contains further short texts in Old English.]

"First Discovery of a Passage to the White Sea," *Gentleman's Magazine* 78/2 (1808), 992-97, 1137-40.

[Translation, notes, and map.]

The Saxon Chronicle, with an English Translation, and Notes, Critical and Explanatory (London, 1823).

[Uses Cotton Otho B.XI (largely destroyed by the fire of 1731), Bodleian Laud Misc. 636, transcripts of Cotton Tiberius A.VI, and Cotton Domitian VIII, and Cotton Tiberius B.I, and Cotton Tiberius B.IV.]

John Conybeare

The Romance of Octavian, Emperor of Rome (Oxford, 1809).
    [Reprinted in *Illustrations of Anglo-Saxon Poetry,* pp. 190-97.]

"An Inedited Fragment of Anglo-Saxon Poetry," *Archaeologia* 17 (1814), 173-75.
    [Reprinted in *Illustrations of Anglo-Saxon Poetry,* pp. 270-73.]

"Account of a Saxon MS. Preserved in the Cathedral Library at Exeter," *Archaeologia* 17 (1814), 180-88.
    [Partially reprinted in *Illustrations of Anglo-Saxon Poetry.*]

"Further Extract from the Exeter Manuscript," *Archaeologia* 17 (1814), 189-92.
    [Reprinted in *Illustrations of Anglo-Saxon Poetry,* pp. 232-35.]

"Account of an Anglo-Saxon Paraphrase of the *Phoenix* Attributed to Lactantius," *Archaeologia* 17 (1814), 193-97.
    [Reprinted in *Illustrations of Anglo-Saxon Poetry,* pp. 224-28.]

"Observations on the Metre of Anglo-Saxon Poetry," *Archaeologia* 17 (1814), 257-66.

"Further Observations on the Poetry of our Anglo-Saxon Ancestors," *Archaeologia* 17 (1814), 267-74.

"Anglo-Saxon Poem on the Battle of Finsborough," in Sir Egerton Brydges and Joseph Haselwood, *The British Bibliographer,* vol. 4 (London, 1814), pp. 261-67.
    [With Latin translation, free English paraphrase, and notes.]

Illustrations of Anglo-Saxon Poetry, edited with additional notes, introductory notices, etc., by William D. Conybeare (London, 1826).
    [Contains selections from various poetic texts, Latin translations, English paraphrases, and literary comments. William D. Conybeare, John's brother, was himself a noted Saxon scholar.]

Thomas Silver

A Lecture on the Study of Anglo-Saxon (Oxford, 1822).
    [Mainly on language, but contains a brief review of literature.]

Robert Meadows White

"Preface" to his edition of the *Ormulum* (Oxford, 1852).
101
[Survey of Anglo-Saxon scholarship from its beginnings. A second edition, published in 1878, was edited by Robert Holt with additions by John Earle.]

John Earle

"A Primitive Old Epic," *Household Words* 17 (1857-58), 459-64.

Gloucester Fragments: 1. Fac-Simile of Some Leaves in Saxon Handwriting on Saint Swithun, copied by Photozincography. . . and published with Elucidations and an Essay; 2. Leaves from an Anglo-Saxon Translation of the Life of St. Maria Ægyptiaca, and a translation and notes (London, 1861).

Two of the Saxon Chronicles Parallel, with supplemental extracts from the others (Oxford, 1865).
[Texts of the versions in CCCC 176 and Bodleian Laud Misc. 636.]

"An Ancient Saxon Poem of a City in Ruins Supposed to be Bath," *Proceedings of the Bath Natural History and Antiquarian Field Club* 2 (1870-73), pp. 259-70.

A Book for the Beginner in Anglo-Saxon (Oxford, 1877).

A Peace of Wedmore (Oxford, 1878).

English Plant Names from the Tenth to the Fifteenth Century (Oxford, 1880).

The Dawn of European Literature: Anglo-Saxon Literature (London, 1884).

"The Beowulf," *The Times* (London), 25 August 1884, p. 6.

"The Ruined City," *Academy* 26 (1884), 29.

"Beowulf I," *The Times* (London), 30 September 1885, p. 3.

"Beowulf II," *The Times* (London), 29 October 1885, p. 3.

A Handbook to the Land-Charters, and other Saxonic Documents (Oxford, 1888).

English Prose: Its Elements, History, and Usage (London, 1890).
> [Contains a brief history of Old English prose with specimens from the eighth to the twelfth centuries.]

The Deeds of Beowulf: An English Epic of the Eighth Century (Oxford, 1892).

"Alfred as a Literary Man," in Alfred Bowker, *Alfred the Great, containing Chapters on his Life and Times* (London, 1899).

The Alfred Jewel: An Historical Essay with Illustrations and Map (Oxford, 1901).
> [Contains comment on the æstel of the Preface.]

Joseph Bosworth

The Elements of Anglo-Saxon Grammar . . . and a Grammatical Praxis with a Literal English Version (London, 1823).

The Origin of the Germanic and Scandinavian Languages and Nations (London, 1836).
> [With a sketch of their literature and short chronological specimens of Anglo-Saxon, Friesic, Flemish . . . originally written as an introduction to his *Dictionary* but prefixed to only a part of the impression. A few copies were printed separately.]

A Dictionary of the Anglo-Saxon Language (London, 1838).
> [Includes a preface on the origin and connection of the Germanic tongues, a map of languages, and the essentials of an Anglo-Saxon grammar.]

A Compendious Anglo-Saxon and English Dictionary (London, 1848).

A Description of Europe, and the Voyages of Ohthere and Wulfstan, Written in Anglo-Saxon by King Alfred the Great; with His Account of the Mediterranean Islands—of Africa—and of the History of the World to the Year B.C. 1413, chiefly taken from Orosius (London, 1855).
> [Contains facsimile from Cotton MS. and from the first part of Lauderdale MS., printed Old English text, literal translation and notes, and a map of Europe in Alfred's time.]

With George Waring, *The Gothic and Anglo-Saxon Gospels in Parallel Columns with the Versions of Wycliffe and Tyndale* (London, 1865).

"Discovery of Anglo-Saxon Manuscripts," *Athenaeum* (1866), 337.

With T. Northcote Toller, *An Anglo-Saxon Dictionary* (Oxford, 1882-98).

Arthur Sampson Napier

"Zu: *Andreas* 1182," *Anglia* 4 (1881), 411.

Über die Werke des ae Erzbischofs Wulfstan, Göttingen dissertation (Weimar, 1882).

Wulfstan. Sammlung der ihm zugeschriebenen Homilien nebst Untersuch-ungen über ihre Echtheit Part 1. Text und Varianten (Berlin, 1883).
   [Part 2 was never published. Not all the homilies are by Wulfstan.]

"A Fragment of Ælfric's *Lives of the Saints*," *Modern Language Notes* 2 (1887), 189-90.

"Bruchstück einer ae Boethiushandschrift," *Zeitschrift für deutsches Alter-tum und deutsche Literatur* 31 (1887), 52-54.
   [Prints a now-missing leaf of Bodleian MS. Junius 186.]

"Ein ae Leben des heiligen Chad," *Anglia* 10 (1888), 131-54.

"The Old-English Poem *The Fates of the Apostles*," *Academy* 34 (1888), 153.

"Ae Glossen zu Isidor's *Contra Judaeos*," *Englische Studien* 13 (1889), 25-27.
   [Continuous interlinear gloss of a copy of Isidore's *De Miraculis Christi* in MS. Bodleian 319.]

"Ae Kleinigkeiten," *Anglia* 11 (1889), 1-10.
   [Short texts on such subjects as Adam, Sarah, Noah, the Virgin Mary, Noah's Ark, etc.]

"A Sign Used in Old English MSS to Indicate Vowel Shortness," *Academy* 36 (1889), 221-22, 254.

"Collation der ae Gedichte im Vercellibuch," *Zeitschrift für deutsches Alter-tum und deutsche Literatur* 33 (1889), 66-73.

"Odds and Ends, III," *Modern Language Notes* 4 (1889), 138-39.
   [On Caedmon's Hymn.]

"Odds and Ends, IV," *Modern Language Notes* 4 (1889), 139.
   [On lines 254-55 of *Andreas*.]

"Ae Miscellen," *Archiv für das Studium der neuren Sprachen und Litera-turen* 84 (1890), 323-27.

    [Prose charms from Bodleian Auct. F.3, 6 and Worcester Cathedral Q.5.]

"Some Points of English Orthography in the Twelfth Century," *Academy* 37 (1890), 133-34.

    [Considers Cotton Vespasian D.XIV and Hatton 38, among other manuscripts.]

"A Passage in the Old English Chronicle," *Academy* 40 (1891), 589.

    [On the entry for A.D. 1086.]

"Bruchstücke einer ae Evangelienhandschrift," *Archiv für Studium der neueren Sprachen und Literaturen* 87 (1891), 255-61.

"Fragments of an Ælfric Manuscript," *Modern Language Notes* 8 (1893), 199-200.

History of the Holy Rood-Tree, A Twelfth-Century Version of the Cross Legend, Early English Text Society 103 (1894).

    [Old English text from Bodleian MS. 343 with facing translation; volume includes two Latin versions and an Old French poetic version.]

With William H. Stevenson, *The Crawford Collection of Early Charters and Documents now in the Bodleian Library,* Anecdota Oxoniensia (Oxford, 1895).

"Two Old English Fragments," *Modern Language Notes* 12 (1897), 53-57.

"Zu *Daniel* 266-7," *Archiv für das Studium der neueren Sprachen und Literaturen* 98 (1897), 397.

"Nachträge zu Cook's *Biblical Quotations in Old English Prose Writers,*" *Archiv für Studium der neueren Sprachen und Literaturen* 101 (1898), 309-24.

    [Further comments on the same subject were published in the same journal 102 (1899), 29-42.]

"Zum ae Boethius," *Beiträge zur Geschichte der deutschen Sprache und Literatur* 24 (1899), 245-46.

"Die ags Fieberbuchwöring (*Archiv* CIV, 123)," *Archiv für das Studium der neueren Sprachen und Literaturen* 104 (1900), 361.

Old English Glosses Chiefly Unpublished (Oxford, 1900).

"Contributions to Old English Literature: I. An Old English Homily on the Observance of Sunday" and "The Frank's Casket," both in *An English Miscellany: Presented to Dr. Furnivall in Honour of his Seventy-Fifth Birthday* (Oxford, 1901), pp. 355-62 and 362-81.

"Zum Archiv CI, s. 313," *Archiv für das Studium der neueren Sprachen und Literaturen* 107 (1901), 105-06.

"The Rule of Chrodegang in Old English," *Modern Language Notes* 18 (1903), 241.

"Notes on the Blickling Homilies," *Modern Philology* 1 (1903-04), 303-08.

"Old English Notes," *Modern Philology* 1 (1903-04), 393-95.

"Contributions to Old English Lexicography," *Transactions of the Philological Society* (London, 1906), 265-358.

"An Old English Vision of Leofric, Earl of Mercia," *Transactions of the Philological Society, 1907-1910* (London, 1910), 180-88.

"The Old English *Exodus,* lines 63-134," *Modern Language Review* 6 (1911), 165-68.

"Two Fragments of Ælfred's *Orosius,*" *Modern Language Review* 8 (1913), 59-63.
  [Prints fragmentary text from Bodleian MS. Eng. hist. e 49.]

The Old English Version of the Enlarged Rule of Chrodegang Together with the Latin Original—An Old English Version of the Capitula of Theodulf Together with the Latin Original—Interlinear Old English Rendering of the Epitome of Benedict of Amiane, Early English Text Society 150 (1916).

W. A. Craigie

"Iraland in King Alfred's *Orosius,*" *Modern Language Review* 12 (1917), 200-01.

Easy Readings in Anglo-Saxon (Edinburgh, 1923).
  [Contains only prose.]

"Interpolations and Omissions in Anglo-Saxon Poetic Texts," *Philologica: Journal of Comparative Philology* 2 (1923-24), 5-19.
  [Notes on *Exodus, Daniel, Christ, Guthlac, Wanderer, Seafarer,* and *Beowulf.*]

"The Meaning of *ambyre wind,*" *Philologica: Journal of Comparative Philology* 2 (1923-24), 19-20.

Specimens of Anglo-Saxon Prose, 3 vols. (Edinburgh, 1923-29).

Specimens of Anglo-Saxon Poetry, 3 vols. (Edinburgh, 1923-31).

"The Nationality of King Alfred's Wulfstan," *Journal of English and Germanic Philology* 24 (1925), 396-97.

J. R. R. Tolkien

"*Beowulf:* The Monsters and the Critics," *Proceedings of the British Academy* 22 (1936), 245-95.
> [This essay was separately issued in London in 1937, 1958, and 1960 and is frequently anthologized.]

"Prefatory Remarks on Prose Translation of *Beowulf,*" in John Clark Hall, *Beowulf and the Fight at Finnsburg* (originally published in London, 1901; this edition ed. Charles L. Wrenn [London, 1940]).

"The Homecoming of Beorhtnoth Beorhthelm's Son," *Essays and Studies by Members of the English Association* 6 (1953), 1-18.

The Old English Exodus: Text, Translation and Commentary, ed. Joan Turville-Petre (Oxford, 1981).

C. L. Wrenn

"The Word 'Goths'," *Proceedings of the Leeds Philological Language Society* 2, part 2 (1929), 125-28.

"Late Old English Rune-Names," *Medium Ævum* 1 (1932), 24-34.

"'Standard' Old English," *Transactions of the Philological Society* (1933), 65-88.

"A Saga of the Anglo-Saxons," *History* 25 (1940-41), 208-15.
> [On Cynewulf and Cyneheard episode, with translation.]

"The Value of Spelling as Evidence," *Transactions of the Philological Society* (1943), 14-39.
> [Reprinted in *Word and Symbol,* pp. 129-49.]

"Henry Sweet," *Transactions of the Philological Society* (1946), 177-201.
[Reprinted in *Word and Symbol*, pp. 150-69.]

"The Poetry of Cædmon," *Proceedings of the British Academy* 32 (1946), 277-95.
[Printed separately (London, 1946) and reprinted in *Essential Articles for the Study of Old English*, ed. Jess B. Bessinger and Stanley J. Kahrl (Hamden, 1968), pp. 407-27.]

Beowulf with the Finnesburg Fragment (London, 1953).

"On the Continuity of English Poetry," *Anglia* 76 (1958), 41-59.
[Reprinted in *Word and Symbol,* pp. 78-94.]

"Saxons and Celts in South-West Britain," *Transactions of the Hon. Society of Cymmrodorian* (1959), 38-75.
[Reprinted in *Word and Symbol*, pp. 16-56.]

"Sutton Hoo and *Beowulf*," in *Mélanges de Linguistique et de Philologie: Fernand Mossé in Memorium* (Paris, 1959), pp. 495-507.
[Reprinted in *An Anthology of Beowulf Criticism*, ed. Lewis E. Nicholson (Notre Dame, 1963), pp. 311-30.]

"Anglo-Saxon Poetry and the Amateur Archeologist," Chambers Memorial Lecture (London, 1962).

"Two Anglo-Saxon Harps," *Comparative Literature* 14 (1962), 118-28.
[Reprinted in *Studies in Old English Literature in Honor of Arthur G. Brodeur*, ed. Stanley B. Greenfield (Eugene, OR, 1963), pp. 118-28. Analyzes references to harps and song in various Old English poems.]

A Study of Old English Literature (London, 1967).

Word and Symbol: Studies in English Language (London, 1967).
[The collected essays of C. L. Wrenn.]

"Some Aspects of Anglo-Saxon Theology," in *Studies in Language, Literature, and Culture of the Middle Ages and Later,* ed. E. Bagby Atwood and Archibald A. Hill (Austin, 1969), pp. 182-89.

Alistair Campbell

The Battle of Brunanburh (London, 1938).

"Two Notes on the Norse Kingdoms in Northumbria," *English Historical Review* 57 (1942), 85-97.

The Tollemache Orosius (British Museum Add. MS. 47967), Early English Manuscripts in Facsimile 3 (London, 1953).

Old English Grammar (Oxford, 1959).

"The Old English Epic Style," in *English and Medieval Studies: Presented to J. R. R. Tolkien on the Occasion of his 70th Birthday,* ed. Norman Davis and Charles L. Wrenn (London, 1962), pp. 13-26.

Contribution on the gloss to *The Vespasian Psalter (British Museum Cotton Vespasian A.i),* Early English Manuscripts in Facsimile 14 (London, 1963).

"Verse Influences in Old English Prose," in *Philological Essays: Studies in Old and Middle English Language and Literature in Honour of Herbert Dean Meritt,* ed. James L. Rosier (The Hague, 1970), pp. 93-98.

"The Use in *Beowulf* of Earlier Heroic Verse," in *England Before the Conquest: Studies in Primary Sources Presented to Dorothy Whitelock,* ed. Peter Clemoes and Kathleen Hughes (Cambridge, 1971), pp. 283-92.

Enlarged Addenda and Corrigenda to the Supplement by T. Northcote Toller to An Anglo-Saxon Dictionary Based on the Manuscript Collections of Joseph Bosworth (Oxford, 1972).

Editor, *Anglo-Saxon Charters I: Charters of Rochester* (Oxford, 1973).

Eric Gerald Stanley

"A Note on *Genesis B, 328*," *Review of English Studies* 5 (1954), 55-58.

"Old English Poetic Diction and the Interpretation of *The Wanderer, The Seafarer,* and *The Penitent's Prayer,*" *Anglia* 73 (1955), 413-66.
    [Reprinted in *Philological Essays: Studies in Old and Middle English Language and Literature in Honour of Herbert Dean Meritt,* ed. James L. Rosier (The Hague, 1970), pp. 458-514.]

With T. D. Kendrick, R. L. S. Bruce-Mitford, H. Roosen-Runge, A. S. C. Ross, and A. E. A. Werner, *Evangeliorum quattour Codex Lindisfarnensis: Musei Britannici Codex Cottonianus Nero D.iv,* 2 vols. (Lausanne, 1956-60).

"The Word 'Alfredian'," *Notes and Queries* 204 (1959), 111-12.

"Hæthenra Hyht in *Beowulf*," in *Studies in Old English Literature in Honor of Arthur G. Brodeur*, ed. Stanley B. Greenfield (Eugene, OR, 1963), pp. 136-51.

"'Weal' in the Old English *Ruin: A Parallel?*" *Notes and Queries* 208 (1963), 405.

"The Search for Anglo-Saxon Paganism," *Notes and Queries* 209 (1964), 204-09, 242-50, 282-87, 324-31, 455-63; 210 (1965), 9-17, 203-07, 285-93, 322-27.

Edited *Continuations and Beginnings: Studies in Old English Literature* (London, 1966).
    [Includes his essay "*Beowulf*," pp. 104-41.]

"Laȝamon's Antiquarian Sentiments," *Medium Ævum* 38 (1969), 23-37.

"Old English '—calla,' 'ceallian'," in *Medieval Literature and Civilization: Studies in Memory of G. N. Garmonsway,* ed. Derek A. Pearsall and Ronald A. Waldron (London, 1969), pp. 94-99.

"Spellings of the *Waldend* Group," in *Studies in Language, Literature, and Culture of the Middle Ages and Later,* ed. E. Bagby Atwood and Archibald A. Hill (Austin, 1969), pp. 38-69.

With A. S. C. Ross, "Glossary to Aldred's Gloss," in T. J. Brown, *The Durham Ritual: A South English Collector of the Tenth Century with Northumbrian Additions (Durham Cathedral Library A.iv.19)*, Early English Manuscripts in Facsimile 16 (London, 1969), pp. 53-92.

"Studies in the Prosaic Vocabulary of Old English Verse," *Neuphilologisches Mitteilungen* 72 (1971), 358-418.

"Some Observations on the A_3 Lines in *Beowulf*," in *Old English Studies in Honour of John C. Pope,* ed. Robert B. Burlin and Edwin B. Irving, Jr. (Toronto, 1974), pp. 139-64.

"Sharon Turner's First Published Reference to *Beowulf*," *Notes and Queries* 22 (1975), 3-4.

The Search for Anglo-Saxon Paganism (Cambridge and Totowa, NJ, 1975).
    [First published in *Notes and Queries* 209 (1964) and 210 (1965).]

"Verbal Stress in Old English Verse," *Anglia* 93 (1975), 307-34.

"Did Beowulf Commit 'Feaxfeng' against Grendel's Mother?" *Notes and Queries* 23 (1976), 339-40.

"How the Elbing Deprives the Vistula of Its Name and Converts It to the Elbing's Own Use in 'Vistula-Mouth'," *Notes and Queries* 24 (1977), 2-11.

"'Sum Heard Gewrinc' (*Genesis B* 317)," *Notes and Queries* 25 (1978), 104-05.

"Geoweorþa: 'Once Held in High Esteem'," in *J. R. R. Tolkien, Scholar and Storyteller: Essays in Memorium,* ed. Mary Salu and Robert T. Farrell (Ithaca, NY, 1979), pp. 99-109.

"The Narrative Art of *Beowulf,*" in *Medieval Narrative: A Symposium,* ed. Hans Bekker-Nielsen, Peter Foote, Andreas Haarder, and Preben Meulengracht Sørenson (Odense, 1979), pp. 58-81.
> [Proceedings of the Third International Symposium Organized by the Centre for Study of Vernacular Literature in the Middle Ages (Odense University, 20 and 21 November 1978).]

"Two Old English Poetic Phrases Insufficiently Understood for Literary Criticism: 'ðing gehegan' and 'seonoþ gehegan'," in *Old English Poetry: Essays on Style,* ed. Daniel G. Calder (Berkeley, 1979), pp. 67-90.
> [Number 10 of the Contributions of the UCLA Center for Medieval and Renaissance Studies.]

"The Date of *Beowulf*: Some Doubts and No Conclusions," in *The Dating of Beowulf,* ed. Colin Chase (Toronto, 1981), pp. 197-211.

"The Scholarly Recovery of the Anglo-Saxon Records in Prose and Verse: A New Bibliography," *Anglo-Saxon England* 3 (1981), 223-62.

"The Prenominal Prefix *ge-* in Late Old English and Early Middle English," *Transactions of the Philological Society* (1982), 25-66.

"The Continental Contribution to the Study of Anglo-Saxon Writings up to and Including That of the Grimms," in *Towards a History of English Studies in Europe,* ed. Thomas Finkenstead and Gertrud Scholtes (Augsburg, 1983), pp. 9-39.

"Alliterative Ornament and Alliterative Rhythmical Discourse in Old High German and Old Frisian Compared with Similar Manifestations in Old English," *Beiträge zur Geschichte der Deutschen Sprache und Literatur* 106/2 (1984), 184-217.

"Notes on the Text of *Christ and Satan*, and on *The Riming Poem* and *The Rune Poem*, Chiefly on *Wynn, Wen* and *Wenne*," *Notes and Queries* 31 (1984), 443-53.

"Unideal Principles of Editing Old English Verse," *Proceedings of the British Academy* 70 (1984), 231-73.

"Ælfric on the Canonicity of the Book of Judith: 'Hit Stent on Leden þus on ðære Bibliothecan'," *Notes and Queries* 32 (1985), 439.

"Notes on the Text of *Exodus*," *Leeds Studies in English* 16 (1985), 240-45.

"Old English Tō-gedēgled: A Ghost Word," *Notes and Queries* 32 (1985), 10.

"The Treatment of Late, Badly Transmittted and Spurious Old English in a Dictionary of That Language," in *Problems of Old English Lexicography*, ed. Albert Bammesberger (Regensburg, 1985), pp. 331-67.

"Notes on the Text of the Old English *Genesis*," in *Modes of Interpretation in Old English Literature*, ed. Phyllis R. Brown, Georgia R. Crampton, and Fred C. Robinson (Toronto, 1986), pp. 189-96.

"Rudolf von Raumer: Long Sentences in *Beowulf* and the Influence of Christianity on Germanic Style," *Notes and Queries* 33 (1986), 434-38.

A Selection of Illustrations from Manuscripts Collected by Richard Rawlinson

Much is said in this volume about the size and diversity of the collections Richard Rawlinson bequeathed to the Bodleian Library. It should be noted, however, that the collection includes not only papers, letters, rare books, and copperplates but also a number of illuminated manuscripts produced in the Middle Ages and the Renaissance. The following are but samples of the artistic treasures Rawlinson collected and preserved.

MS. Rawl. D. 939, Part I
New Testament Scenes, The Annunciation (c. 1370)
Reproduced by permission of the Bodleian Library.

MS. Rawl. G. 185, fol. 43ᵛ
The Derby Psalter (14th c.)
Reproduced by permission of the Bodleian Library.

MS. Rawl. G. 185, fol. 81ᵛ
The Derby Psalter (14th c.)
Reproduced by permission of the Bodleian Library.

MS. Rawl. liturg. d. 6, fol. 1
Private Prayerbook of Vladislav, Prince of Poland (c. 1470)
Reproduced by permission of the Bodleian Library.

MS. Rawl. liturg. b. 1, fol. 233
Missal, Initial C(oncede), English (Whitby, 14th c.)
Reproduced by permission of the Bodleian Library.

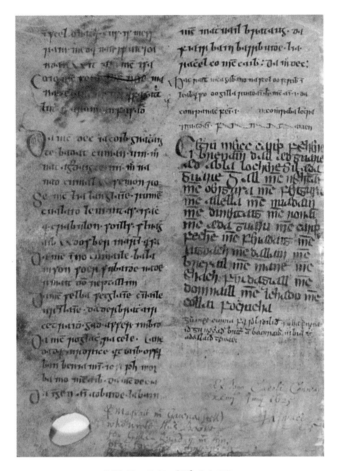

MS. Rawl. B. 486, fol. 75ᵛ
Colophon at end of Macgawan's "Six Ages of the World"
Reproduced by permission of the Bodleian Library.

MS. Rawl. D. 939, Part II
Occupations of the Months
December, Feasting (late 14th c.)
Reproduced by permission of the Bodleian Library.

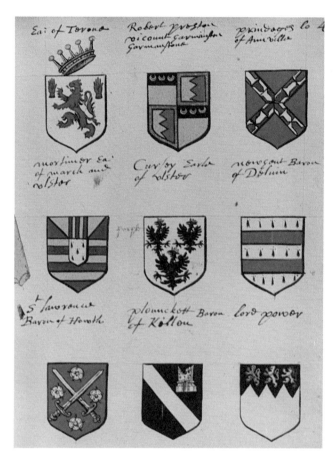

MS. Rawl. B. 69, fol. 40
Irish Heraldry: Arms of Irish Families of the Period of Charles I (17th c.)
Reproduced by permission of the Bodleian Library.

Richard Rawlinson and the Chandlers

"I know you are a universal collector" wrote Edward Umfreville in a manuscript[1] he presented to his friend Richard Rawlinson, whose collections in the Bodleian Library defeat the most persistent attempts at analysis. Macray, searching for Rawlinson's interests and purpose in collecting, indicated the peculiar strength of the collections—seventeenth-century history, heraldry, biography, and topography—but he hastened to refer to their "omnigenous" character "so that students of every subject now bury themselves in their stores with great content and profit."[2] Another writer saw no point in seeking for an explanation which did not really exist, remarking perfunctorily that Rawlinson *"avait au plus haut degré l'amour de la curiosité: ses collections étaient nombreuses, mais confuses."*[3] It is easy to avoid the problem and conclude that Rawlinson collected for the love of collecting, for the pride of possession; but such an explanation does not account for the extreme generosity he exhibited in lending his curiosities to contemporaries, many of whom failed to return them,[4] nor for his final bequest. The waste-paper trade of the eighteenth century may perhaps supply a slightly more satisfactory solution.

The waste-paper monger of the eighteenth century was a common enough figure for Hogarth to include in his cartoons, chanting "waste paper for shops."[5] The stamp duty on newspapers made it economical for traders to buy up unsold sheets of books and even to use the pages when stitched. Pope's reference to the popular undignified use of learned tomes

> … twelve of amplest size
> Redeem'd from tapers and defrauded pies[6]

is well known, and John Radcliffe, a Southwark chandler, is said to have become interested in book collecting through seeing so many manuscript and printed leaves used for wrapping the articles of his trade.[7] Rawlinson was well aware of the problem.[8] Tanner wrote to him describing his joy at finding "part of the John Stow's MS. written with his own hand," adding sadly, "I fear that a good deal of it has been destroyed by rats, mice and women putting it under pies."[9] Rawlinson himself wrote to Brett exulting over the calamity which had befallen a work attacking the Non-jurors: "I have seen Dr. Rye's book which I believe has grown scarce, not for its value, but like some others, the Impression has supplied the Pye shops and Trunk makers for some time."[10] Unfortunately the traders were not always so discriminating in their choice of material, and much of Rawlinson's energy was consumed in the twofold task of searching their stocks and preserving useful documents from their counters. Rawlinson would have endorsed Sir Thomas Phillipps's announcement of the principle on which he had constructed his massive collection:

> In amassing my collections of Mss. I commenced with purchasing every-thing that lay within my reach to which I was instigated by reading vari-ous accounts of their destruction. . . . My chief desire for preserving vel-lum Mss. arose from witnessing the increasing destruction of them by goldbeaters; my search for charters and deeds by their destruction in the shops of gluemakers and tailors.[11]

All Rawlinson's activities at auctions and in booksellers' shops, his obse-quious attentions at the deathbeds of other collectors,[12] and his relentless search after stray papers, become more comprehensible when interpreted as a campaign waged against the waste-paper merchants rather than as a symptom of advanced bibliomania. The purchase of Gandy's papers (1734),[13] what Morant described as the "refuse of William Holman's papers" (1752),[14] Thomas Hearne's collections (1747),[15] and the Thurloe state papers (1751),[16]—to name only the more spectacular hauls—probably preserved many of the papers from being discarded to the grocers. The interesting vol-ume of the Alexander Pope-Cromwell correspondence[17] and the papers of Sir Thomas Browne[18] were almost certainly acquired from Curll, whose in-terest in manuscripts expired immediately he printed them.

Distinct from the preservation of papers from the traders was Rawlin-son's search among those already in their possession. It was a task for which he was eminently suited. He had no regard for elegant dignity and did not hesitate to pursue his investigations personally. He probably kept before him the example of his model Anthony Wood, who, his nephew reported, "used to rake in the Boghouses for papers thinking to find something of scandal."[19] Specialized knowledge, of hands and contents, such as Rawlinson pos-sessed, was indispensible and brought a large dividend. There was an ele-ment of luck and uncertainty which whetted Rawlinson's appetite, but when successful in identifying valuable papers he could purchase them for little more than they cost the trader, who bought them by weight. Regard-less of the consumption of his own time and energy, no one was more pleased than Rawlinson at making a good bargain. Attached to such discoveries was a certain publicity which Rawlinson loved to court; the learned world had reason to be grateful to him for his devotion and perseverance, and its interest had been aroused by the novelty of the rescue. Immediately he had recovered the Pepys papers he displayed some of them before the Society of Antiquaries.[20] It was the best way of securing allies for the fight with the chandlers.

Rawlinson opened the struggle before he went abroad in June 1720. On 21 March 1719 Hearne recorded that Rawlinson "hath procurid many MSS. Papers of Mr. Nich. Lloyd that wrote ye Hist. and Poetical Dictionary, among w[ch] is an Account of Mr. Lloyd's and his Father's life."[21] Hearne welcomed the acquisition of the manuscripts which now number seven separate volumes and was willing to admit that Lloyd "was a good scholar and there may be some good things in the papers you speak of."[22] Rawlinson was not slow to make full use of the papers. His edition of Aubrey's *The Natural History and Antiquities of the County of Surrey* was almost ready for the press when he recovered the papers, and he mentioned Lloyd who, he maintained, would have secured a greater reputation had his papers "lately retrieved from waste paper" been published.[23]

On Rawlinson's return from abroad in April 1726 he resumed his searches with greater vigor. His straitened circumstances resulting from his brother Thomas's debts made the quest more attractive as the main means of enlarging his collections. Richard Roach's papers, now bound into ten volumes, probably came to him as a reward for his industrious searches. It was through Hearne that we learn of the discovery. Roach had been a fellow of St. John's, Rawlinson's old college,

> but expelled for non-residence about 1700. Dr. Rawlinson hath found some papers of his of a surprising nature. He had the character of a learned honest man, but (it seems) was of an unsettled head...dyed a Millenarian. Among the said papers are letters from learned men in the Latin tongue from whence may be perceived that Dr. Blake, Dr. Knight &c. were not averse to the Philadelphian notions; but as they have seen their errour Dr. Rawlinson has some thoughts of committing them to the flames.[24]

Rawlinson could not bring himself to destroy the papers after their earlier escape; as a non-juring bishop he may have been afraid to keep such documents in his possession, for at the end of the year he sent them to the Bodleian through Hearne, giving the latter permission to study and transcribe the papers. Hearne was equally chary of reading the heretical author "looked upon as a sort of Madman" and dispatched them to the safe keeping of Mr. Fisher.[25]

Rawlinson's respect for the papers of scholars with opinions differing from his own can be observed again in his recovery of the Presbyterian Robert Fleming's papers. In a postscript to a letter to Brett he announced that "the other day I discovered amt a large heap of paper, papers lately belonging to a presbyter and teacher one Fleming."[26] The purchase must have been made some time between 21 July 1735 when the letter was dated and 7 August when the postscript was added. Fortunately, among some fragmentary accounts, an entry dated 8 August records Rawlinson's payment of £6. 15s. for the manuscripts,[27] an extremely cheap acquisition.

After 1735 and the conclusion of the sales of Thomas's books, Rawlinson was once more able to devote more time to scholarship and, having undertaken a continuation of Wood's *Athenae Oxonienses,* visited Oxford frequently. It was in 1738 on one of these visits to Oxford that he recovered the papers of Archbishop Sancroft which are now among his collections. Sancroft's papers had always fascinated Rawlinson. He was tireless in his searches for them at Lambeth and in his request for loans from Lord Oxford,[28] and much of his correspondence with Thomas Tanner centered on the archbishop's papers in the latter's possession. He waited for Tanner's bequest of manuscripts to arrive at Oxford and complained to Brett that "since they were neither catalogued nor digested I could not then make the use I intended hereafter of them. Amt them are several of Archbp. Sancroft which I shall look narrowly into."[29] During the next few years "he took much pleasure in Oxford amt Archbp. Sancroft's Mss."[30] and transcribed whole volumes personally; but to his delight his bookseller friend and agent, Fletcher of the Turl, was able to put him in contact with some of the originals. Rawlinson annotates one of the Sancroft manuscripts in his possession "15 August 1738. This original collection of papers relating to Archbp. Sancroft and his affairs I purchased from Mr. Fletcher Bookseller in the Turl in Oxford who had them with other Books &c. from Bp. Tanner's executors."[31] A week later he announced his triumph to Brett:

> By means of a friend I have met with several papers once the property of Archbp. Sancroft some relating to his private affairs, others to the Kentish part of his province, testimonials for pluralities, petitions for benefices &c. most endorsed by his own hand. They like many other papers were retrieved from waste at little more than the weight price.[32]

London proved an equally profitable hunting ground. Rawlinson had been abroad when the sale of Sir John Cooke's books and papers took place in Bristol in February 1722.[33] Nearly twenty years later he recorded his good fortune to Rawlins:

> Last week I met with a collection of ecclesiastical causes, several of notes, which formerly belonged to Sir John Cooke, Advocate General and Dean of the Arches. They were sold by his nephew's widow to support pyes, currants, sugar, &c., and I redeemed as many as came to 12s. at 3d. a pound, which I intend to digest and bind up. Amongst the rest are the causes of Bp. Watson, the Duchess of Cleveland with the whole process, sentence, original letters &c.[34]

Cooke's papers now number ten volumes; twice as many of bishops Compton and Robinson were recovered by Rawlinson two years later:

> I lately rescued from the grocers and chandlers &c. a parcel of papers once the property of Compton and Robinson, successively Bps. of London. Amongst those of the first were original visitation and subscription books, letters and conferences during the apprehensions of Popery amongst the clergy of this diocese, remarkable intelligences relating to Burnet and the Orange court in Holland in those remarkable times before 1688, minutes of the proceedings of the Commissioners for the Propagation of the Gospel and a great variety of other papers. Amongst those of Bp. Robinson, numbers of the originals relating to the transactions at the treaty of Utrecht, copies of his own letters to Lord Bolingbroke and originals Lord Bolingbroke, Lord Oxford, Electress and Elector of Hanover, Ormonde, Strafford, Prior &c.; letters from the Scots deprived bishops to Compton and variety of State papers. They belonged to one Mr. [Anth] Gibbon lately dead, who was principal secretary to both the aforementioned prelates.[35]

In the same letter—and perhaps from the same source—Rawlinson spoke of his rescue of some of Archbishop Wake's papers:

> A gent last week met with some papers of Archbp. Wake's at a chandler's shop; this is unpardonable in his executors as all his Mss were left to Christ Church, But quaere whether these did not fall into some servant's hands who was ordered to burn them and Mr. Martin Folkes ought to have seen that done. They fell into the curate's hands of St. George's, Bloomsbury.[36]

The papers, now contained in two volumes,[37] were of great interest to contemporaries especially to those who, like the oriental scholar Thomas Hunt, had had an opportunity of consulting the main bulk of the collection in Christ Church: "I think I know his handwriting,"[38] he wrote to Rawlinson, and congratulated him on the recovery of the manuscripts.

Two more volumes of papers[39] belonging to Edward Meredith, a Jacobite exile in Italy, were recovered in 1743. Rawlinson, enumerating the treasures he had purchased, added in a letter to Rawlins:

> There are also originals of the Duke of Perth's, Berwick's, F. Sanders, Sabran, &c. and a sketch of the life of James II, an original renunciation of Popery by one John Gordon a Jesuit, and other uncommon papers which I rescued from the chandlers.[40]

To the same scholar he announced that "a few days since I retrieved some MSS. which belonged to the late Mr. Orme a non-juring clergyman by the neglect of his widow fallen into a Presbyterian bookbinder's Hands." Robert Orme died 14 January 1734,[41] and on 24 March, sometime before 1737, Rawlinson paid £1. 5s. 6d. for his papers, as the erased fragmentary accounts disclose.[42] The manuscripts may have been lent and lost or perhaps were mistaken by Rawlinson and are hidden among his manuscripts under a disguise, but the entry reveals his eagerness to secure manuscripts relating to his fellow Non-jurors from the clutches of the chandlers.

The last triumph Rawlinson secured, and a fitting climax to his efforts, was his acquisition of some of Samuel Pepys's papers in 1749. Rawlinson was deeply interested in Pepys, not only because of the important position he filled in the Admiralty under Charles II and James II, but because he had been a Non-juror and a frequent visitor at the Mitre tavern kept by Richard's grandfather, Daniel Rawlinson.[43] In April 1749 Thomas Bowdler, whose father had worked with Pepys, sent a letter to his fellow Non-juror Rawlinson:

> I congratulate you on the purchase you have made and whenever I come next to town I will take the liberty to wait on you for probably by seeing only the covers of the MSS. I might give a guess whether they are Mr. Pepys; not that I have any great doubt of their having been his from the circumstances of the letters to and from him. Had you told me from what quarter you got them it would have given me some light into the affair.... Mr. Pepys by his will left his books and MSS. to Magd. Coll. Cam. and they are now to be seen though some people say they have not had fair play since they have been there.... I cannot guess where these papers have been all this time.... My father had himself a pretty large collection of MSS. relating to naval affairs, among them some original books of ye office; whether they are of any use is more than I know, but I know he kept them in nice order and valued them much. As my brother took to the sea service my father gave him all those naval books and papers, and he still has them and I believe would be glad to dispose of them ... tho'

by the short account you give me of those you have bought I almost suspect they were his and that you bought them from somebody he has employed to sell them. The original letters, the numbers on ye covers & the
empty covers all answer very well to those my brother had. If they were
his I fancy you have a valuable collection for a little money.... P.S. The
more I think of it the more I am convinced they were his.[44]

The gradual development from suspicion to certainty in Bowdler's letter is
convincing, and a few months later he furnished Rawlinson with more details concerning Pepys and the manuscripts Rawlinson had acquired: "I neither know whose they were or how my father got them. I well remember he
esteemed them much and I heartily wish you had had them all but I doubt
those which are lost were most worth keeping."[45] Bowdler's next letter
ended all doubt as to the origin of the papers and hinted at the way in which
Rawlinson had gained possession of them:

> When I first heard the fate of my father's naval papers I was as you may
> imagine a good deal vexed for he had put them in very exact order and
> thought them a collection of some value and I think he could not but be
> in some measure a judge of such things. Had the whole collection fallen
> into your hands I should have been well content, but I doubt many of
> them are destroyed. Pray Sir does the Catalogue mention the titles of all
> the Books and papers or only of the books? There were a great many pa-
> pers tyed up in bundles and I suppose the Catalogue can hardly mention
> the titles of both those. I once looked into one or two bundles. I thought
> there seemed to be some curious things. If you think ye Capt. has still
> any of them by him, I presume you may have them if you will send a let-
> ter to him by the post saying that you hear he has such things to dispose,
> of which you should be glad to buy. If you don't care to write in your
> own name you can make use of any other; the direction is to Capt.
> Bowdler at Canterbury. I should imagine the person at whose house they
> [the MSS.] were lodged could tell you whether the Capt. sold all or only a
> part. I am sorry this affair is known at Cambridge; the mention of it here-
> after will be no great credit to the Bowdlers.[46]

Rawlinson took Bowdler's advice and noted writing to the Captain on 19
August 1749.[47] We are as anxious to know the result of the inquiry as was
Thomas Bowdler,[48] but there is no evidence to show that the manuscripts,
which now amount to nearly a hundred volumes, were acquired in two
blocks. Rawlinson was delighted with his good fortune and his success in
rescuing the manuscripts from the dealers. He informed Rawlins:

> I have purchased some part of the fine collection of Mr. Pepys, secretary
> to the Admiralty during the reigns of King Charles II and King James II.

> Some are as old as King Henry VIII. They were collected with a design
> for a Lord High Admiral, such as he [Pepys] should approve, but these
> times are not yet come and so little care was taken of them that they were
> redeemed from *thus et odores vendentibus.*[49]

He wrote frequent detailed letters to his Cambridge friend Dr. Richardson concerning the papers and received equally detailed replies to his inquiries about those contained in Magdalene College.[50] The discovery of the papers caused something of a stir in the learned world. Some were shown before the Society of Antiquaries;[51] many were lent to Carte and subsequently endorsed "Mr. Carte has seen this";[52] and George Vertue "was well pleased with a view of" the state of Tangier[53] and referred to Rawlinson's recovery of the manuscripts in his notebooks.[54] The importance of Rawlinson's haul has been confirmed by Pepys's latest biographer[55] and by the use which has been made of the documents for naval history.[56]

Rawlinson realized that his task was not complete; his work in preserving papers from the destructive hands of the dealers cannot but be admired, but he could not rest there. What was to happen after his decease? Would the safety of the papers he had so carefully and with so much difficulty preserved be imperilled again? Would someone less conscientious and knowledgeable than himself discard what might be considered unimportant? The weapon Rawlinson was to use was binding. Rawlinson's bindings are notoriously ugly. Unlike his brother he was responsible for few of the books bearing the Rawlinson arms;[57] it was extravagant—the money was, in his opinion, far better spent purchasing additional manuscripts—and in some cases it was harmful.[58] Nevertheless it was impossible to leave much of the material he had saved from the chandlers in its original condition; to do so would almost certainly ensure its destruction. He declared his policy quite freely to Rawlins: "The better to preserve letters and strengthen them I put all sizes first by dates and then each of them within a single sheet of paper and with these precautions and strengthened thus it is hoped they will be of no use to chandlers &c., the sad fate of many valuables."[59] Again he wrote: "I go on digesting and binding up my papers as I think you should Dr. Charlett's correspondence least these kinds of things should be lost or disregarded by those who come after us."[60] Bindings in an old parchment lease is the only way to "rescue them from the shops."[61] His second weapon, in addition to binding, was his bequest of his manuscripts and annotated printed books, which included all he had rescued from the chandlers, to the Bodleian Library. While his collections there were not safe from the demands of parsonages[62] and Oxford colleges,[63] there was no danger that the manuscripts recovered from chandlers would return to the shops.[64]

We cannot leave Rawlinson and the chandlers in perpetual enmity. Rawlinson disliked their practices and probably their trade; but like capital and labor, the two parties soon discovered that their aims and interests were identical. With a little cooperation and trouble, the chandlers realized that Rawlinson's passion paid them an immediate profit, and the arrangement turned out to be mutually advantageous. Rawlinson's own methods were not above reproach. His treatment of the leases for binding his treasures exasperate the modern archivist, and the bibliographer is equally at a loss to understand why he preferred incunabula to blank leaves as endpapers. He sent Brett an old paper and the instruction: "If of no other use than to light your pipe, as such freely use it."[65] Rawlinson had something in common with the opportunist chandlers, and, as well as being their best customer, was probably one of their best suppliers of waste paper. His eagerness to digest and bind his papers caused him to discard what he considered unimportant. "I am digesting and putting together my MSS.," he wrote to Rawlins, "and am gleaning my large collection in order to contract my compass and throw out a great quantity of chaff, for we collectors are insensibly overwhelmed with learned paper buried in dust."[66] He blandly declared: "As in all collections there must necessarily be a quantity of rubbish, I shall begin and sift them [MSS.] and contract my quarters."[67] We are forcibly reminded of his treatment of some of his brother's books during the auction sales. Writing to Hearne, he announced: "I am now clearing off my rubbish books by tale, or at worst, weight,"[68] and later added that the prices bidders were prepared to pay for imperfect Caxtons were so "incredibile trifling that [for] those [books] that are bulky, the chandlers and the grocers are the best chapmen."[69] The entries in the auction accounts for sales of waste paper were far from being few or insignificant[70] and might almost justify our calling Rawlinson the chandlers' ally. Rawlinson's collaboration with the chandlers is amply compensated for by the treasures he preserved from their stores; his activities, besides adding to his fame, may perhaps exonerate him from charges of stealing manuscripts and books from other libraries and collections.

Notes

This article originally appeared in the *Bodleian Library Record,* 4 (1953), 216-27, and is reproduced here, with slight modification, with the permission of Dr. Brian J. Enright and of the *Bodleian Library Record.*

[1]MS. Rawl. C. 317. init.

[2]W. D. Macray, *Annals of the Bodleian Library 1754-55* (Oxford, 1890), p. 234.

[3]*Nouvelle Biographie Générale depuis les temps les plus reculés* jusqu'a nos jours, ed. J. C. F. Hoefer, 46 vols. (Paris, 1857-66), 41.731.

[4]MS. Rawl. C. 811. Many of the entries recording loans are endorsed "lost."

[5]A. Dobson, *William Hogarth,* new and enlarged edition (London, 1907), p. 16.

[6]*The Dunciad,* 1.156.

[7]S. de Ricci, *English Collectors of Books and Manuscripts (1530-1930) and Their Marks of Ownership* (Cambridge, 1930), p. 117.

[8]It was not a problem peculiar to the eighteenth century. Leland commented on the use of the books from the monastic libraries "some to scour their candlesticks, and some to rub their boots; some they sold to grocers and soapsellers, and some they sent oversea to the bookbinders, not in small numbers, but at times whole ships full to the wondering of foreign nations." Hazlitt emphasized that the pulping-mill had been as busy as the printing press and that recently war had added "a new danger of indiscreet zeal in salvage" (C.T. Flower, "Manuscripts and the War," *Transactions of the Royal Historical Society,* 4th ser., 25, p. 15).

[9]MS. Rawl. lett. 30, fol. 27 (29 August 1735).

[10]MS. Eng. th. c. 33, fol. 446 (12 December 1746).

[11]"Preface" to Phillipps's catalogue; quoted in de Ricci, p. 117.

[12]E.g., John Blackburne, Henry Gandy.

[13]MSS. Eng. th. c. 33, fol. 24; c. 32, fol. 34.

[14]MS. Rawl. lett. 27c, fol. 145; John Nichols, *Literary Anecdotes of the Eighteenth Century,* 9 vols. (London, 1812-15), 2.705.

[15]MS. Rawl. D. 1167.

[16]MS. Rawl. C. 989, fol. 169.

[17]MS. Rawl. lett. 90.

[18]MSS. Rawl. D. 108, 109, et seq.

[19]MS. Rawl. lett. 114*, fol. 248. An anecdote strangely reminiscent of *The Dunciad,* 1.144.

[20]BL. Add. MS. 5151, fol. 310.

[21]*Remarks and Collections of Thomas Hearne,* ed. C. E. Doble, D. W. Rannie, and H. E. Salter, 11 vols. (Oxford, 1886-1915), 6.321 (O.H.S.). Hereafter cited as Hearne, *Collections.*

[22]MS. Rawl. lett. 114*, fol. 131c.

[23]J. Aubrey, *The Natural History and Antiquities of the County of Surrey,* 5 vols. (London, 1719), 5.140.

[24]Hearne, *Collections,* 10.404 (15 April 1731).

[25]Hearne, *Collections,* 11.9 (22 December 1731). About the same time Hearne noted: "Dr. Rawlinson met lately with a book (among some rubbish) printed in black letter, and intitl'd De neutralibus et mediis, grosly inglyshed Jacke of both sydes . . . London . . . 1562" (Hearne, *Collections,* 11.7).

[26]MS. Eng. th. c. 33, fol. 235.

[27]MS. Rawl. J. 8°. 4, fol. 23v.

[28]*Report on the Manuscripts of His Grace the Duke of Portland Preserved at Welbeck Abbey,* Royal Commission on Historical Manuscripts, 6 vols. (London, 1899-1931), 6.29 (16 May 1730).

[29]MS. Eng. th. c. 33, fol. 8 (4 December 1736).

[30]MS. Eng. th. c. 34, fol. 493 (11 November 1739).

[31]MS. Rawl. lett. 59.

[32]MS. Eng. th. c. 34, fol. 261 (22 August 1738).

[33]Mus. Bibl. III. 8°. 2.

[34]MS. Ballard 2, fol. 28ᵛ (13 July 1739).

[35]MS. Ballard 2, fol. 59 (24 June 1741).

[36]MS. Ballard 2, fol. 59 (24 June 1741).

[37]MSS. Rawl. A. 275 and D. 730.

[38]MS. Rawl. lett. 96, fol. 323 (1 February 1751).

[39]MSS. Rawl. D. 21 and lett. 71.

[40]MS. Ballard 2, fol. 83 (25 June 1743).

[41]Hearne, *Collections,* 11.156; H. Broxap, *The Later Nonjurors* (London, 1924), p. 315.

[42]MS. Rawl. J. 4°. 4, fol. 239.

[43]For the connections between Pepys and members of the Rawlinson family, see: *The Diary of Samuel Pepys,* ed. Robert Latham and William Matthews, 11 vols. (Berkeley and Los Angeles, 1979-83), esp. 10.349 and 11.241.

[44]MS. Rawl. lett. 114*, fol. 66 (17 April 1749).

[45]MS. Rawl. D. 923, fol. 280 (10 July 1749).

[46]MS. Rawl. lett. 114*, fol. 65 (5 August 1749).

[47]MS. Rawl. C. 811, fol. 14.

[48]MS. Rawl. D. 293, fol. 291 (24 August 1749).

[49]MS. Ballard 2, fol. 115 (25 January 1750).

[50]MS. Rawl. J. 4°. 31, fol. 106 (5 July 1749); MS. Rawl. lett. 114*, fol. 285 (10 June 1749); MS. Rawl. lett. 114*, fol. 287 (23 August 1749); MS. Rawl. C. 811, fol. 24 (26 August 1749).

[51]BL. Add. MS. 5151, fol. 340 (13 April 1749). In the original minute book of the Society of Antiquaries under that date appears the record: "Dr. Rawlinson showed two MSS. recovered from being made wast paper, formerly part of the collection of Samuel Pepys. There were in the same parcel, above 200 original MSS. relating to the navy, and probably belonging to the public, which falling into ignorant hands have been sold for wast paper, as appear from the covers still remaining."

[52]MSS. Rawl. A. 170 (19 May 1749) and A. 464.

[53]MS. Rawl. D. 916.

[54]*The Note Books of George Vertue Relating to Artists and Collections in England,* ed. Katharine A. Esdaile, Giles S. H. F. Strangways, and Sir Henry M. Hake, 6 vols. (Oxford, 1930-47), 5.75.

[55]A. Bryant, *Samuel Pepys* (Cambridge, 1938).

[56]C. H. Firth, *The Mariner's Mirror: The Journal of the Society of Nautical Research,* vol. 3, p. 18.

[57]C. Davenport errs in ascribing the binding to Richard Rawlinson *(English Heraldic Book-stamps* [London, 1909], p. 323).

[58]MSS. Rawl. D. 863, fol. 117; Rawl. lett. 27ᶜ, fol. 155.

[59]MS. Ballard 2, fol. 94 (28 April 1744).

[60]MS. Ballard 2, fol. 131 (27 June 1743).

[61]MS. Ballard 2, fol. 155 (9 June 1744).

[62]Macray records the return of two parish registers from the Rawlinson collection (*Annals*, p. 309).

[63]Magdalen unsuccessfully applied for the return of a copy of the statutes of the college in 1839 (Macray, *Annals*, p. 339).

[64]The Library was not above making money from waste paper (Macray, *Annals*, p. 313), and some of the Rawlinson printed books appear to have been disposed of in the sales of duplicates. Autographs and annotations were no obstacle but were cut out and pasted in copy-books. Cf. the treatment of Tanner's volumes (MS. Autogr. c. 7.).

[65]MS. Eng. th. c. 34, fol. 261 (22 August 1738).

[66]MS. Ballard 2, fol. 134 (12 July 1743).

[67]MS. Ballard 2, fol. 131 (27 June 1743).

[68]MS. Rawl. lett. 9, fol. 22 (5 February 1730).

[69]Hearne, *Collections*, 9.36 (6 March 1731).

[70]In September and October 1732, he received sums totalling £30 from "Mr. Dunning for waste paper and imperfect books."

The Later Auction Sales of Thomas Rawlinson's Library: 1727-34

I

Over fifty years ago W. Y. Fletcher, in a paper read to the Bibliographical Society,[1] drew attention to the disposal of the libraries of the brothers Thomas and Richard Rawlinson. Since then new materials have come to light concerning the later sales of the books of Thomas Rawlinson, whom Dibdin dubbed "the Leviathan of book collectors" and de Ricci the owner of "the largest library as yet sold in England and, with the Heber library, the largest sold to the present day."[2] This investigation has been prompted by the discovery of considerable numbers of Thomas Rawlinson volumes on the shelves of many libraries today;[3] the distinctive diamond-shaped auction ticket, bearing a number, can quickly be checked against the sixteen catalogues, and can establish, with as much certainty as de Ricci's "hardly noticeable marks of ownership,"[4] yet another stage in a book's pedigree. Why were so many books dispersed (a particularly perplexing question when we find that it was Dr. Richard Rawlinson, as eager a bibliophile as his brother, who organized the later sales)? Is it possible to learn how eighteenth-century book-auctions, especially those taking place in London coffee-houses, were conducted?

As early as 1716 Hearne wrote to his friend, Thomas Rawlinson: "Your Collection of Books is admirable. I hope they will be kept together after your death."[5] Unfortunately his wish was not fulfilled, for Thomas lacked skill in administering the Rawlinson family estates,[6] and soon his eagerness for collecting bibliographical rarities and his search for the perfect copy involved him in considerable debt.[7] In a belated attempt to re-establish the family fortunes Thomas aggravated his woes, for it was reported that he

> had put his Money into the South Sea Stock, and was one of those that
> lost all by that wicked Scheme, in which so many Thousands were

utterly undone...this...was what ruin'd his Fortune, and forced him to run so much in debt, and was the principal occasion of all his Miseries.[8]

It is significant that the first of the sales of Thomas's duplicates began the year following the general collapse.

The auctions were a bitter blow for the enthusiastic collector, and he annotated one of his books, which mentioned the wealth of his collections, with the lugubrious gloss: "God knows for his sinns on sale."[9] Yet the plan was well conceived, as many of the creditors were book-collectors willing to take payment in kind, as Thomas explained to Hearne: "W[t] ever attend me, I never meant You should lose by me....I hope You were acquainted always You might have w[t] books You pleas'd upon y[e] Account, for so other Creditours have had."[10] These sales[11] realized a useful £2,409,[12] and, as Hearne pointed out, the position was far from irredeemable:

> Had he lived some Years longer (w[ch] he might have done by the Course of nature, for he was not, I think, more than 45 or 46 Years of Age), 'tis probable he might have extricated himself, & lived comfortably. For an Estate (I am told, of six hundred Pounds per an.) came to him a few months since by the Death of his Mother, and he had begun to sell his Books in order to pay his Debts, and printed several Catalogues...in w[ch] are many rare, excellent, & uncommon Books, tho' the chief of his Collection was not comprehended in these Catalogues.[13]

There was still a chance that the "chief of his collection," the choicest printed books and all his manuscripts, could yet be saved, for many creditors like Hearne refused to embarrass their friend, while others, if they resented Thomas's "loving to be very free in his Discourse (for as he was born to the Freedom of an English Man, so he said he would make use of it),"[14] would be content to draw interest from what appeared to be a safe investment as long as the Rawlinson family prestige remained high in the City.[15]

The fate of the remainder of the library was sealed by Thomas's "fateful marriage." Richard remarked in sketching his brother's biography:

> In 1724, he married Amy, the daughter of Mr....Frewin who had been first a servant to a Coffee House in Aldersgate Street and afterwards to himself, to the great grief and scandal of himself, family, friends and acquaintance, and indeed to the hastening of his own death.[16]

This catastrophic marriage undermined the creditors' confidence,[17] and Hearne agreed that Thomas's anxiety at being constantly pestered hastened his death:

> The immediate cause of it was a great Concern he had upon account of his Debts, which were very considerable. For after his marrying M[rs] Amy

Frewin, that was a Servant to him, his Creditors were very angry with him, and united to give him trouble. . . . But notwithstanding the Justness of the Debts, I am of the opinion that such as were not under an urgent necessity should have been less violent towards him, especially Booksellers, for whom he had done eminent service. For, being a Man of a brave, noble Spirit, and being a great Lover of Books, in wch I never knew any one whatsoever better skill'd, he took all opportunities of being present at, or at least giving Commissions at, Sales and Auctions, and by his high bidding he strangely advanced the Prices of Books, wch he likewise did in Booksellers' shops, so that I have heard it said long ago (and I am of the same Mind) that the booksellers ought to erect a Statue to him. And yet so ingratefull were they that one of them arrested him for an inconsiderable Sum . . . wch was the beginning of his troubles, and occasion'd him to keep in . . . to the impairing of his Health.[18]

Since 1720 Dr. Richard Rawlinson had been travelling in Europe collecting antiquities as far afield as Sicily and Malta, but when he heard of the death of the family banker and of possible financial reverses he decided to return to England. It was while he was in Genoa that he learned of the death of his brother, but he saw no great reason for haste or alarm. As Thomas had had no children the entailed family estates under the terms of their father's will automatically devolved upon Richard,[19] and it was only natural that he would have expected Thomas to have entrusted what remained of the library to his care. It must have been a cruel blow for him to realize when he returned to England that neither estate nor library was safely in his grasp. As Thomas grew weaker, one of his non-juring friends, William Ford,[20] saw his opportunity not only to intercede on Mrs. Rawlinson's behalf but also to line his own pocket. In May 1725 he "sought Mr. Ward of the Temple's opinion about cutting off the entail" of the Rawlinson estates only to be told that it could be effected by a "common recovery."[21] The advice was immediately taken,[22] for Thomas was sinking fast; only two days before he died he signed a will[23] making over all the family property to Ford (whom he paid liberally for his trouble as executor) to be held in trust for possible heirs of his marriage. Hearne accurately summarized the will:

> He hath ordered all his Books to be sold, in order to pay his Debts, that he hath left 120. . .libs. per an. to his Wife during Life, that he hath left only two Legacies . . . and that he hath died . . . ten thousand libs. in debt.[24]

Not only was Richard not mentioned either as regards the estate or the library, but this "barbarously framed" will made the younger brother's task as difficult as possible. Hearne reported: "D^r. Richd Rawlinson . . . blames his late Brother Thomas to the last degree for his Marriage, docking the entail of the paternal Estate, &c., by wch the D^r. is so very much injured."[25] Richard immediately challenged the validity of the will, and in November 1726 Hearne wrote fervently hoping "to hear of a Compromise with respect to your Late Brother's Affairs. If Things come to the Lawyers, God knows when there will be an end."[26] Richard explained his difficulties to his friend Thomas Rawlins, remarking of his brother's widow:

> Tho' of a good name, Frewen, she came to T[homas] R[awlinson] from an adjoyning Coffea House's service, and after tryal, and pretence of pregnancy was admitted to his bed, afterwards by the force of Gin, broke his heart, drunk so much herself, that no Child was got before, or after his death, tho' endeavours, if fame lyes not, were not wanting. The marriage was clandestine, if any, and the Preist [sic] and witnesses both ran their Country when the next heir [Richard Rawlinson himself] came from abroad, but our good Civilians alledging that she was owned as wife during her husbands life, and in his will, and by that a dowry due to her, it was thought fit to drop the controversy, and by the perswasion of Creditors, to save themselves, and no body else, Dr. R[awlinson] was perswaded to administer, and luckily for that end, the Executor [William Ford] dies, choked with beans and bacon, and one of his Sons (a conscientious man tho' a chief contriver of the Will) pined away in a consumption, and a third broke his neck at a hunting Match. All these removed the Widow comes in next, and Dr. R. is flattered that a plundered Library (for so it really was) would make him amends for giving her 300 pds, and £140 per annum durante vita, commencing Lady Day 1725.[27]

To Thomas Deacon,[28] who had become one of the beneficiaries of the will, Richard Rawlinson outlined his struggle:

> You will know, S^r, excuse these resentments, as you can't be insensible how ill I have been used...I could not, S^r, seal up, before I answer'd an objection which at so great a distance might arise in your mind, and that is the time since this bequest in August 1725, to which I return yt the will was disputed (as it ought to have been yet) for near a year while indispositions &c kept me abroad, that Mr. Ford's death at ye latter end of 1726 both hastened and delayed an agreement, that it removed him out of the way, & deprived him of the sweet morsel he had swallowd in imagination, that circumstances obliged, as well as ignorance how to proceed, the supposed widow for a sum to relinquish her claim, and this was not concluded til 1727, and this agreement much to my loss, but ill advis'd I took on me the administration and have done gratis what others would have paid mercenaries for.[29]

The agreement referred to, dated 18 January 1727,[30] was between Richard Rawlinson and John Tabor who, by marrying the widowed Mrs. Rawlinson, had "gained all her rights." It stated explicitly that it aimed at eliminating the expense and delay which a legal contest would cause while the estate was being bled white paying interest to creditors. As the executor to Thomas Rawlinson's will had died intestate, Tabor agreed to support Richard's claim to a life interest in the estate and to disregard both Thomas's recoveries and his will, provided that Richard would acquiesce in the provision already made for Thomas's widow and indemnify both her and Tabor from Thomas's debts. Richard was to pay the creditors by selling Thomas's personal effects, which Tabor, lacking bibliographical skill, considered were at least "worth a great deal." Tabor was determined not to be cheated and arranged that either he or his deputy should be present when the inventory was taken (for which a time-table was sketched out), while the doors of London House, where Thomas's books lay, were immediately fitted with two sets of locks. The books were to be sold by auction (the manuscripts to be disposed of in a single sale); Richard was to have the option of buying if he was willing to pay the price offered by the highest bidder; but Tabor was to be informed in good time of the dates of each sale, and had the right to attend them, inspect the books, and note the prices. It was only if the auctions did not satisfy the debts that portions of the estate could be mortgaged or sold.

In this document lies the explanation of the enigma why Richard, himself a most eager book-collector, had to dispose of his brother's magnificent collection. Hearne at first could not understand why Richard ignored his plea: "I wish you may preserve his whole Collection of MSS. together, and not part with them, to say nothing of the principal of his printed Books."[31] It also explains the second problem, why Richard, to all appearances in charge of the auctions, was forced to buy at the actual sales instead of using the simpler and more economical method of withholding those items he required. And the third difficulty—the apparent folly of releasing over fifty thousand books and a thousand manuscripts in less than seven years—becomes more comprehensible; it was only then that Richard could begin to control the landed property and that the troublesome interference of Tabor would be terminated.[32]

On 12 February 1727 Hearne reported:

> D[r] Rawlinson...Tells me, that the Business of settling the accommodation about his late brother, is at last finished, and the administration is granted to him of his said Brother's Will, and he is now with all speed entering on the Execution of it, as he hopes to the satisfaction of his brother's creditors, and perhaps, he says, more to his honour than the usage shewed to him may deserve. But as he intends to act with all justice, he doubts not but that Providence, w[ch] has already so visibly appeared in his

Black Ink

5 pints of raine water, halfe a pound
of galls bruised, halfe a pound of lumbrick gum
5 ounces of green copperas let it stand a
fortnight together before it y putt over the
fire stir it every day, let it simmer halfe
an hour over a gentle fire but not
boyl

Red Ink

a pint of middle beer, a pint of beer
vinegar, 2 ounces of brazil, a nobb
of Alum boyl them a quarter of an hour
then strain them off, then boyl them
again putt an ounce and halfe gum
boyl them togetter till all y dissolved
and then you may use it as you
may please

Richard Rawlinson's Recipes for Black and Red Ink. MS. Muniments LXXXVII, 281, St. John's College, Oxford. Reproduced by permission of the President and Fellows of St. John's College, Oxford.

favour, if he may presume to judge the removal of two the chief contrivers against him to another state to be such, the same will, he hopes, yet interpose in his favour.[33]

For Rawlinson the next seven years were fully occupied in arranging ten sales of his brother's library. We may indeed be grateful to Rawlinson for the care with which he recorded the slightest expense in a three shilling "Paper account Book"[34] in case of future disputes or claims by Tabor, for by so doing he has left us an almost day to day record of ten prominent eighteenth-century book-auctions.

The accounts for the period covering the first sale (or the seventh in the main series), on 2 March 1727, read, in part:

[fol. 3ʳ]

1726/7	Expences	£	s–	d
2. Feb.	For a Paper account Book	0–	3–	0
3.	for sweeping Chimnys	0–	1–	0
	Two Grates, 2 pʳ of Tongs, Shovels, Pokers, &c, and a branch of six brass Candlesticks for the Library	2–	17–	6
8.	For a Sack of Coles and small Cole for yᵉ Library	0–	3–	5½
	Pᵈ a Porter a days work for cleaning 2 small rooms	0–	2–	6
9.	Given to Mr. Dixon for a gratification in Chadds affairs	3–	3–	0
	Paid for a Bond of Indemnification	0–	5–	0
	Pᵈ for a Ream of Paper as by receipt	0–	14–	0
10.	For Mopps, Brushes and Brooms	0–	7–	7
	Pᵈ half of the Lease Money for drawing up	0–	10–	6
	Pᵈ Mr. May rent due last Michaelmass	47–	10–	0
13.	Pᵈ for dusting Clothes for the books	0–	1–	0
14.	Pᵈ the Joyner for mending the floor	0–	2–	0
	Pᵈ the Glazier for mending the windows as by recpᵗ	0–	5–	11
17.	A Sack of Coles	0–	3–	3
18.	A Chaldron of Coles, Carriage, and Shooting as by receipt	1–	14–	8
do.	A dozen pound of Candles as by receipt	0–	5–	6
do	for two pairs of Snuffers	0–	0–	6
do.	Pᵈ Mr. Thompson for a weaks work in the Library as p rect.	0–	10–	0
	Pᵈ John Matthews a Porter for one days work in the Library	0–	1–	6
20.	Paid for two earthern Candlesticks for the Library	0–	0–	2

21.	Pᵈ for Coles for the Library as p receipt	1–14– 8
	Pᵈ for Charcole	0– 0– 2½
23.	Pᵈ for a Cole Basket	0– 0– 9
do.	for Past and an Earthern Candlestick	0– 0– 2
25.	Pᵈ Mr. Minshull for taking Catalogues as by receipt	3–13– 6
	Pᵈ Mr. Halsey for taking Catalogues as by receipt	1–11– 6
	Pᵈ John Matthews Porter as by receipt	0– 9– 0
	Pᵈ another Porter	0– 6– 0
28.	Pᵈ for a Cord for the Branch of Candlesticks and Sizzors	0– 0– 4
do.	for a lock and Key to yᵉ Garrett	0– 1– 4
do.	for a Hinge to the Inner door on the great Stairs	0– 0– 6
March 1.	for Six brass Sconces for the Library	0– 8– 6
2.	Pᵈ Mr. Minshull for a pint of Ink	0– 1– 0
	Pᵈ for half a dozen bottles of wine	0–10– 0
	Pᵈ for three dozen of Chairs as by receipt	1–13– 0
3.	Pᵈ Mr. Mishull for Pens, and Sand	0– 0– 7
	Pᵈ Mr. Morgan for four Standishes	0– 0– 8
4.	Pᵈ for Boxes for the Money	0– 0– 5
	Pᵈ Richard the Porter for a week due this night	0–12– 0
	Pᵈ John the Porter for a week due this night	0– 9– 0
	Pᵈ Mr. Halsey for taking Catalogues &c as by recᵗ.	2– 5– 9
	Pᵈ Mr. Minshull for a lock to his desk and packthread	0– 1–10

Richard Rawlinson decided to hold the sale at London House, where his brother had lodged and kept his books, partly, no doubt, to economize on transport costs but primarily, one suspects, so that the repair and furnishing of his own future residence could be met out of the expenses allowed for preparing for the auction. The preparations were somewhat simplified by the Catalogue[35] which Thomas had compiled before he died.[36] This classified the books roughly by the subject, and gave three- and four-line detailed descriptions—an unusual feature at a time when single-line entries were the rule. But Richard took care to advertise the sale, and welcomed patrons who, like Lord Oxford, inspected the books at London House before the sale began, longing "for some choice rarities."[37]

A short note prefixed to one of the Rawlinson manuscripts[38] in the Bodleian Library addressed to the Mr. Minshull mentioned in the accounts draws attention to the actual record which he kept of purchasers' names and prices paid while the auction was in progress. He employed a curious method, opening the account with the buyer of the first folio, leaving a space which he judged to be sufficient for that individual's subsequent purchases, and then inserting the buyer of the second and successive folios. He often miscalculated, and had to make a double column for Lord Coleraine's purchases; and he started anew at the beginning of each day's sale. The absence of a consecutive enumeration of the volumes, the long Continuation added by Richard,[39] and the complexities of the subject and size divisions resulted in chaos and confusion. Sales of "Epistolae" were mixed up with those of "Cicero," "Theologia" overlapped "Ius Civile," while records of bids for "Poetae quarto" volumes had a disconcerting habit of appearing among "Rhetores." It is not surprising to find frequent errors noted in Minshull's auction record, and Richard himself realized how unsatisfactory his brother's system was when he came to organize later sales.

Lord Coleraine[40] was by far the most considerable purchaser, but Minshull's record reveals that the deference paid to Blackbourne, Sloane, Bacon, and Maittaire was not wasted. Richard's name was mentioned but once, and then only to be immediately obliterated, for he thought it wiser to spend £8 on seventy-one items discreetly under assumed names, as a comparison of his manuscript entitled "Books bought by me in my brother's auction"[41] with Minshull's record reveals. Apart from his wish to raise the bidding, he wanted to save books that were either financially or sentimentally valuable, or perhaps he may have thought the prices absurdly low and hoped to improve them by resale.[42] In the middle of the sale Richard wrote to Hearne remarking that "trifles sell extravagantly, but good books indifferently"[43]—a not unfavorable report when compared with his criticisms of later sales.

Declaring himself anxious to hold the next auction before Parliament rose[44] so as to attract book-collectors in the House, Rawlinson opened the eighth sale (26 April 1727) less than a month after the seventh had closed. It was held at Bedford Coffee House in Covent Garden, well known as an auction sale-room and not far from London House. The accounts reveal many of the obscure features of the coffee-house auction:[45]

[fol. 4^r]

1. April	P^d Mr. Halsey for Cataloguing the Books in the Library	1–12– 6
do.	P^d John Matthews for Porterage and marking a week	0– 9– 0
do.	P^d Samuel Lowndes for marking Books in the Library	0– 6– 0
	Given to Mr. Blackbourne for a Catalogue allowed to Mr. Bedell by Mr. Tabor's permission and desire	0– 2– 6
	P^d Robinson for cataloguing one hundred Books	0– 1– 6

15.	P^d Mr. Cooke the bookbinder remaind^r of his bill for Catalogues	0–15– 6
do.	P^d Mr. Reiley the printer on acc^t of the Catalogue as p rect.	6– 6– 0
do.	P^d Sam. Lowndes for marking the Books	0– 6– 0
do.	P^d John Matthews for Porterage and marking the Books	0– 9– 0
do.	P^d Mr. Halsey for cataloguing	1–11– 6
do.	P^d Mr. Greated for cataloguing 1000. Books	0–15– 0
	P^d Mr. Porteous for catalog. & marking 700: Books	0–12– 0
18.	Paid Mr. Nutt for advertising last auction in Daily Post as p rec^t.	3– 0– 0
21.	Paid Davis's Porter for bringing Sacks & carr. Catal- [sic]	0– 1– 0
do.	Paid postage for Catalogues by the penny post	0– 4– 3
22.	P^d Mr. Reiley the Printer the remainder for the Catalogue	7–14– 0
do.	P^d Cart, Coach, Candles, Porters, drink &c	0– 7–10$\frac{1}{2}$
do.	P^d for letters with Catalogues by the penny post	0– 0– 9
29.	Paid Mr. Greated for cataloguing and writing 4. Nights at y^e auction	0–12– 2
	Paid John Matthews for his Porterage & his sons attendance during the time of the Sale	0–12– 0
May 1.	P^d the Joyner Sudbury for shelving a room at Bedf. Coff. House	2– 2– 0
2.	P^d Mr. Elliott for binding 3 pieces of Giordano Bruno—12°	0– 3– 0

Rawlinson charged a shilling for the catalogue,[46] which contained short single-line descriptions of 2600 books, unclassified but quickly identifiable by a running number. Particular rarities were printed in black letter, and were distributed judiciously throughout the twenty nights' sale to maintain interest.

Only two purchasers can be identified. One was a creditor John Anstis, Garter King of Arms, who sent a receipt for 41s. to cover his purchases,[47] and the other was Rawlinson himself, who laid out £23 on 120 items, among them an illustrated edition of Virgil's *Aeneid* costing 11 guineas.[48] Prices entered in Crynes's copy of the catalogue were low, Caxton's *Caton distichis* going for 13s. The highest bid was £11. 16s. for Pliny's *Natural History* printed by J. de Spira at Venice in 1469. Rawlinson was disappointed, and Hearne apologized for his mistaken optimism: "Mr. Murray told me the books in your last Auction in general sold well; but it seems by your Letter, that the contrary is true, for wch I am sorry."[49]

Rawlinson spent the next five months in preparing for the rapid sequence of four new sales, in which ten thousand items were sold, and confessed to Blackbourne that he had more than enough to employ his time.[50] Hearne wrote sympathetically:

> I know the trouble and hurry you are in, and wish all possible success. But I fear there are underminers, such too as may possibly seem friends. But I need not tell you (who know the world so much) any news of this kind. I am a perfect Recluse, and yet know too much of insidious doings.[51]

Rawlinson's principal difficulty concerned the inefficient auctioneer, Charles Davis,[52] and his letter to one of Tabor's agents reveals how limited he was by the terms of the agreement:

> I then mentioned [Rawlinson wrote], that if Mr. Tabor knew of any contract with Mr. Davis (which tho' a stranger to, I am not unwilling to comply with) for time spent in preparing the last Catalogue in which himself as well as others think he has some merit, it is necessary that as formerly he should be so good as to send me such a complyance und' his hand: If he be of a different opinion, I should be glad to know as much, that I may regulate my conduct not to give unwarily any offence, and yet to take proper measures for the ballance of the account between Davis and myself, either by gentle, or if those are insufficient, more rough methods; let the event be what it will I am not conscious that he is able to do me, or the books any disservice, I never thought it in many [sic] mans power so far to undervalue a commodity in itself valuable, as to hinder its sale when peoples eyes are open that design to be purchasers; nor do I, speaking without any prejudice, think he did us any service in the two auctions, or had any other interest but his own in view, this my reservedness to him upon all occasions as well as my uneasiness at his garbling the books is a full proof of, and yet granting this, tho' I am sorry, yet if others are pleased I do not repent of having complyed, even against my own judgement, but as the step we are now going to take seems to be of some consequence, I am cautious of proceeding but joyntly with all parties concerned, that none may have the least reason to think themselves aggriev'd, or their interest hurt by any litigious proceeding, without which, or a compliance with his terms, I don't flatter myself with any compliance, but what the Law will oblige him to, which will not only be a trouble to me, but an expence to the administration: as you have generously and frequently interested your self in this affair, I believe you will not scruple giving Mr. Tabor your opinion by whose directions I shall pursue: I don't pretend to give my advice, or foresee what may be the consequences of this step, my resolution is not to allow the six guineas insisted on without a written commission from Mr. Tabor, or can I be answerable for what malice, and a disappointed avarice may effect.[53]

The accounts for this period, besides revealing Rawlinson's general preparations for the future sales, show that Tabor forced him to agree to the auctioneer's demands:

[fol. 6^r]

June 3.	Paid Mr. Halsey for Cataloguing of Books	1–	0–	0
	P^d Mr. Greated for Cataloguing books	0–	6–	8
	P^d Saml Lowndes for marking books in the Library	0–	6–	0
	P^d John Matthews for porterage and marking books	0–	9–	0
12.	Letter to Ld Colerane by penny post and past	0–	0–	4

[fol. 7^r]

23.	P^d the Smith's bill for work done in the Library	0–	6–	6
28.	P^d Mr. Preist the Joyner for work done in the Library, as by Bill affidavit and receipt	5–	4–	3
July 3.	P^d Mr. Porteous for a bundle of Pens	0–	1–	0
5.	P^d Insurance for the books to Xmass next	0–10–	0	
8.	P^d Mr. Porteous for cataloguing M.S.S. and books	0–18–	0	
21.	P^d Mr. Halsey for two copies of Catalogues of the Manuscripts with paper	1–11–	6[54]	
26.	P^d Mr. Blackbourn expences at the Tavern in treating Ld Coleranes steward, as he said, by Mr. Tabors ord^r	0–	4–	0

[fol. 8^r]

Aug. 2.	Paid Mr. Taber for an M.S. taken out of pawn	5–	5–	0
7.	P^d for Red Ink to mark the Catalogue	0–	0–	3
19.	P^d Mr. Davis for selling books at London House	22–	1–	0
do.	P^d Mr. Davis for selling books in Covent Garden	21–	0–	0
	P^d Mr. Davis for attendances as by Mr. Tabors verbal and written consent given 1st August 1727	6–	6–	0
26.				
do.	P^d Mr. Reily for printing title page, contents, and conclusion of K. Edw. VI. Liturgy &c as by receipt	0–15–	0	

The last item is somewhat alarming. After his return from abroad, Rawlinson specialized in facsimile printing,[55] skilled enough to deceive Hearne,[56] and while Rawlinson's efforts might be primarily directed toward making the text of the book complete, if the work was performed as skilfully as his other printing it might still mislead the most critical eye.

For the ninth auction (16 October 1727) Rawlinson returned to the rooms his brother had made use of in St. Paul's Coffee House, nearer to London House than Covent Garden. Charles Davis had been replaced as auctioneer by Thomas Ballard, assisted by Anthony Barker, and the conditions of the sale as announced in the catalogue[57] were slightly more in favor of the promoters. The following entries in the accounts are of particular interest:

[fol. 8ʳ]

Octob. 2.	Pᵈ for packthread, postage of penny post letters wᵗʰ Catalogues	0– 2– 0	
16.	Pᵈ for some wooden steps for the Library	0– 7– 0	
28.	Pᵈ Sam. Lowndes for attendance at auction &c	0– 7– 0	
do.	Pᵈ Tho: Powell for work in Library and at auction	0– 9– 0	
do.	Pᵈ Mr. Greated for writing at the auction	0–18– 0	
Nov. 9.	Pᵈ at the Tavern expences at the end of the auction	1–17– 0	
10.	Pᵈ Mr. Cooke Bookbinder for stitching Catalogues and other expences necessary to the auction beginning at St. Pauls Coffea House on Octob. 16. 1727	2–10– 8	
do.	Pᵈ Mr. Ryleys Servᵗ. for overrunning last half sheet of Catal	0– 2– 0	
13.	Pᵈ Mrs. Hoole & Brewer for paper for IXᵗʰ Catalogue	10–19– 6	
do.	Pᵈ Mr. Bowyer for printing 8 sheets & ¹/₄ of ye same	14– 2– 6	

[fol. 9ʳ]

Nov. 16.	Pᵈ Richard the Porter for carrying 22. Sacks of books at 4ᵈ p sack to the auction at Sᵗ Pauls Coffea House began 16. Octobʳ 1727	0– 7– 4	
23.	Pᵈ Mr. Nutt for advertisement of the last auction beginning at Sᵗ Pauls Coffea House 16. Oct. 1727	3–18– 0	
24.	Pᵈ Mr. Bubb for a Ham for the treat of the Book buyers at the end of the last auction	0– 7– 0	
Decemb. 4.	Pᵈ Mr. Ballard for selling the books of 20. Nights Sale beginning Octob. 16. 1727. & other expences	19–10– 0	

Of the 3200 lots of this twenty-night sale Rawlinson himself bought three hundred (nearly a tenth) for just under £33, the most expensive item being a 1542 Greek New Testament costing 19*s*. No other purchaser's name has been recorded, but the prices noted in Crynes's copy of the catalogue were disappointing. Thomas Baker, the Cambridge antiquary, wrote that he was "sorry for Dʳ Rawlinson's sake, that his Brother's last Books have gone so low."[58]

Scarcely a fortnight after the ninth auction, Rawlinson opened the tenth (22 November 1727) lasting twenty-two days and putting 3,520 books on the market. Hearne was amazed to receive the catalogue: "Curious & valuable Books" there were, but he hastened to add "indeed there is (as I understand) such a Glut of Books at this time in London, that I fear it will lessen the Sale."[59] The accounts covering the sale include the following items.

[fol. 9ʳ]

Nov. 18.	Pᵈ the Porter for carrying the books of the Auction at Sᵗ Pauls Coffea House beginning 22. Novemb	0–	6–	0
30.	Pᵈ Mr. Morris for stopping the Bible sold to him by Joh. Matthews stoln out of the Library	0–	1–	6
1 Decemb.	Pᵈ Mr. Riley printer in part for the Catalogue of an auction beginning 22. Novemb. at St. P. Coffea H	6–	6–	0
2.	Pᵈ Mr. Wagstaffe for writing at the auction	0–	12–	0
do.	Pᵈ Charles Merryman for attendance at Library & auct.	0–	9–	0
do.	Pᵈ Samˡ Lowndes for attendance &c	0–	7–	6
21.	Pᵈ Tavern bill for entertaining the gentlemen after the auction	2–	9–	0
27.	Pᵈ Mr. Cooke the Bookbinders bill for work done for the last auction as by recᵗ.	2–	16–	7

[fol. 8ᵛ]

23. Decembʳ.	Paid Mr. Nutt for advertisements in the auction beginning Novembʳ 22.	4–	13–	0

[fol. 10ʳ]

1727/8 Jan. 6.	Pᵈ Mr. Riley the Printer the remainder of his bill for the Catalogue beginning 22. Novembʳ 1727	4–	15–	0
13.	Pᵈ Mr. Ballard for selling the books of XXII Nights Sale and other expences of the auction began on Novemb. 22. as by receipt	21–	9–	0

Rawlinson annotated his copy of the catalogue with the names of the purchasers as well as the prices paid,[60] revealing many creditors taking advantage of his permission to take settlement in kind. Maittaire and West made considerable purchases, and Oliver Acton bought as many as 190 lots.[61] Hearne reported that Lord Oxford bought not only many "ordinary printed pieces" but also, at £10. 12s., the third Rawlinson copy of *Antiquitates Ecclesiae Britannicae,* "(Wᶜʰ was Archbishop Parker's own book)...a price (as the Dʳ says) much below its value, as he also says the other two went much too low."[62] By far the most numerous purchases were made by Rawlinson's non-juring colleague Tireman, who, as a comparison of the annotated catalogue and the Rawlinson list[63] reveals, was acting as the Doctor's agent.

The consistently high prices which Hearne's publications maintained in the sale[64] are spectacular, for Thomas Rawlinson, who acted as Hearne's London agent,[65] possessed many copies. In the middle of the sale Hearne wrote amicably to Rawlinson:

> I do not at all doubt but you will act with the Friendship that hath always past between us, and I return you my thanks for your design of keeping up the Prices of my books, in order to wch I send you the several Prices (what you desire) of what I have published since Leland's Itin....I would fain have those baulked, that exspect [sic] great Bargains from the falsely supposed great numbers.[66]

But in spite of stipulating "that no person shall put in for a folio for less than a shilling, quarto and octavo than 6d," Rawlinson could not hide his disappointment at the yield of the sale.[67] Thomas Baker commiserated with his friend,[68] and Hearne lamented:

> Tis a very great sign (among many others) of the great decay of Learning that whimsical & nonsensical books bring greater Prices in these Auctions than books of true worth & learning wch are sold at mean rates, not so much often as their binding came to.[69]

To Rawlinson he wrote: "I am very sorry to find you have such bad usage, when you act so very honourably. But I am too sensible, that booksellers and others are in a Combination against you."[70]

The accounts for the eleventh and twelfth sales (22 January and 18 March 1728) can be taken together as completing the series of sales at St. Paul's Coffee House from October 1727 to April 1728:

[fol. 10^r] 1727/8

Jan. 13.	P^d the Porter for carrying the books of 15. days sale to the auction Room	0– 4– 0
10. Jan.	P^d Insurance Office for one year for Lond. House	1– 0– 0
26.	P^d Mr. Reiley in part for printing the Catalogue of the auction begun 22. Jan. 1727/8	6–18– 0
27.	P^d Charles Merriman for attendance at Library & auction	0– 9– 0
do.	P^d Saml Lowndes for attend. at Library and auction	0– 7– 6
February 2.	P^d the Porter for carrying the remainder of the books	0– 1– 9
8.	P^d Mr. Reiley the remainder for Catalogue	3–18– 0
21.	P^d for the entertainment at the Tavern for the Book buyers at ye auction ending this day	2– 5– 0

22.	P^d Mr. Wagstaffe for writing twenty two days the last auction at St Pauls Coffea House	1–13– 0
[fol. 9ᵛ]		
24. Feb. 1727/8	Paid for Mr. Nutt for Advertisements of the auction of 22. January	1– 7– 0
[fol. 10ᵛ]		
12. March 1727/	P^d Mr. Ballard for 22. Nights Sale and Candles for the auction beginning 22. January 1727/8	21– 9– 0
[fol. 11ʳ]		
15.	P^d the Porter for carrying fourteen days sale of the auction beginning 18. March 1727/8	0– 3– 6
16.	P^d Mr. Reily for printing the catalogue of the auction beginning 18. March 1727/8	10– 6– 6
19.	P^d Mr. Cooke for stiching and sowing [sic] of Catalogues. and work done for the auction beginning 22. January 1727/8	2–10– 1
1. April.	P^d Mr. Atkinson in full for selecting the books of the first auction at London House as p^r rect	2– 2– 0
2.	P^d Porterage for the remainder of the Books to St. Pauls Coffea House of the auction of 18. March	0– 3– 0
6.	P^d Mr. Wagstaffe for writing 18 days at ye auction	1– 7– 0
13.	P^d the Expences at the Tavern being the last night of the auction	2– 0– 6
15.	P^d Mrs. Nutt for advertisements of auction of March 18	8–11– 0
27.	P^d Porterage for books return'd of last auction	0– 0– 6
30.	P^d John Hopkins for the use of shelves of St. Pauls Coffea House from 16. Octob^r. 1727 to this day	1–17– 6
[fol. 13ʳ]	1728/9 Jan. 23. P^d Mr. Cooke bookbinder for books bd for the auction began 18. March 1727/8	2–13– 8

Hearne thanked Rawlinson for the catalogues of the eleventh sale, which he distributed among his Oxford colleagues,[71] though he characteristically pointed out a mistake. It was a compliment to the accuracy of the catalogues that Hearne treated them as works of scholarly bibliography and could only find one error. Only one purchaser in the twenty-two-night sale can be traced—Oliver Acton, who bought 131 of the total 3,510 lots; all but two of these cost him less than a pound.[72]

Rawlinson's annotated copy of the catalogue of the twelfth sale, in which 3,840 items were sold in twenty-four nights, reveals few new names among the buyers. Hearne gave the wrong impression of the success of the sale as a whole when he complained that one book "was sold in this Auction for twenty six shillings, tho' 'tis not worth above six pence,"[73] for Rawlinson only received £151 from his agent.[74] He had one consolation, as Hearne, probably quoting from one of his letters, reported about this time:

> D[r] Rawlinson bought several Books himself of very good value out of some of the Auctions of his late Brother's books, and he hath told me…
> that he hath not let slip any book with the valuable MSS. notes of learned men, as J. Casaubon, Heinsius, Faber, and my Friend D[r] Thomas Smith.[75]

William Brome too wrote to Richard: "Glad I am to hear that you took care to purchase the choicest books in y[r] Brothers Library."[76]

After settling the bill for the six months' use of the Coffee House rooms Rawlinson informed one of his agents: "I am preparing what remains of the Library for the publick, who cannot be said in the prizes [sic] to have done justice to the memory of him who is gone, or answer'd the expectations of …R[ichard] R[awlinson]."[77]

A year, however, was to elapse before the next auction took place, and during this time, as the accounts reveal, two clerks were continually employed organizing the library; bookbinders were paid substantial sums for repairing damaged items; and insurance was carefully maintained. In May 1728 John Anstis wrote that he was still willing to take books in lieu of the sum Thomas Rawlinson owed him.[78]

On 13 April 1729 Thomas Baker wrote wishing Rawlinson every success in the thirteenth auction,[79] which was to begin on 21 April, and adding that he had sent a copy of the Catalogue to Dr. Middleton, Protobibliothecarius of the University of Cambridge: "The Dr. has a public Purse and, I hope, may be a good Customer. My Purse is not so deep as my desires, but yet I shall be tempted to stretch it."[80] The accounts reveal little novel in the organization of this the largest sale Rawlinson had yet held, comprising four thousand lots and lasting twenty-six nights at St. Paul's Coffee House:

[fol. 13[r]]
April 11. P[d] Mr. Reily for printing the Catalogue of books to
        begin to sell 21st. inst. at 1–10–0 p Sheet
        7 Sheets   10–12– 6
[fol. 14[r]]
June 3.   P[d] Mr. Wagstaffe for writing twenty six days at the
        auction began 25. April past   1–19– 0

Attention was focused on another copy of the *Antiquitates Ecclesiae Britannicae:* "Our last Matthew Parker," Rawlinson announced,

> now takes his fate. I am told there is a latent Commission of 50 libs. for it from France, but I hope England will not lose such a treasure, tho' I can't well afford to be the master of it.[81]

Hearne and Baker found the price beyond their pockets,[82] and their bitterness at the thought that the rarity might leave England has a curiously modern flavor. Their fears were unnecessary, for Hearne later reported:

> D[r] Rawlinson tells me it is well known at London that L[d] Oxford has the last copy of Matthew Parker, and…that since this, he has lent it to D[r] Drake, whose Edition is very near finished…If my L[d] Oxford hath it, it is in good hands, and he gave full enough for it, much more than it is worth."[83]

In general, however, the auction was disappointing, and on the day it ended Rawlinson described himself as one

> who lead[s] no very pleasant life from my Brothers creditors, when they find most of his effects so ill answer expectations: books are rather a charge than advantage with the expences attending their keeping, sale &c so that I am forced to be importunate from my own affairs.[84]

Six months later, on 24 November 1729, the fourteenth auction opened at St. Paul's Coffee House, to last eighteen nights and dispose of another 2,700 items. Some of the arrangements are revealed in the accounts:

[fol. 14[r]]

Octob. 3.	P[d] Mr. Brewer stationer for Paper	20– 0– 0
Nov. 21.	P[d] Mr. Reily in part for printing the Catalogue beginning the 24th instant I say in part	5–17– 0
2. Decemb.	P[d] Mr. Cooke for binding books for auction	0–16– 5$^{1}/_{2}$
do.	To Mr. Cookes servants for dispatch	0– 1– 0

[fol. 15[r]]

22.	P[d] Eliz Heath for eighteen days attendance by her Son at the auction	0– 9– 0
23.	P[d] Reily in full for printing the last Catalogue of Books	4– 1– 3
31.	P[d] fire office Policy to Xmass 1730	1– 0– 0
1729/30 1. Jan.	P[d] Mrs. Hool and Brewer for Paper in full as by rec[t]	19– 1– 0
20.	P[d] Mr. Nutt for advertisements in the Daily Post for the two last auctions as p rect	8– 5– 0

Rawlinson was displeased with the yield from the sale and replied angrily to Hearne, who had tactlessly expressed his joy "to hear...that your Books go at great Rates."[85] Rawlinson challenged him:

> If you have any inclination to undeceive yrself as to the last Sale, all the Catalogues in Mr. Crynes' hands are on demand for your view, so far are the prizes from being high, yt I know of Commissions from Oxford four times larger than the books fetched.[86]

II

Since 1727 Rawlinson had disposed of the greater portion of his brother's vast collection, and in the three-year interval before the next sale was held he attempted to satisfy creditors. He reviewed the situation to John Griffin, who still awaited payment of his legacy:

> As far as I have gone in the disposal of my late Brother's effects I need not mention the success, a too high value at first unskillfully, I hope without ill design, made, the greatest Glutt of books for these last years brought to market that ever was known, the Library I fear in some measure pillaged, as severall curiosities are not to be met with formerly known to be there, our effects as much undervalued in the sale as overrated in the estimate, and more debts appearing than at first loaded with a growing interest, with what care and parsimony I have executed the trust I appeal to all, and am ready when called on to justify myself.[87]

A year later he attempted to convince Thomas Deacon, to whom Griffin had left his legacy:

> Either the valuation was preposterous, books are much fallen, or depraedations have been made by the Executour [Ford] and his son (whose character I shall not enlarge on, as they are cum aliis gone to their place) so that I can almost assure you, except the MSS, pictures, prints, &c rise not very high, the chance of legatees is but small...which I'll prove from books, and in so fair and clear a manner that there shall remain no doubt of the justice with which I have acted.[88]

While Rawlinson had reasons for deceiving the two legatees, he knew that Tabor was in a position to know the truth and complained to him that "the great glutt of books now at market, and what is more particular the sale of above 1200 valuable Manuscripts very much sink my spirits, and in this I doubt not you'll sympathize."[89] He blamed the rival auctions of Woodward (11 Nov. 1728) and Freind (2 Jan. 1729) for "the fall of price in the old Editions, now sunk below their bindings."[90] Rawlinson, the protagonist in the struggle against the waste-paper merchants,[91] was not feigning displeasure when he declared to Hearne:

> Many of my Brother's very old books, such as now remain by Caxton, Wynkyn de Word, are imperfect, the prices people will now give for these is so incredible trifling, that [for] those that are bulky the chandlers and Grocers are the best chapmen.[92]

Two years before he had written that he was "now clearing off my rubbish books by tale, or at worst weight,"[93] and in September and October 1732 he received nearly £30 "of Mr. Dunning for Wast paper and imperfect Books."[94]

As well as clearing up business connected with earlier sales, such as reminding the Reverend Mr. Reynolds, an Exeter schoolmaster, that the books bought many years before were still unpaid for and uncollected,[95] Rawlinson, according to a report of Hearne, was in April 1732 "very busy in digesting and drawing a Catalogue of his late brother Thomas's pamphlets, which he calls the most important part (what I much wonder at) of his Collection."[96] Rawlinson had complained that Thomas had made the task difficult: "Had my late Brother only bound up wt was really curious, he had saved me much trouble."[97] Although in January 1733 he admitted that he was still organizing the pamphlets,[98] no such sale materialized; it is possible that he came to an understanding with Tabor that it would not be an economical proposition to sell them and absorbed them into his own collections instead, for at his death he was in possession of the prodigious number of twenty thousand.

Routine work in the library in preparation for the next sale continued. Charles Merryman replaced Samuel Lowndes as clerk at the weekly wage of nine shillings, and he in turn was followed by Charles Harrison, who till his death remained with Rawlinson acting as his amanuensis. Thomas Rawlinson's bookcases were disposed of,[99] and many of his books rebound. Rawlinson's attempts to complete imperfect books are disconcerting. On 20 July 1730 he "Pd Mr. Reily for printing some leaves and a Title to Proctors History of Sr Thomas Wyatts rebellion as p rect 0–10–9,"[100] and the accounts for 14 April 1731 record "Pd Mr. H. Parker for printing one leaf of the *Successi d'Inghilterra dopo la morte d'Odoardo sesto* as p rect 0–2–6." Rawlinson had experienced some difficulty in obtaining a perfect copy of the latter work and apologized to Lord Oxford: "I blush for the trouble I gave you by Mr. Maittaire about Guilio Rossi's *Successi d'Inghilterras,* of which I now hear there is a copy in Bodley's Library."[101]

In July, 1731, Rawlinson informed Hearne:

I am preparing for a conclusion next winter, and hope before that is over to do you justice, which has been always more in my inclination than power, as I have been oft bullyed by Bond Creditors, and even blamed, however rational the design, for permitting Book Creditors to buy out at Sales.[102]

It was, however, October, 1732, before he could write to Wright, one of his agents: "I am preparing for another sale of my Brothers books, and hope to finish this season."[103] The Accounts reveal a new attempt to attract buyers from the universities:[104]

[fol. 21ʳ]		
Sept. 11.	Pᵈ for Advertisemnt. in yᵉ Daily Advertiser	0– 2– 0
14.	Pᵈ Mr. Parker in full for printing a Catalogue of the auction to begin on 13. Novemb. 1732 eight pounds eight shill. as p rect	8– 8– 0
15.	Pᵈ Mr. Taylor the Bookbinder for stiching three hundred Catalogues	0– 6– 0
30.	Pᵈ Poole Bookbindʳ for stiching Catalogues	0– 6– 6
Octob. 19.	do. Pᵈ carriage of Catalogues to Oxfd & Cambridge	0– 1– 6
[fol. 22ʳ]		
Nov. 4.	Pᵈ for three advertisements in yᵉ Daily Advertiser	0– 6– 0
17.	Pᵈ Matth. Poole Bookbinder for binding books in the auction beginning 13ᵗʰ instant	3–10– 6
18.	Pᵈ Charles Harrison for attendance in the Library & writing five nights at auction	0–14– 0
Do.	Pᵈ Porter for attendance at Auction	0– 3– 0
Dec. 16.	Pᵈ Tho: Hedges for attendance twenty four nights at the auction	0–12– 0
29.	Pᵈ one years Insurance at the Fire Office	1– 0– 0
30.	Pᵈ Rich. Williams Porter for Carrying the books to and from the auction	0– 7– 0
[fol. 24ʳ]	1733/34	
Febr. 5.	Pᵈ Mr. Nutt for advertisements of the last Catalogue as p rect	4–19– 0

Rawlinson opened the fifteenth sale, which comprised 3,500 lots and was to last twenty-six nights, beginning 13 November, at St. Paul's Coffee House after a hard day's research with Wagstaffe in the Tower of London.[105] More than six hundred items "marked B" in Rawlinson's copy of the catalogue were "sent at their request to the Public Library at Oxford," probably as a gift.[106] For his own use in issuing facsimile editions he bought a 1563 edition of the Thirty-Nine Articles and Laud's Speech of 1637 in the Star Chamber.[107] The only other purchaser that can be identified was Oliver Acton, who bought eighteen items, the highest price being nine shillings for a copy of Dart's *Canterbury*.[108] If duplicates of books sold in earlier sales can be assumed to be almost identical in condition, prices had dropped considerably, and Rawlinson thought them "a reproach to the Age." Hearne tactlessly wrote: "I was also told that a very great part of your late Auction was all sold at one lump...I hope your Auction brought you a good sum of Money."[109] He probed for more information ten days later: "I hear of prized copies of your last Auction Catalogue wch looks as if the Books were all sold single, & not (as I was told) the greatest part at a lump."[110] At this Rawlinson could contain himself no longer:

> How false it is y^t a great part of my last auction was sold at once let the prized Catalogue wth Mr. Crynes demonstrate: of printed books...there will be no more Catalogues, of the MSS prints & pictures you'll soon hear."[111]

In 1727 Hearne had fervently wished that "the D^r may preserve his whole Collection of MSS together."[112] While Rawlinson hoped to purchase many items, he could not prevent the auction, but determined to minimize the damage caused by the dispersal of the collection. "Dr. Rawlinson tells me," Hearne reported,

> that he designs to cut in copper & print, tho' never publish, some specimens of several hands of the most antient, fair, and best MSS. in his late Brother's library. I cannot see of what use this can be, but I must forbear giving my frank opinion to him.[113]

Hearne seemed equally shortsighted when Rawlinson offered him the loan of any of his Brother's manuscripts: "a year or less will determine their fate...and transcripts...such as you make, can never be useless."[114] Under the terms of the agreement he could not allow Hearne to print any extracts until after the sale, and the antiquary noted peevishly: "Such restrictions I cannot come into...so I had rather wave it."[115] Undaunted by this rebuff Rawlinson informed Le Neve that among the manuscripts "are severall Heraldical whose worth your self will be more capable of judging of, than I am qualifyed to do, and a view you may command whenever you please."[116] Thomas Palmer took the opportunity to consult parts of the collection while it was still intact, copying extracts concerning Somerset and Devon from a manuscript "in the possession of Mr. Rawlinson, 1729."[117]

Perhaps Rawlinson was not so altruistic as might at first appear, for by lending out manuscripts he hoped to obtain expert opinion which could be included in the sale catalogue—the third and, for Rawlinson, the most important method by which the memory of the famous collection could be preserved. As early as February, 1727, Hearne noticed the preparation of the Catalogue, "a province he [Rawlinson] himself hath undertaken,"[118] basing it on Thomas's list.[119] Despite his own thorough acquaintance with the collection, he was anxious to make it as perfect a description as possible, and in July, 1727, he had two copies[120] made of his brother's list which he then sent for Hearne's inspection. He may have been disappointed that the latter only kept it three days,[121] but Anstis, who received the list next, suggested some alterations,[122] while Le Neve corrected many of the entries.[123] For the description of the oriental items Rawlinson relied on Theocharis Dadichi, whom he "esteem'd...greatly for his incomparable Parts, and excellent Learning, particularly in the Eastern Languages, of which he was a great Master."[124] Apart from correcting and rearranging his brother's catalogue Rawlinson succeeded in adding fifty hitherto unrecorded items to the original list. Maittaire, who received an advance copy of the catalogue, declared:

> The method of the catalogue pleases me much: it can't be call'd prolix, for 'tis instructive and necessary. As to w[hethe]r [it] is proper to mention the gentlemen who have assisted you in it, I should think 'twould be better in English, since most of the notes and observations, in the Catalogue, are in that language. However if your opinion inclines more to Latin, you need seek for no other pen but your own. Your compliment on mine is more friendly than true.[125]

Rawlinson was proud of the result, and in sending Hearne "some odd things for his walks" enclosed part of his

> Brother's Catalogue of M.S.S. in whose description I have been as particular as possible, that it may be of use to posterity,[126] if they can discover into whose possession any article may come.... Of these catalogues I print but few, as purchasers in this ware are not numerous, and where I have any hopes I post the sheets as they are printed, and am advised on that score to publish but a few days before I sell, as otherwise Catalogues are lost, and then the loss not to be repaired: you may be pleased to shew it to Mr. Crynes and friends tho' I have am [sic] not sanguine in my expectations from your parts.[127]

From Oxford Crynes had written: "I shall endeavor to recommend some of the MSS. to ye Vice-Can: for ye [Bodleian] Library."[128] The reception from Cambridge was less encouraging, and Baker returned his copy

> after I had show'd it to 2: or 3: Friends, who seem to be of opinion there is no bidding for MSS, without viewing them, & seeing the Contents. Thus much I can discern without a view, that it is a very extraordinary Collection for a private Person.[129]

The auction opened on 4 March 1734, when 1020 manuscripts were sold in an eleven-night sale followed by eight hundred printed items left over from previous sales and disposed of immediately afterwards in five nights. Several entries in the accounts are of interest:

[fol. 25ʳ] 1733/4

Febr. 27.-	Paid Mr. Say the printer for printing my Brothers Catalogue of MSS. &c to be sold 4. March by auction and some paper as per rect	11–	18–	0
1. March	Pᵈ Taylor Bookbinder for stiching Catalogues	0–	4–	0
March 4.	An advertisement in the Daily Advertiser	0–	2–	0
April 6.	Pᵈ Rich. Williams the Porter for carrying books to the auction room, and bringing the unsold back	0–	9–	0
9.	Pᵈ Mr. Poole for binding books putt into the Catalogue of the last auction	4–	15–	0

[fol. 26ʳ]

June 12.	Pᵈ Mr. Cooke for binding books in the last auction	2–	6–	8
2. Aug.	Pᵈ Tho. Hedges for attending the last auction seventeen Nights	0–	8–	6
6.	Pᵈ a Porter for bringing down all the wast paper from the Garrett	0–	8–	6

[fol. 27ʳ]

Octob. 12.	Pᵈ Richards for bringing wast from the Garrett	0–	1–	6
Nov. 20.	Do Pᵈ Mr. Ballard expences of Sale of the MSS.	22–	7–	0
23.	Pᵈ Mr. Dawson Stationers bill for printing paper for Catalogues	8–	14–	0

[fol. 29ʳ] 1735

June 20.	Pᵈ Mr. Nutt for advertisements of the Catalogue of MSS began in March 1733/34	3–	0–	0
24.	Pᵈ Mr. Anthony Barker for writing attendance before, at, and after the Sale of the MSS. for the collecting of mony, shewing and delivering the MSS. and books as p rect	9–	4–	0

The sale attracted prominent book-collectors, and the names of Lord Coleraine, Joseph Ames, Browne Willis, and Thomas Carte appear in Rawlinson's annotated catalogue as purchasers.[130] James West secured a magnificent copy of Bede's *Historia Ecclesiastica* for only £4,[131] and the bargains collectors acquired became a by-word. Hearne noted ruefully:

The MSS. in Dʳ Rawlinson's last Auction…went extraordinary cheap, and those that bought had great pennyworths.…My friend Mʳ Brome… in a letter to the Dʳ says, that he cannot but wonder at the low rates of most of the MSS., and adds that had I been in place I should have been tempted to have laid out a pretty deal of money, without thinking my self at all touched with Bibliomania.[132]

Rawlinson agreed with Hearne: "You justly remark that the Tast of the Town is very different from the Age of Sunderland, Somers &c.,"[133] but instead of resentment he showed only a desire to assist scholarship, sending one of his annotated catalogues to Thomas Brett

> as somewhat uncommon. If any of the MSS. I have bought would be of use to you, command the loan, I have therefore mark'd them, and y' you may judge at how low an ebb learning runs, have given you the prices.[134]

Rawlinson bought two Colchester Corporation books and four days later presented them to the mayor of that town;[135] but his purchase of almost a third of the total number of manuscripts through his agent Tireman did not pass without angry comment, as he informed Hearne: "I don't know whether I mentioned Mr W[est]'s disgust at my purchases last auction, tho' he knew, and all the company supported me in it, that as a creditor I had a right equal to any other."[136] Many of the items endorsed "Not here" or "lost" in the annotated catalogue are now to be found among his collections in the Bodleian.

After sixteen sales all that now remained of Thomas Rawlinson's library were his pictures and prints. After paying "Tho: Witham 12s. for cleaning pictures and lackering the frames,"[137] Richard Rawlinson disposed of his brother's collection of paintings in a two-day sale, beginning 4 April 1734:

[fol. 25ʳ]
April 30. Pᵈ Mr. Spurrett poundage for selling pictures at
           1ˢ & 6ᵈ in yᵉ pᵈ for 27–7–0   2– 1– 0
[fol. 26ʳ]
July 4.   Pᵈ Mrs. Parker for printing a Catalogue of my
           Brothers pictures   1– 3– 0

Rawlinson himself was the largest single purchaser, many of the works then sold being now in the Bodleian. As a curiosity Rawlinson reprinted the catalogue after the sale inserting the price each item fetched.[138]

At the end of the first catalogue of paintings appeared the note: "A Catalogue of Mr. Rawlinson's prints and some MSS. missing in the last sale and of others discovered since is now in the press and will be ready for sale early next winter." As early as 1732 Rawlinson had been inquiring about the Catalogue of his brother's prints,[139] and the accounts[140] for 13 May 1735 record a payment "To Mr. Overton for appraising the Prints and drawings two days 2–12–6." Overton's manuscript,[141] dated 9 May 1735, comprised 122 items in folio and 383 in quarto, and the prices, recorded in a simple code, amounted to £55. Baker was surprised at the news of another sale, if misinformed as to its contents: "I wish you success in your next Sale of Books," he wrote in May, 1735, "I thought the last Auction had been really the last."[142] Rawlinson welcomed an inquiry about the prints[143] and spent half a guinea at the Rose Tavern "about the affair of the Prints";[144] but there is no record of an auction having taken place, and the prints were either sold privately like the medals[145] or, more probably, absorbed into Richard's own collections, for the more spectacular of his collection of prints now in the Bodleian belonged originally to Thomas.

When the library had been sold, Hearne remarked: "Dr Rawlinson by the Sale of his brother's books hath not raised near the money expected. For, it seems, they have ill answered, however good books, the MSS. worse."[146] Although generally suspicious, Hearne did not question this statement, though it seems possible that Rawlinson might have been spreading unduly pessimistic propaganda to his brother's creditors. Yet when Oliver Acton's account, comprising the steady purchase of heraldic and genealogical materials at nearly every auction between 1718 and 1740 is studied, the uniformly low prices he paid at the Rawlinson sales are too consistent to be coincidental.[147]

It is easy to overrate the value of Thomas Rawlinson's collections; he possessed many important items, but he was boasting when he told Hearne that the collections he had made at the cost of £2,000 were, in 1712, worth at least £8,000. Thomas's treatment of his library may account for many low prices. On occasions he could have books bound magnificently, but generally he used a rather unattractive covering which was not proof against the dust and cobwebs of London House. Hearne noted how the Bridges books, sold in 1726, "go very high, being fair Books, in good Condition, & most of them finely bound," adding that "People are in love with good Binding more than good Reading."[148] Many prospective buyers may have shared Oldys's fierce resentment against Thomas's practice of breaking up and rearranging bound volumes of tracts, so that he "confused and dispersed" what "some curious men had been pairing and sorting half their lives to have a topic or argument complete;"[149] and Thomas's habit of annotating books with disparaging and, in some cases, abusive remarks may have decreased the value of a considerable number.[150] Richard Rawlinson's efforts to reprint missing leaves show that some of the books were imperfect; some were fit only for the waste-paper merchant, and others were returned by disillusioned buyers who would be unwilling to make purchases in subsequent sales.[151] William Stuart spoke for many when he wrote:

I thank you for the Catalogue, and sh^d be glad of any opportunity of shewing my respect for an Old Friend; but in my former purchases, I have bin so unhappy to find many of the Books imperfecte, most of 'em foul, and some of 'em even misrepresented; that I am afraid to venture again.[152]

Like Heber, Thomas Rawlinson believed that "no gentleman can be without three copies of a book, one for show, one for use and one for borrowers," but Heber himself would have "smiled at his [Thomas's] duplicates, quadruplicates, and multiplied specimens of a single edition."[153] When the library came to be sold, the first copy might secure its price, but the market collapsed when the second and subsequent copies appeared.

When Richard Rawlinson came to dispose of his brother's books he found himself hampered by the arrangements made before he secured the administration and had to submit to Tabor's direction even when he had no confidence in him. When he first inspected the library he was surprised that he did "not find so many Leidger books &c., as has been imagined, of Classicks few of Antiquity;" and "as to Missals and beautifull miniatures" he thought them less numerous than his own collection.[154] He soon began to suspect the collections had been "pillaged"[155] and "plundered"[156] by the Commissioners of Appraisement, particularly Maittaire who

> would not rob on the road, and yet would perhaps clandestinely borrow a book or medal, and think his honour no way impeached.... Maittaire has been observed at the time of their Commissions to enter empty and return loaded from London House, that several covers of the books of the old Editions...have been discovered in odd parts of the Library, behind other books, but the valuable contents gelt.... The D^r [Rawlinson] is unwilling to expose Mr. M's character, and yet cannot but insist upon some sort of justice, such as clearing by oath in Chancery, a request (says the D^r) an honest man will not refuse, no more than a knave decline.[157]

Maittaire denied the charges,[158] but Rawlinson remained unconvinced and drafted what appears to have been an advertisement for a newspaper:

> Whereas between the death of Thomas Rawlinson, Esqr. in August, 1725, & the time of granting Administration in January 1726/7 it is more than suspected, that some curious books, &c. have been embezzled; which, for the better conveyance were sometimes cut out of the covers. To the end therefore, that the publick may be in part convinced of the great wrong done to all concerned: this is to give notice that at the end of another catalogue which will soon be published, the titles of those covers & other particulars will be printed. And it is hoped, that whoever may be thereby enabled to give any light towards a farther discovery, will, for the

common sake of all Lovers of Learning, be so good as to do it by a Letter directed to London house.[159]

Rawlinson later regretted having allowed creditors to take payment in kind at the auctions, "a priviledge which the law forbids,"[160] for they were well known to each other and probably combined to keep prices down. Hearne spoke of a "combination of Booksellers" against Rawlinson, while Crynes had "heard that ye booksellers combined and wou'd receive no commissions,"[161] and complained that through using a London bookseller he lost two items which had sold well below the price he was prepared to pay: "Had I thought so many delicate books cou'd have gone off at such prizes, I wou'd have attended not only the last but all ye former Catalogues in Person."[162] Rawlinson had reason to complain to Hearne:

> I know of Commissions from Oxford four times larger than the books fetched, and even some for wch commissions were sent were thrown aside, and not executed by the booksellers to whom they were trusted; such knaves, such enemies are they to ye interest of yt Man, to whom they ought to erect even a statue.[163]

The booksellers would not be obliged to Rawlinson for flooding the market, but even without their opposition he would have been unfortunate. At the time he was selling his brother's books important sales such as the St. Amand, which coincided with the fourteenth Rawlinson sale, and the Keill, which clashed with the tenth, drew away many would-be purchasers, while others like the Grey, Freind, and Woodward sales, which occurred in the intervals between the Rawlinson sales, produced that "Glutt" of books which Hearne considered had been responsible for the collapse of prices. Hearne was correct in using the word "Bibliomania"[164] as a novel expression when a copy of Caxton's *King Arthur and his Knights* (bought by Quaritch in 1895 for £1,950) went for £2. 4s. 6d.

Perhaps the search for the reasons for the disappointing yield can be carried too far. In any age the release of over thirty thousand lots, comprising perhaps fifty thousand volumes,[165] and over a thousand manuscripts in seven years would have brought down prices and saturated the market. Oldys spoke of Thomas Rawlinson as "the greatest collector of books in our time who has made his collections public."[166] The response of the eighteenth century to the novelty must not be condemned too lightly, for it did not completely disregard the warning on the title-page of one of the catalogues: *Qui non credit, cras credat.*

Notes

This article originally appeared in *The Library,* Transactions of the Bibliographical Society, 11 (1956), 23-40, 103-13 and is reproduced here, with slight modifications, with the permission of Dr. Brian J. Enright and the British Library.

[1]"The Rawlinsons and Their Collections," *Transactions of the Bibliographical Society,* 5 (1899), 67-84.

[2]S. de Ricci, *English Collectors of Books and Manuscripts (1530-1930) and Their Marks of Ownership* (Cambridge, 1930), p. 45.

[3]Printed items have been found in many of the bequests and purchases of the Bodleian Library; the British Library; Cambridge University Library; Christ Church, Exeter, and Queen's College, Oxford; the Evelyn Library, now deposited at Christ Church, Oxford; the Earl of Leicester's Library, Holkham; the Hunterian Library, Glasgow University; and the Durham University Library. Mr. J. B. Oldham found sixty items out of a collection of seven thousand in Shrewsbury College Library that belonged to the Rawlinson brothers (*Transactions of the Shropshire Archeological Society,* 51 [1941-43], 69). The manuscripts are easier to trace and appear in the Rawlinson and other collections in the Bodleian Library; the British Library (Harleian, Sloane, and Additional collections); the John Ryland's Library; and the R. Garrett Library, Baltimore. Not infrequently, manuscript items appear in sale catalogues, e.g., Sotheby 23 (1952), no. 531; Goldschmidt 93 (1951), 127, no. 313; and Grafton 287 (1952), 191, no. 577. Unless otherwise stated, all the manuscripts mentioned in this article are in the Bodleian Library, Oxford. Dates throughout are given in the old style except that the year is taken as starting on 1 January. When old and new style over-lap, old style date precedes slash, new follows.

[4]De Ricci, *English Collectors of Books and Manuscripts,* p. 2.

[5]MS. Rawl. lett. 33, item 37 (21 September 1716).

[6]The estates were in a poor state of repair when his father died, but Thomas's direction was apathetic. He showed interest only when he dealt with the etymology of the place name of one of his Warwickshire estates which "Dugdale slubbers over" (*Remarks and Collections of Thomas Hearne,* ed. C. E. Doble, D. W. Rannie, and H. E. Salter, 11 vols. [Oxford, 1886-1915], 5.345. Hereafter cited as Hearne, *Collections*).

[7]He borrowed £420 from Christopher Bateman, a bookseller in Little Britain (St. John's College, Oxford, Muniment R. 303), and another £200 from John Humphreys in 1720 (St. John's College, Oxford, Muniment R. 306). I am grateful to the President and Scholars of St. John's College, Oxford, for permission to quote from the Muniments and Account book in the possession of The College and the Librarian, Mr. H. M. Colvin, for his assistance.

[8]Hearne, *Collections,* 9.20 (4 September 1725), quoting William Oldisworth's conversation.

[9]Ch. Ed., *The relation of a journey into England and Holland in the years 1706, 1707... by a Saxon physician* (London, 1711), p. 40. The Bodleian copy is 8° c. 63 Jur.

[10]Hearne, *Collections,* 8.338 (25 February 1725).

[11]A list by F. Madan of all the sales with shelfmarks of the complete set of catalogues in the Bodleian Library is appended to Mr. Fletcher's article (n. 1 above) in *Transactions of the Bibliographical Society,* 5 (1899), 85-86.

[12]W. Y. Fletcher, "The Rawlinsons and their Collections," p. 69.

[13]Hearne, *Collections,* 9.19 (4 September 1725).

[14]Hearne, *Collections,* 9.20 (4 September 1725).

[15]Thomas Rawlinson's father had been Lord Mayor of London (1705) and Master of the Vintner's Company.

[16]MS. Rawl. J. 4°. 4, fol. 149. The certificate of the marriage is now MS. Rawl. J. 4°. 4, fol. 151.

[17]Thomas's father's will was constructed to oblige his heir to redeem a large mortgage on the family estates "by a wife's fortune." Richard Rawlinson sarcastically remarked to Brett: "In order to this my elder brother married his servant" (MS. Eng. th. c. 35, fol. 47 [10 July 1740]).

[18]Hearne, *Collections,* 9.19 (4 September 1725). Some of Thomas's friends thought that his wife had hastened his death more directly: Maittaire reported that "he was perfectly raving and in a strange delirium for many hours before he died" (Hearne, *Collections,* 9.23 [10 September 1725]); and "Mr. Anstis let drop a word, that he wish'd she had not poyson'd Mr. Rawlinson" (Hearne, *Collections,* 9.23 [10 September 1725]).

[19]For a detailed study of trusts for contingent remainders see H. J. Habakkuk, "Marriage Settlements in the Eighteenth Century," *Transactions of the Royal Historical Society,* 4th ser., 32 (1950), 15-30.

[20]Ford is mentioned in J. H. Overton, *The Nonjurors, Their Lives, Principles and Writings* (London, 1902), p. 478.

[21]St. John's College, Oxford, Muniment R. 228. Blackstone defined the common recovery as "fictitious proceedings introduced by a kind of *pia fraus* to elude the statute *de donis* which was found so intolerably mischievous and which yet one branch of the legislature would not then consent to repeal; . . . these recoveries however clandestinely begun are now become by long use and acquiescence a most common assurance of lands and tenements, so that no court will suffer them to be shaken or reflected on, and even acts of Parliament have by a sidewind countenanced and established them" (W. Blackstone, *Commentaries on the Laws of England,* four books [London, 1765], 2.117.

[22]St. John's College, Oxford, Muniments R. 194, 209, and 216.

[23]Somerset House, Farrant Folio (22 January 1727).

[24]Hearne, *Collections,* 9.23 (10 September 1725).

[25]Hearne, *Collections*, 9.135 (20 May 1726).

[26]MS. Rawl. lett. 3, item 161 (7 November 1726).

[27]MS. Ballard 2, fol. 139 (18 August 1743). See also MS. Ballard 2, fol. 92 (1 August 1741).

[28]For a complete study see H. Broxap, *A Biography of Thomas Deacon, the Manchester Nonjuror* (Manchester, 1911).

[29]MS. Rawl. lett. 85, fol. 49 (27 July 1731).

[30]Counterpart St. John's College, Oxford, Muniment R. 204.

[31]MS. Rawl. lett. 32, fol. 9 (21 February 1726/7).

[32]Tabor had frequently to be consulted about manuscripts thought to be stolen (MS Rawl. lett. 85, fol. 11 [10 July 1729]) or in pawn (Accounts [2 August 1727]). In 1741 Rawlinson said that he did not possess the accounts, "they lying before the Master" (MS Ballard 2, fol. 92 [1 August 1741]).

[33]Hearne, *Collections,* 9.270 (reporting a letter of 2 February 1727).

[34]This is now MS. St. John's College, Oxford, 268.

[35]The Bodleian copy is now Crynes 806.

[36]Hearne, *Collections*, 9.274 (19 February 1727).

[37]Hearne, *Collections,* 9.275 (19 February 1727).

[38]MS. Rawl. D. 661. In cataloguing this manuscript W. D. Macray remarked erroneously: "Of this auction there does not appear to be any record in print."

[39]About this time Rawlinson wrote to Le Neve: "The affairs I am at present embarrassed in, are some obstacle to more composed studies, and I am obliged to be more acquainted with title pages than the more usefull parts, the insides of Books, a vast variety, I see, which create an equal confusion" (MS. Autogr. c. 7, fol. 13 [23 March 1726/7]).

[40]1693-1749: in 1754 Rawlinson was able to return the compliment by attending the sale of Coleraine's books.

[41]MS. Rawl. D. 1200, fol. 1.

[42]Some bear several auction tickets, e.g., 8° Rawl. 943.

[43]Hearne, *Collections,* 9.287 (17 March 1726/7).

[44]MS. Rawl. lett. 85, fol. 2 (11 April 1727).

[45]In this, as in later extracts, I have omitted recurring items which do not add new information.

[46]He sent a copy to Thomas Brett (MS. Eng. th. c. 30, fol. 13 [30 May 1727]). The Bodleian copy is Crynes 806.

[47]MS. Rawl. lett. 30, fol. 52 (22 July 1727).

[48]MS. Rawl. D. 1200, fol. 4^v.

[49]MS. Rawl. lett. 32, fol. 21 (1 August 1727).

[50]MS. Rawl. lett. 85, fol. 11 (9 July 1727).

[51]MS. Rawl. lett. 32, fol. 22 (19 August 1727).

[52]Davis was still selling books in 1740. Rawlinson was in possession of his catalogue for a sale then as well as his accounts (Mus. Bibl. III. 8°. 65).

[53]MS. Rawl. lett. 85, fol. 3^v (24 July 1727).

[54]It is interesting to note that the catalogue of the manuscripts sold seven years later was so far advanced. The copies are now MSS. Rawl. C. 937 and D. 885.

[55]Notably the reprint of the 1637 edition of Archbishop Laud's Speech in the Star Chamber and the rare Latin 1563 edition of the Thirty-Nine Articles.

[56]Hearne, *Collections*, 11.147 (14 January 1733).

[57]The Bodleian copy is Crynes 807. Thomas Baker distributed copies at Cambridge (MS. Rawl. lett. 30, fol. 103 [12 October 1727]).

[58]Hearne, *Collections*, 9.370 (reporting a letter of 12 November 1727).

[59]MS. Rawl. lett. 32, fol. 24 (20 November 1727).

[60]Mus. Bibl. III. 8°. 33.

[61]MS. Rawl. D. 716, fol. 16.

[62]Rawlinson later gained possession of the book at Lord Oxford's sales, and it came with his other annotated printed books to the Bodleian (now 4° Rawl. 593). Thomas's note— "Collated & I think perfect"—and the auction number—"477"—inserted on the flyleaf and corresponding with the catalogue entry indicate that it is the identical copy Hearne described (*Collections*, 9.374).

[63]MS. Rawl. D. 1200, fol. 12.

[64]Cf. Hearne's satisfaction at the ninth sale (*Collections,* 9.370 [16 November 1727]).

[65] I. G. Philip, "Thomas Hearne as a Publisher," *Bodleian Library Record,* 3 (1951), 154.

[66] MS. Rawl. lett. 32, fol. 28 (27 November 1727).

[67] In Rawlinson's interleaved copy of the catalogue of the sale (Mus. Bibl. III 8°. 33) are receipts totalling £212 for sums from the auctioneer.

[68] MS. Rawl. lett. 30, fol. 105 (13 January 1728).

[69] Hearne, *Collections*, 9.375 (27 November 1727).

[70] MS. Rawl. lett. 32, fol. 28 (27 November 1727).

[71] MS. Rawl. lett. fol. 30 (8 January 1727/8).

[72] MS. Rawl. D. 716, fol. 21^v.

[73] Hearne, *Collections*, 9.408; see also Hearne, *Collections*, 10.4.

[74] Mus. Bibl. III 8°. 33.

[75] Hearne, *Collections*, 10.14 (20 May 1728). Many of these items are now among the Rawlinson printed collection in the Bodleian Library.

[76] MS. Rawl. lett. 31, fol. 262 (11 September 1728).

[77] MS. Rawl. lett. 85, fol. 4^v (27 April 1728).

[78] MS. Rawl. lett. 30, fol. 56 (21 May 1728).

[79] MS. Rawl. lett. 30, fol. 126 (13 April 1729).

[80] MS. Rawl. lett. 30, fol. 126 (13 April 1729). The Bodleian copy of the catalogue is now Crynes 807.

[81] Hearne, *Collections*, 10.119 (10 April 1729).

[82] Hearne, *Collections*, 10.128 (7 May 1729).

[83] Hearne, *Collections*, 10.169. The book was lot 3520 and was sold for £45. It later came into Joseph Sandford's possession, and he presented it to the Bodleian in 1750. It is now A. 19.9. Th. and bears a note by Owen that Rawlinson had confirmed that it was the copy sold in 1729.

[84] MS. Rawl. lett. 85, fol. 9 (20 May 1729).

[85] MS. Rawl. lett. 32, fol. 48 (18 December 1729).

[86] MS. Rawl. lett. 9, fol. 31 (5 February 1729/30).

[87] MS. Rawl. lett. 85, fol. 28 (19 March 1730).

[88] MS. Rawl. lett. 85, fol. 48^v (27 July 1731).

[89] MS. Rawl. lett. 85, fol. 39^v (12 January 1731).

[90] MS. Rawl. lett. 85, fol. 50 (27 July 1731).

[91] See "Rawlinson and the Chandlers," *Bodleian Library Record*, 4 (1953), 216-27.

[92] MS. Rawl. lett. 27c, fol. 162^v (6 March 1731/2).

[93] MS. Rawl. lett. 9, fol. 32 (5 February 1729/30). MS. St. John's College, Oxford, 268, fol. 2^v (28 February 1727) records: "Rec^d from Mrs. Osborne Tallow Chandl. for wast pap^r 0-2-6."

[94] MS. Rawl. lett. 9, fol. 4^v (16 September and 6 October 1732).

[95] MS. Rawl. lett. 85, fol. 54 (2 November 1731).

[96] Hearne, *Collections*, 11.51 (25 April 1732).

[97] MS. Rawl. lett. 27c, fol. 155^v (31 January 1731/2).

[98] MS. Rawl. lett. 27c, fol. 165 (25 January 1732/3).

[99]"1731/2 1 Jan Allowed according to Mr. Tanner a sworn broker's valuation for six walnutt Tree small cases—3–0–0 and for an India Cabinet—2–0–0" (MS. St. John's College, Oxford, 268, fol. 3^v).

[100]One copy of the work, sold in the fourteenth sale (lot 2297), fetched a guinea; another, sold three years later in the fifteenth sale, fetched only four shillings.

[101]*Report on the Manuscripts of His Grace the Duke of Portland Preserved at Welbeck Abbey*, Royal Commission on Historical Manuscripts, 6 vols. (London, 1899-1931), 6.29 (16 May 1730).

[102]MS. Rawl. lett. 27c, fol. 147 (20 July 1731).

[103]MS. Rawl. lett. 85, fol. 65 (5 October 1732).

[104]Rawlinson sent a copy to Tanner (MS. Rawl. lett. 30, fol. 16 [18 April 1732]). The Bodleian copies are Mus. Bibl. III 8°. 9 and Crynes 808.

[105]MS. Eng. th. c. 32, fol. 99 (14 November 1732).

[106]Mus. Bibl. III. 8°. 9.

[107]Letter to Crynes (MS. Rawl. lett. 114^x, fol. 100a [6 January 1733]).

[108]MS. Rawl. D. 716, fol. 33^v.

[109]MS. Rawl. lett. 32, fol. 140 (11 January 1732/3).

[110]MS. Rawl. lett. 32, fol. 142 (21 January 1732/3).

[111]MS. Rawl. lett. 27c, fols. 165 (25 January 1732/3). An entry in the accounts for 31 December 1733 reads: "P^d for insurance of my Brothers books M.S.S. prints and pictures to Xmass 1734 1–0–0" (MS. St. John's College, Oxford, 268, fol. 24^r).

[112]Hearne, *Collections,* 9.275 (19 February 1727). At first, Rawlinson tried to sell the collection as a block, but even Lord Oxford could not comply with such a condition (Hearne, *Collections*, 9.375 [27 November 1727]).

[113]Hearne, *Collections,* 10.26 (5 July 1728). The actual plates and prints Rawlinson prepared are now in the Bodleian Library.

[114]Hearne, *Collections,* 10.105 (9 March 1728/9).

[115]Hearne, *Collections,* 10.105; see also Hearne, *Collections*, 10.101.

[116]MS. Autogr. c. 7, fol. 13 (23 March 1727).

[117]Royal Commission on Historical Manuscripts, Sixth *Report* (London, 1877-78), p. 347. The manuscript was bought by Rawlinson and is now MS. Rawl. B. 298.

[118]Hearne, *Collections*, 9.275 (19 February 1727).

[119]The list is now MS. Rawl. D. 902.

[120]MS. St. John's College, Oxford, 268, fol. 7^r.

[121]MS. Rawl. lett. 32, fol. 353 (28 January 1728/9).

[122]MS. Rawl. D. 902, init.

[123]MS. Rawl. D. 902, passim.

[124]MS. Rawl. lett. 96, fol. 130 (9 February 1743/4). Dadichi sometimes annotated the actual manuscript, e.g., MS. Rawl. Classics 2.

[125]MS. Rawl. lett. 29, fol. 91 (15 January 1733/4).

[126]William Oldys treasured his copy (J. Yeowell, *A Literary Antiquary. Memoir of William Oldys...* [London, 1862], p. 2 [29 June 1737]), but posterity appreciated the catalogues of the printed collections rather more, and regretted that Rawlinson was unable to publish the

"very pompous and... usefull Catalogue of the whole Library of his late Brother" which he once contemplated (Hearne, *Collections*, 10.26 [5 July 1728]). Although the catalogues were devoid of illustrations and index, unlike some contemporary lists, they were used frequently as works of reference, e.g., by F. Blomefield, *An Essay Toward a Topographical History of the County of Norfolk*, 11 vols. (London, 1805-10), 1.477; and by J. Ames, *Typographical Antiquities* (London, 1749), pp. 71, 77, 468. George Mason was anxious to complete his set (J. Nichols, *Illustrations of the Literary History of the Eighteenth Century,* 8 vols. [London, 1817-58], 4.555 [21 April 1785]).

[127] MS. Rawl. D. 390, fol. 99 (3 January 1733/4). As a result of Rawlinson's care, over a third of the manuscripts can be identified in many libraries today.

[128] MS. Rawl. lett. 29, fol. 300 (18 January 1729/30).

[129] MS. Rawl. lett. 30, fol. 252 (10 March [1734]).

[130] Mus. Bibl. III. 8°. II.

[131] Now MS. Douce 368.

[132] Hearne, *Collections*, 11.389 (9 November 1734); see MS. Rawl. lett. 31, fol. 325 (9 April 1734).

[133] MS. Rawl. lett. 32, fol. 175 (7 March 1734/5).

[134] MS. Eng. th. c. 33, p. 9 (19 April 1734). Brett replied: "The reverend Mr. Peg, Vicar of Godmersham... ye Bearer hereof, is my very good Friend. He is a great lover of Books... Upon w[ch] Account I communicated to him ye Catalogue of Manuscripts you were so kind to send me. He has a great Desire to see some of those which are yet unsold w[ch] if you will be so kind as to lend him I will be answerable for ye Return of them again safe to you" (MS. Rawl. lett. 114[x], fol. 77 [20 July 1734]). On 24 July he lent him seven items and sent another, about Chaucer, to Brome (MS. Rawl. lett. 31, fol. 325 [9 April 1734]). Another lent to Hearne was stolen from his study (MS. Rawl. C. 811, fol. 2[v] [5 March 1735]).

[135] MS. Rawl. D. 863, fol. 117 (8 March 1733/4).

[136] MS. Rawl. lett. 27c, fol. 179 (31 August 1734). Some of the items Rawlinson missed at the sale he later regained at the sales of Le Neve and Murray.

[137] MS. St. John's College, Oxford, 267, fol. 3 (27 April 1734).

[138] A copy of the first catalogue is Crynes 808, and the reprint is bound in MS. Rawl. C. 937. The Accounts record: "1734 30 April Recd then of Mr. W[m] Spurrett the produce of my Brothers pictures sold by auction twenty-seven pounds, seven shillings. 11 June Recd from Dr. Mead for the picture of Petrus Aegidius fifteen pounds fifteen shillings" (MS. St. John's College, Oxford, 268, fol. 4[v]).

[139] MS. Rawl. lett. 114[x], fol. 218 (12 January 1731/2).

[140] MS. St. John's College, Oxford, 268, fol. 29[r]. Receipt. Muniment R. 292.

[141] MS. Rawl. D. 879.

[142] MS. Rawl. lett. 30, fol. 199 (22 May 1735).

[143] MS. Rawl. D. 879, init.

[144] MS. St. John's College, Oxford, 268, fol. 29[r] (13 May 1735).

[145] MS. St. John's College, Oxford, 268, fol. 5[v]. Sold 25 April 1735 for £1–14s.–0d.

[146] Hearne, *Collections,* 11.390 (10 November 1734).

[147] MS. Rawl. D. 716. See H. B. Wheatley, *Prices of Books: An Inquiry into the Changes which have Occurred in England in Different Periods* (London, 1898), p. xi.

[148] Hearne, *Collections*, 9.92 (15 February 1725/6).

[149]*A Literary Antiquary. Memoir of William Oldys*, p. 101.

[150]Richard tried to erase some of his brother's slighting remarks, e.g., 4° Rawl. 172.

[151]Minshull noted many such in the record of the seventh auction (MS. Rawl. D. 661).

[152]MS. Rawl. lett. 29, fol. 439 (26 April 1729).

[153]C. I. and M. A. Elton, *The Great Book-Collectors* (London, 1893), p. 214.

[154]Hearne, *Collections,* 9.275.

[155]MS. Rawl. lett. 85, fol. 28 (19 March 1730).

[156]MS. Ballard 2, fol. 139 (18 August 1743).

[157]Hearne, *Collections*, 10.168 (21 August 1729).

[158]MS. Rawl. lett. 29, fol. 395 (26 April 1735).

[159]MS. Rawl. poet. 174, fol. 103. The threat to print a list of missing books in the catalogue was never carried out.

[160]MS. Rawl. lett. 85, fol. 50 (27 July 1731). See also Hearne, *Collections*, 8.338 and 10.438.

[161]MS. Rawl. lett. 29, fol. 296 (13 November 1729).

[162]MS. Rawl. lett. 29, fol. 300 (18 January 1729/30).

[163]MS. Rawl. lett. 9, fol. 31 (5 February 1729/30).

[164]Hearne, *Collections*, 11.389 (9 November 1734).

[165]Hearne, *Collections*, 9.187 (31 August 1726). De Ricci put the total collection—the complete sixteen sales—at 200,000 volumes (*English Collectors of Books and Manuscripts,* p. 45).

[166]*A Literary Antiquary. Memoir of William Oldys,* p. 101.

Bibliographies

Works Published by Richard Rawlinson

The following are listed in chronological order. Volumes for which Rawlinson admitted responsibility are preceded by *.

*The Life of Mr. Anthony a Wood, Historiographer of the Most Famous University of Oxford (London [Oxford], 1711).

Proposals for Printing by Subscription the Antiquities and History of the Two Antient Foundations and Colleges of Winchester and Eton (London, 1711).

*The University Miscellany: or, More Burning Work for the Oxford Convocation, 2nd ed., corrected (London, 1713).

*The Chorographical Description, or, Survey of the County of Devon, with the City and County of Exeter. Collected by Tristram Risdon (London, 1714).

A Continuation of the Survey of Devonshire. By Tristram Risdon (London, 1714).
  [This and the previous item were re-issued in London in 1723.]

*The Jacobite Memorial: Being a True Copy of the Letter sent to Mr. Broadwater, Mayor of Oxford. With the Proceedings of that Loyal University and City relating thereunto. In a Letter from a Gentleman of Magdalen College, to his Friend in London (London, 1714).

*The Laws of Honour: or a Compendious Account of the Ancient Derivation of all Titles, Dignities, Offices, &c. as well Spiritual as Temporal, Civil or Military (London, 1714).
  [Another edition was published in London in 1726.]

*Miscellanies on Several Curious Subjects: Now first Published from their Respective Originals (London, 1714).

The Oxford Packet (London, 1714).

Pietes Universitatis Oxoniensis on Obitum Sereniasimmae Reginae Annae at Gratulatio in Auguetiasimi Regis Georgii Inaugurationem (Oxford, 1714).

Exequiae Clarissimo Viro Johanni Radcliffe M.D. ab Oxoniensi Academia Salutae (Oxford, 1715).

A Full and Impartial Account of the Oxford-Riots...In a Letter from a Member of the University to his Friend in London (London, 1715).

Mr. William Lilly's History of his Life and Times, from the Year 1602, to 1681. Written by himself (London, 1715).

Some Memoirs of the Life of John Radcliffe M.D., 2nd ed. (London, 1715).
[Two letters published on p. 107.]

The Antiquities of the Cathedral Church of Worcester, By that Learned Antiquary, Thomas Abingdon, Esq: To which are added, The Antiquities of the Cathedral Churches of Chichester and Lichfield (London, 1717).
[Another edition was published in London in 1723.]

The Conduct of the Reverend Dr. White Kennet, Dean of Peterborough, From the Year 1681, to the Present Time. Being a Supplement to his Three Letters to the Bishop of Carlisle, Upon the Subject of Bishop Herks. By an impartial hand. 2nd ed. (London, 1717).

The History and Antiquities of the Cathedral Church of Rochester (London, 1717).
[Another edition was published in London in 1723.]

The History and Antiquities of the City and Cathedral-Church of Hereford (London, 1717).
[Another edition was published in London in 1717.]

The Inscriptions upon the Tombs, Grave-stones, &c. in the Dissenters Burial Place near Bunhill-Fields (London, 1717).

Memoirs of the Life of that Learned Antiquary, Elias Ashmole, Esq: Drawn up by Himself by way of Diary (London, 1717).

Opera Posthuma Latina, Viri Doctissimi et Clarissima Roberti South, S.T.P. (London, 1717).

Posthumous Works of the Late Reverend Robert South D.D. Containing Sermons on Several Subjects (London, 1717).

Proposals for Printing by Subscription "Antiquitates & Athenae Etonenses," or the History and Antiquities of the Famous College of Eton. By an impartial hand (London, 1717).

*A Survey of Staffordshire. Containing, the Antiquities of that County…*by Sampson Erdeswicke (London, 1717).

Petri Abaelardi, Abbatis Ruyensis et Heliossae, Abbatissae Parancletensie Epistise A prioris Editiones Erroribus purgatae, A cum Cod. MS. collatae Cura Ricardi Rawlinson (London, 1718 [1717]).
  [Another edition was published in Oxford in 1728.]

A Dissertation upon the most Celebrated Roman Poets. Originally written in Latin by Joseph Addison, Esq; Made English by Christopher Hayes, Esq (London, 1718).

To the Reverend the Clergy and Gentlemen of the County of Middlesex (London, 1718).
  [Printed questionnaire.]

To the Reverend the Clergy and Gentlemen of the County of Oxford (London, 1718).
  [Printed questionnaire.]

The Antiquitie of Berkshire. By Elias Ashmole, Esq. 3 vols. (London, 1719).
  [Another edition was published in London in 1723.]

The History and Antiquities of the Cathedral-Church of Salisbury and the Abbey-Church of Bath (London, 1719).
  [Another edition was published in London in 1723 and still another in London in 1728.]

The Natural History and Antiquities of the County of Surrey. Begun in the year 1673, by John Aubrey, Esq; F.R.S. and continued to the present time. 5 vols. (London, 1719).

Proposals for an enlarged edition of Norden's *Description of Middlesex* (London, 29 February 1719/20).

The English Topographer: or, An Historical Account… of all the Pieces that have been Written relating to the Antiquities, Natural History, or Topographical Description of any Part of England…. By an impartial hand (London, 1720).

Speculi Britannae Pars Altera: or, A Delineation of Northhamtonshire.... By John Norden (London, 1720).

"Extracts of the Memoirs from the Dutch Gazatte."
   [MS. J 4°.1, fol. 351. *Memoirs of John Ker* (London, 1726).]

A Catalogue of Choice and Valuable Books...being the Sixth [really the seventh] *Part of the Collection made by Tho. Rawlinson.*
   [Catalogues for the eighth through sixteenth sales were also published in London between 1727-34.]

The History of That Most Eminent Statesman, Sir John Perrott... Now First Published from the Original Manuscript (London, 1728).

*A New Method of Studying History....*By M. Langlet du Fresnoy; made English by Richard Rawlinson. 2 vols. (London, 1728).
   [Another edition was published in London in 1728 and still another, now entitled *A New Method of Studying History, Geography, and Chronology,* was published in London in 1730.]

A Week's Conversation on the Plurality of Worlds. By M. Fontenelle. Translated by William Gardiner, Esq. 2nd ed. *To which is added, Mr. Secretary Addison's Oration, made at Oxford, in Defense of the New Philosophy* (London, 1728).

Copy of a Bull taken from the Door of St. John Baptist's Church in the City of Valletta in the Isle of Malta. Ex Autographo. Penes Ricardum Rawlinson (London, 1729).

A Speech Delivered in the Starr-Chamber, on Wednesday, the xiv of June MDCXXXVII • at the Censure of John Bastwick, Henry Burton, & William Prinn; Concerning Pretended Innovations in the Church. By William L. [Laud] Archbishop of Canterbury.
   [Originally published in London in 1637; reprinted in London, c. 1729.]

Viri Eruditissmi Theophili Downes, A.M. Coll. Baliol, Oxon. olim Socii, De Clypeo Woodwardiano Strucurae Breves (London, 1729).

The Dimensions of St. Peter's Church at Rome, and St. Paul's Cathedral at London; as taken in the Year 1725 (London, c. 1730).

Pictures Rawlinsoniansis: Being a Collection of Original Paintings of Tho. Rawlinson (London, 1734).

Works Published Posthumously

The Deed of Trust and Will of Richard Rawlinson, of St. John Baptist College, Oxford, Doctor of Laws, Containing his Endowment of an Anglo-Saxon Lecture, and other Benefactions to the College and University (London, 1755).

Works Which Rawlinson May Have Published or Helped to Publish

Posthumous Works of the Learned Sir Thomas Browne, Kt. M.D. (London, 1712).

The Life of that Learned Antiquary, Sir William Dugdale (London, 1713).

The Antiquities of St. Peter's, or the Abbey-Church of Westminster. 2nd ed. with Supplement (London, 1715).

Works Consulted in the Preparation of This Volume

Allibone, S. Austin. *A Critical Dictionary of English Literature and British and American Authors.* 3 vols. (Philadelphia, 1902).

Ames, J. *Typographical Antiquities* (London, 1749).

Aubrey, J. *The Natural History and Antiquities of the County of Surrey.* 5 vols. (London, 1719).

Bayne-Powell, Rosamund. *Eighteenth-Century London Life* (New York, 1938).

_____. *Travellers in the Eighteenth Century* (New York, 1972).

Blomefield, F. *An Essay Toward a Topographical History of the County of Norfolk.* 11 vols. (London, 1805-10).

Broxap, Henry. *A Biography of Thomas Deacon, the Manchester Nonjuror* (Manchester, 1911).

_____. *The Later Nonjurors* (Cambridge, 1924).

Bryant, A. *Samuel Pepys* (Cambridge, 1938).

Carpenter, Edward. *The Protestant Bishop: Being the Life of Henry Compton, 1632-1713, Bishop of London* (London, 1956).

Carpenter, Humphrey. *J. R. R. Tolkien: A Biography* (London, 1956).

Carter, John. *Books and Book Collectors* (London, 1956).

Clark, Andrew, ed. *The Life and Times of Anthony Wood.* 2 vols. (Oxford, 1892).

Clark, Donald Lemen. *John Milton at St. Paul's School: A Study of Ancient Rhetoric in English Renaissance Education* (New York, 1948).

Craster, Edmund. *History of the Bodleian Library* (Oxford, 1952).

Cunliffe, Lynette Rawlinson. *The Rawlinsons of Furness* (Kendal, 1978).

Davenport, C. *English Heraldic Bookstamps* (London, 1909).

Defoe, Daniel. *A Tour through the Whole Island of Great Britain.* 2 vols. (New York, 1968).

de Ricci, S. *English Collectors of Books and Manuscripts (1530-1930) and their Marks of Ownership* (Cambridge, 1930).

Doble, C. E., D. W. Rannie, and H. E. Salter, eds. *Remarks and Collections of Thomas Hearne.* 11 vols. (Oxford, 1886-1915).

Dobson, A. *William Hogarth,* new and enlarged edition (London, 1939).

Douglas, David C. *English Scholars 1660-1730.* Revised edition (London, 1951).

Elton, C. I., and M. A. Elton. *The Great Book-Collectors* (London, 1893).

Emden, Alfred B. *An Oxford Hall in Medieval Times* (Oxford, 1968).

Emmison, F. G. *Tudor Secretary: Sir William Petre at Court and at Home* (London, 1961).

Enright, Brian J. "The Later Auction Sales of Thomas Rawlinson's Library: 1727-34," *The Library,* Transactions of the Bibliographical Society 11 (1956), 23-40, 103-13.

_____. "Richard Rawlinson and the Chandlers," *Bodleian Library Record* 4 (1953), 216-27.

_____. "Richard Rawlinson: Collector, Antiquary, Topographer" (Doctoral thesis, Oxford University, 1955).

Esdaile, Katherine A., Giles S. H. F. Stangways, and Henry M. Hake, eds. *The Notebooks of George Vertue Relating to Artists and Collections in England.* 6 vols. (Oxford, 1930-47).

Evans, Joan A. *A History of the Society of Antiquaries* (Oxford, 1956).

Firth, Charles H. *The School of English Language and Literature: A Contribution to the History of Oxford Studies* (Oxford, 1909).

Fitzgerald, Percy. *The Book Fancier* (London, 1887).

Fletcher, W. Y. "The Rawlinsons and Their Collections," *Transactions of the Bibliographical Society* 5 (1899), 67-84.

Flower, C. T. "Manuscripts and the War," *Transactions of the Royal Historical Society,* 4th ser., 25.

Foster, Joseph. *Alumni Oxonienses: The Members of the University of Oxford 1500-1714.* 4 vols. (Oxford, 1891-92).

Fussner, F. Smith. *The Historical Revolution* (London, 1962).

Godley, A. D. *Oxford in the Eighteenth Century* (London, 1908).

Green, John Richard. *A Short History of the English People.* 4 vols. (New York, 1903).

Greenfield, Stanley B., and Fred C. Robinson, eds. *A Bibliography of Publications on Old English Literature* (Toronto and Buffalo, 1980).

Habakkuk, H. J. "Marriage Settlements in the Eighteenth Century," *Transactions of the Royal Historical Society,* 4th ser., 32 (1950), 15-30.

Hebdomadal Council Papers (Oxford, 1910).

Hebdomadal Council Papers (Oxford, 1911).

Historical Register of the University of Oxford…With an Alphabetical Record of University Honours and Distinctions, 1220-1900 (Oxford, 1900), with Supplements.

Hoefer, J. C. F., ed. *Nouvelle Biographie Générale depuis les temps reculés jusqu'a nos jours.* 46 vols. (Paris, 1857-66).

Hollis, Christopher. *Eton* (London, 1960).

Holmes, Geoffrey. *The Trial of Dr. Sacheverell* (London, 1973).

Hopkinson, M. R. *Anne of England* (New York, 1934).

Hunter, Michael. *John Aubrey and the Realm of Learning* (London, 1949).

Kirby, Paul F. *The Grand Tour in Italy* (New York, 1952).

Kirk, John Foster, ed. *A Supplement to Allibone's Critical Dictionary of English Literature and British and American Authors.* 2 vols. (Philadelphia, 1902).

Latham, Robert, and William Mathews, eds. *The Diary of Samuel Pepys.* 11 vols. (Berkeley and Los Angeles, 1979-83).

Lathbury, Thomas. *History of the Nonjurors* (London, 1845).

Lindsay, Phillip. *For King or Parliament* (London, 1949).

Macaulay, Thomas B. *A History of England in the Eighteenth Century* (London, 1980).

Macray, W. D. *Annals of the Bodleian Library 1754-55* (Oxford, 1890).

_____. *Catalogi Codicum Manuscriptorum Bibliotahecae Bodleiane Partis Quintae Fasciulus Primus [-Quintus] Ricardi Rawlinson...*(Oxford, 1862-1900).

Marshall, Dorothy. *Eighteenth-Century England* (London, 1962).

McLynn, Frank. *The Jacobites* (London, 1985).

Mead, William E. *The Grand Tour in the Eighteenth Century* (New York, 1914).

Mirrlees, Hope. *A Fly in Amber* (London, 1962).

Nichols, John. *Illustrations of the Literary History of the Eighteenth Century.* 8 vols. (London, 1817-58).

_____. *Literary Anecdotes of the Eighteenth Century.* 9 vols. (London, 1812-15).

Ollard, Richard. *Pepys: A Biography* (New York, 1975).

Overton, John Henry. *The Nonjurors, Their Lives, Principles and Writings* (London 1902).

Palmer, David J. *The Rise of English Studies* (London, 1965).

Parkes, Joan. *Travel in England in the Eighteenth Century* (London, 1925).

Philip, Ian. *The Bodleian Library in the Seventeenth and Eighteenth Centuries* (Oxford, 1983).

──────── . "Thomas Hearne as a Publisher," *Bodleian Library Record* 3 (1951).

Pinkham, Lucille. *William III and the Respectable Revolution* (Cambridge, 1954).

Rawlinson, Richard. *The Deed of Trust and Will of Richard Rawlinson, of St. John Baptist College, Oxford, Doctor of Laws, Containing his Endowment of an Anglo-Saxon Lecture, and other Benefactions to the College and University* (London, 1755).

──────── . *Diaries.* 10 vols. (Unpublished. 1720-26), Bodleian Library.

Roscoe, E. S. *Robert Harley, Earl of Oxford* (London, 1902).

Rosenbach, A. S. W. *Books and Bidders* (Boston, 1927).

Shield, A., and A. Lang. *The King Over the Water* (London, 1907).

Stanhope, Philip H. *History of England.* Vol. 1 (London, 1836).

Stukeley, W. *The Family Memoirs of the Rev. William Stukeley* (Durham, 1882-87).

Tompson, Richard S. *The Atlantic Archipelago* (Queenston, 1986).

Trease, Geoffrey. *The Grand Tour* (New York, 1967).

Warnicke, Retha M. *William Lambarde, Elizabethan Antiquary, 1536-1601* (London, 1973).

Weidhorn, Manfred. *Richard Lovelace....* Twayne's English Authors Series 96 (New York, 1970).

Wheatley, H. B. *Prices of Books: An Inquiry into the Changes which have Occurred in England in Different Periods* (London, 1898).

Yeowell, J. *A Literary Antiquary. Memoir of William Oldys...* (London, 1862).

Appendix 1

The following essay is included essentially as written. It is a lively account of the tea trade in the seventeenth and eighteenth centuries, and concerns a company originally founded by members of the Rawlinson family. However, the author might have traced the origin of the firm further back than he did. In fact it was founded in 1650 by Daniel Rawlinson (1614-79) under the sign of the Three Sugar Loaves and Crown. This is the same Daniel who was keeper of the Mitre Tavern and whose son, Sir Thomas Rawlinson, was the father of Richard. Since Sir Thomas was preoccupied with civic responsibilities, Daniel left the business on his death to his nephew, also named Daniel (1654-1701). This second Daniel was the father of the Reverend Robert Rawlinson of Charlwood and the grandfather of the Sir Thomas Rawlinson (1710-69) with whom Mr. Rutter begins his account. The firm continues to operate but is located now not in Creechurch Lane but at 52-58 Weston Street, London SE1 3QJ.

At the Three Sugar Loaves and Crown: The Origin of the Firm

In Creechurch Lane, off Leadenhall Street, stands an old shop with a sign such as the merchants of the City were wont to display two centuries ago: three golden sugar-loaves surmounted by a golden crown. Standing there with its face to the formidable mass of the new Cunard House, Number Fourteen is like a little old lady, robust and kindly but rooted in tradition, surveying the younger generation. But she keeps abreast of the times, as old ladies do today. Within the shop, you may buy anything from sugar to cigars, from Trinidad chocolate to Jamaica rum, from tea to treacle (which in the cellar below you may see oozing sleekly from barrels into tins), but although the broad, scarred, oaken counter and the gigantic tea-canisters tell of an older day, there is nothing out-of-date in the methods of those who serve you. They are alert and modern. Their watchword is "Empire Goods." And they are proud to remember that their firm has sold its goods to the citizens of London under fourteen sovereigns without a break.

The Sign of the Three Sugar Loaves and Crown. Photo C. 86.1. Reproduced by permission of the Guildhall Library, City of London.

A tradition handed from generation to generation gives 1650 as the year in which Davison, Newman and Co. was founded. The earliest printed reference to the firm, which was then Thomas Rawlinson, is in Henry Kent's Directory for 1736, which mentions "Rawlinson, Thomas, grocer, Fenchurch Street./Ray, Walter, grocer, Fenchurch Street."

Thomas Rawlinson was a great-great nephew of Dan Rawlinson, the friend of Pepys and keeper of the Mitre Tavern in Fenchurch Street, and is not to be confused with his great-uncle of the same name who was Lord Mayor of London in 1706. Thomas was apprenticed to Walter Ray in 1725. He became a freeman of the Grocers' Company in 1734, and Master in 1747. His father, the Reverend Robert Rawlinson, was for thirty-five years Rector of Charlwood, Surrey, of which he was left the presentation by his father, Daniel, in 1701.

Walter Ray served his apprenticeship as a grocer with one Paul Garnier from 1699 to 1706 and became a warden of the Grocers' Company in 1724. That he was in Fenchurch Street as early as 1714 we know from the following invitation to the funeral of his sister:

> You are Desired to Accompany the Corps of Mrs. Margaret Rawlinson, late wife of the Reverend Robert Rawlinson, from the Dwelling House of Mr. Walter Ray in Fenchurch Street, to the Parish Church of St. Dionis Backchurch, on Thursday the 9th of December, 1714, at Six of the Clock in the Evening.
> And bring this Ticket with you.[1]

Walter Ray took his nephew Thomas into his business after the usual seven years' apprenticeship, and the young man did the next best thing to marrying his employer's daughter; since his employer had no daughter he married his niece, Dorothea Ray, who was his own first cousin.[2] Walter Ray bequeathed to Thomas Rawlinson his "houses in ffenchurch Street except the House wherein I now do dwell," which he left to his wife, but on condition that "she do not suffer any Tea Coffee or Chocolate to be sold in the said house or shop belonging to it without the Consent and Approbation of my Nephew Thomas Rawlinson." The lease of this house also went to Thomas after his aunt's death.

Thus it is clear how the business came into Thomas Rawlinson's hands. It may well have had a founder earlier than Walter Ray, who probably himself took it over from his master Paul Garnier, while Garnier may have had it from Samuel Conyers, to whom he was apprenticed in 1691. This is conjecture, but it is certain that Thomas Rawlinson carried on the business in his own name after Ray's death in 1737. An early document relating to the firm is a receipt (now in the possession of Sir Ambrose Heal) dated February 20, 1740, from Thomas Rawlinson, "at the Three Sugar Loaves and Crown in Fenchurch Street," to Mrs. Bennett (whose husband was a partner in Gosling's Bank) for

12 lb fine plaine chocolate @ 4/4	£2-12-0	
Box	0-0-6	
	£2-12-6[3]	

Another receipt in the possession of the firm shows that the business was still "Thomas Rawlinson" in 1745, while a trade card in the collection of Sir Ambrose Heal shows that an offshoot of the firm, Lumley and Ray, was at that time in business near Crutched Friars, Mark Lane, trading under the sign of the Tea-Tub, and having apparently borrowed the Rawlinson sign as well. This Ray may have been a nephew of Walter Ray, and so Thomas Rawlinson's brother-in-law. It was about the same time, also, that the Rawlinsons' connection with the Davison family began.

Davison and Newman

More than one member of the Davison family became associated with Thomas Rawlinson, but the most prominent was Monkhouse Davison, who was admitted to the Grocers' Company as a freeman by redemption in 1738. He was a son of Isaac Davison, of Cowdall Hall, Cumberland, and, since the Rawlinsons had been established for generations in Lancashire and Westmorland, it is probable that the two families were united by ties of friendship before the business alliance began.

The exact date when Davison's name was added to Rawlinson's is not certain, but that the style of the firm was "Rawlinson and Davison" by 1753 is clear from an old check of that year, while an engraved copper plate shows that they were "Dealers in Coffee, Tea, Chocolate, Snuff, etc." The connection must have begun, however, several years before, since in 1756 we find Mainplaise Davison being credited with the sum of £3,500, the cost of ten years' boarding and lodging the men:[4] a reminder of the days when it was customary for the apprentices and storemen to live under the same roof as their masters.

By this time the firm had developed an extensive foreign trade. For example, the old ledgers show that from March to November 1755 transactions (chiefly in spices) with a customer in Rotterdam amounted to no less than £53,000.

An agreement dated 1764 shows that Abram Newman (who married into the Davison family) was taken into partnership in that year (he had become a freeman of the Grocers' Company by redemption in 1761) and the firm then traded as "Rawlinson, Davison and Newman."

In 1753 the Lord Mayor, Edward Ironside, died soon after his accession to office and Thomas Rawlinson—said to be among the six aldermen in the picture of "Benn's Club," now in the possession of the Goldsmiths' Company—was elected in his place for the remainder of the year. He was knighted in 1760 and in the same year he bought Stowlangtoft Hall, near Bury St. Edmunds, the property including the whole parish, of which he was Lord of the Manor. Here he lived in the later years of his life, but he died in his house in Fenchurch Street on December 3, 1769. Sir Thomas Rawlinson was buried at Haughley, Suffolk, to which place his wife had been carried subsequent to her burial at All Hallows, Staining. This, save for the tower,[5] has been demolished. A swordrest of his, showing his arms, once in All Hallows, Staining, may still be seen in All Hallows, London Wall, while another, a finely carved specimen, is in the Hall of the Grocers' Company.

Sir Thomas left one son, Walter, and one daughter, Susannah. The son, (Sir) Walter Rawlinson, married Mary, daughter of Sir Robert Ladbroke, Lord Mayor in 1746-47, and became a partner in the banking firm of Ladbroke, Son, Rawlinson & Parker, carried on at "The Phoenix" in Lombard Street. Although he was a freeman of the Grocers' Company, and Master in 1773, he did not take any active part in the business after his father's death, and the firm became "Davison, Newman and Company (late Sir Thos. Rawlinson)," the trade name which is preserved to this day.

How careful the firm was in accepting new customers may be seen from the following correspondence:

From Mr Daniel Sunstead, of Yarmouth, to
Messrs Davison, Newman and Company.

Sir,   August 23, 1786.

I am recommended to your House by Messrs Butler and Hammond, 50 Cheapside. Indeed I can never be a great Customer, but I intend to be a good one, that is to say I wish to be well served, and I mean to pay well. I have only a little retail trade, and therefore must have prime goods, at present I want only a HGSD of good 6d. sugar, and quality must be good whatever the price is, I suppose 52/- or 53/-. It must be a clean dry sugar, not what I have. Pray do the best in your power for me. If you think it's likely to be cheaper in a short time I wish to wait awhile, but if it is at the lowest Beg you will send it. My Common way of payment is to send a Bill when I Received the goods. When lumps are low and safe shall be glad to know. If you are fearful about the money, Mr Hammond will be answerable for it; he is now at my house and beg you will use me well for his sake that he may have credit by his recommendation and am Sir,

Your hble servent
Daniel Sunstead.

The firm's somewhat uncompromising reply was as follows:

August 25, 1786.

Sir,

We are favoured with yours of the 23rd ordering a Hhd of 6dy. Sugar and saying that you can go as high as 52/- or 53/- per cwt. Now as this will only purchase the lowest Scaliable Tip and it being your first order we cannot think of executing it, besides we should be glad to know with what Grocer in this place you formerly did Business with as we are not fond of taking recommendations from people in another line of business unless they find it convenient to remit with their orders—Annexed we trouble you with a list of the different articles we sell we deal as we like to sell Grocery in a general way; Sugar alone being a bare Commodity.

We are,
Your most hble Servants,
Davison, Newman and Co.

The list referred to, though lengthy, is worth quoting to show the extensive range of the firm's business at this time:

Almonds of all Sorts	Figs, Turkey
Anniseeds	Figs, Faro
Barley, French	Ginger, White
Barley, Pearl	Ginger, Black
Blues of all Sorts	Ginger, Ground
Brimstone Roll	Hairpowder
Brimstone Flour	Hartshorn Shavings
Carraway Seeds	Hartshorn, Burnt
Carriander Seeds	Isinglass, whole
Chocolate, plain	Isinglass, beat
Chocolate, vanilla	Macaroni
Cinnamon	Mace
Cirton	Millett Seed
Cloves	Morrells
Cocoa Shells	Mustard, Durham
Coffee, Turkey	Nutmegs
Coffee, Jamaica	Nuts, Pistachoa
Confectionery of all Sorts	Pepper, Black
Currants	Pepper, Ground
Dates	Pepper, White

Pepper, Long	Salt Petre
Pepper, Jamaica	Salt Prunella
Plums, French	Senna
Plums, Gammaroon	Snuff of all Sorts
Prunellas	Starch, Poland
Prunes	Starch, common
Raisons of all Sorts	Snuff of all sorts
Rice, whole	Teas of all Sorts
Rice, ground	Truffles
Saffron	Vanilla
Sago	Vermicelli[6]
Salloop	

In 1777 Davison and Newman & Co. admitted into partnership three of their clerks, among them William Thwaytes, who was to become the sole owner of the firm. It is said that none of these gentlemen invested more than £500 in the business, whose capital, even then, was £80,000.

Monkhouse Davison died in 1793, at the age of eighty, and Abram Newman followed him six years later. In the "Annual Register" for 1799 appears the following note:

> March 8th. Died at his house in Fenchurch Street, Abram Newman, Esq. He was one of the richest citizens of London, and a happy instance of the wonderful powers of accumulation by the steady pursuit of honourable industry. Without speculation or adventure he acquired £600,000 as a Grocer. He retired from trade about four years ago, but so forcible was his habit that he came every day to the Shop, and ate his mutton chop at 2 o'clock (the good old city hour) with his successors.
> To each of his two daughters he left £100,000.

Both Monkhouse Davison and Abram Newman were buried in one tomb in All Hallows, Staining. Their monument is now in that fine old City Church, St. Olave's, Hart Street. It is surmounted by a symbolic figure of commerce, in flowing draperies, reclining, fitly and with a surprising air of comfort, on several bales of tea.

The Boston Tea Party

Tea has been an important part of the firm's business ever since its inception, and one of the traditions is that Davison and Newman shipped the tea which was thrown into Boston Harbor on the fateful evening of December 16, 1773, the prelude of the American War of Independence.

It is unnecessary to recount in detail the events which led the citizens of Boston to boycott the tea. Their chief grievance was that while the duty on paper had been suspended the duty on tea had been retained, and on the arrival of the ship *Dartmouth* in Boston Harbor on November 29, 1773, this notice was posted up all over the town:

NOTICE CONVENING MEETING
OF NOVEMBER 29, 1773
Friends! Brethren! Countrymen!

That worst of plagues, the detested Tea, shipped for this Port by the East India Company, is now arrived in the Harbour; the Hour of Destruction, or manly Opposition to the Machinations of Tyranny, stares you in the Face; every Friend to his Country, to himself and to Posterity, is now called upon to meet at *Faneuil Hall*, at nine o'clock, THIS DAY (at which time the Bells will ring), to make a united and successful resistance to this last, worst and most destructive measure of administration.

This appeal brought together a large concourse of people and it was re-solved that "the tea should be returned to the place from whence it came," without payment of the duty. The same afternoon Francis Rotch, the owner of the *Dartmouth*, and Captain Hall, the master, were "convented" by the citizens and charged not to land the tea, at their peril.

It is clear from the log of the *Dartmouth* that Captain Hall had been expecting trouble. On Sunday, November 28, after the ship had come to anchor in the harbor "under the Admiral's stern," it appears that

At 10 at night two Customs-House Officers were boarded upon us by the Castle, we being the first ship ever boarded in this manner, which hap-pened on account of our having the East India Company's *accursed dutiable Tea* on board.

On the following night, after the meeting, a guard of twenty-five men went on board the *Dartmouth* to see that the tea was not landed. The con-signees—Richard Clarke and Sons, Benjamin Faneuil, Joshua Winslow, and Thomas and Elisha Hutchinson (sons of the governor)—were called upon to send the tea back to England. They replied that it was "entirely out of their power" to do so, and suggested storing it until they could send to London for further advice. But the colonists were determined that the tea should not be landed. Every night the guard went on board the *Dartmouth*. Similar action was taken with two other ships, the *Eleanor* and the *Beaver*, which arrived with further consignments of tea.

Meanwhile Captain Hall began to unload the remainder of his cargo and continued to do so from day to day. The colonists were insistent that the

Dartmouth must take the tea back to England, and, seeing that Mr. Rotch "rather lingered in his preparations," they again summoned him before them. His reply to their demand was that "it would prove to his entire ruin to comply and he should not do it."

At last, on December 16, the colonists lost patience. What happened is best related by the *Dartmouth's* log:

> Thursday, December 16. This 24 hours rainy weather; town meeting this day. Between 6 and 7 o'c. this evening came down to the wharf a body of about 1,000 *people*; among them were a number *dressed and whooping like Indians.* They came on board the ship, and after warning myself and the Customs-House Officer to get out of the way they unlaid the hatches and went down the hold, where was eighty whole and thirty-four half chests of Tea, which they hoisted upon deck, and cut the chests to pieces, and hove the Tea all overboard, where it was damaged and lost.[7]

The tea on board the *Eleanor* and the *Beaver* was destroyed in a similar manner.

Now one of the traditions of the firm had been that they actually shipped part of this historic tea. Unfortunately there was no definite evidence to show that they were trading with the American colonies at this period. A short time ago, however, in an old chest that contained papers dating back two centuries, an interesting document was found. It contains a record of the sale of tea on behalf of Davison and Newman by their agent Henry Lloyd, of 5 Long Wharf, Boston. It is headed "Messrs Davison and Newman, their Sterling acct. Crt. with Henry Lloyd" and signed "Boston, N. E. July 7th, 1773. Errors Excepted. Henry Lloyd." One side of the account shows the amounts received from the sale of tea consigned by the firm between January 1772 and July 1773; the other side shows payments made by Mr. Lloyd on behalf of the firm. Among these items is the entry:

> May 13, 1773. To 2 Bills drawn by Francis Rotch on Haley a Hopkins dated 5th inst at 30 Days sight in fav. Leonard Jarvis, viz:
>
> | | | |
> |---|---|---|
> | 1 Bill for | £120 | |
> | 1 do. | £100 | £220. |

This entry proves that Rotch was carrying tea for the firm in May 1773. Consequently there was a very strong presumption that the tea which was thrown into Boston Harbor from Rotch's ship six months later had also been shipped by Davison and Newman.

On the other hand it was found that the East India Company's papers, which are still in the Records Department of the India Office, made no mention of any consigners other than the Company itself; but the Warehouse Ledgers of the East India Company, which might have given more details, have been destroyed. The firm, however, possesses delivery notes which show that Davison and Newman were in the habit of buying tea direct from the Company at this period and shipping it to its customers in America and elsewhere.

Some light is thrown on the matter by an old book, *Tea Leaves*,[8] which deals with the Boston Tea-Party. This is an extremely rare work, of which there is no copy in the British Museum Library.

By an Act of Parliament, passed on May 10, 1773, "with little debate and no opposition," the East India Company, on exportation of its teas to America, was allowed a drawback of the full amount of English duties, binding itself only to pay the three-pence duty, on its being landed in the English colonies. In accordance with this Act, the Lords Commissioners of the Treasury gave the Company a license (August 20, 1773) for the exportation of six hundred thousand pounds, which were to be sent to Boston, New York, Philadelphia, and Charleston, S.C., the principal American ports.

In anticipation of this the Directors of the East India Company approached the leading London merchants who were in the tea trade to ascertain their views as to the exportation of the tea. Messrs Davison and Newman made the following reply:

> Sir,
>
> Upon considering the exportation of teas by the Company, having no direction or power from our correspondents at Boston or New York, to make terms, we decline offering any recommendation in the present state of the affair, at the same time think our thanks are due to you for your readiness in attending to any propositions we might make. We are, respectfully,
>
> Yours most obt. servts.
DAVISON and NEWMAN.
>
> Fenchurch Street *July* 15, 1773.
> Edwd Wheeler, Esqr. Deputy-Chairman.[9]

The plan finally adopted by the Directors of the East India Company was to ship the tea themselves to agents in America who were friendly to the administration, and the event proved that Davison and Newman displayed no little acumen and foresight in declining to ship tea which, they had reason to fear, would be boycotted by the irate colonists.

But among the Treasury Board Papers in the Public Record Office an exceedingly important document has come to light showing that, after the trouble seemed to have blown over, the firm began to ship tea to Boston again and that sixteen chests of this tea, consigned in the brigantine *Fortune* early in 1774, was the cause of a second and unrecorded Boston Tea Party. When the news reached England the firm petitioned the king in the following terms:

> To the Kings most excellent Majesty
> The humble Petition of Peregrine Cust James Bradley Charles Herries Robert Thornton William Greenwood Monkhouse Davison and Abraham Newman all of the City of London Merchants:
> Sheweth—
>
> That your Petitioners Monkhouse Davison and Abraham Newman have for many Years past dealt and traded in buying large Quantities of Teas at the India Company's Sales in London and selling the same by Wholesale and also in shipping and sending the same to the British Colonies in America for Sale there.
>
> That your said Petitioners in December One thousand seven hundred and seventy three in the ordinary Course of such their Trade shipt on board a Brigantine or Vessel called the Fortune—commanded by Benjamin Goreham then lying in the River Thames bound for Boston in the Province of Massachuset's Bay in North America Sixteen Chests of Tea consigned to Henry Lloyd a Merchant there.
>
> That the said Ship arrived in the Harbour of Boston on Sunday the Sixth of March One thousand seven hundred and seventy four laden with Goods and Merchandizes of various kinds (amongst which were the said Sixteen Chests of Tea) upon Freight and about Eight o'Clock in the Evening of the next Day being the Seventh of March the said Ship being then at a Wharf in the Harbour of Boston aforesaid a great Number of Persons all of whom were unknown to the Captain and many of them disguised and dressed and talking like Indians armed with Axes and Hatchets with Force and Violence entered on board the said Vessel and broke open the Hatches and proceeded to rummage the Hold and hoisted out twenty eight chests of Tea (amongst which were the before mentioned Sixteen Chests of Tea) upon the Deck of the said Vessel and there with Hatchets Axes and Clubs broke open the said Chests and emptied and threw the Tea in to the Water whereby the same was wholly lost and destroyed.
>
> That in December One thousand seven hundred and seventy three your Petitioners Peregrine Cust James Bradley Charles Herries Robert Thornton and William Greenwood underwrote a Policy of Insurance on the said Sixteen Chests of Tea for several Sums of Money amounting together to Four hundred and eighty Pounds which Sum by reason of the Loss of the said Tea they have paid to your Petitioners Monkhouse Davison and Abraham Newman the Assured in the said Policy.

That the said Tea with the Charges and Premium of Insurance thereon was of the Value of Four hundred and seventy two Pounds Two Shillings and Ten Pence Sterling as by the Invoice thereof made and sent therewith dated the Twenty third Day of December One thousand seven hundred and seventy three appears.

That your petitioners are prepared with proper Evidence fully to prove the Matters aforesaid.

That by an Act of Parliament passed in the present Sessions intitled "An Act to discontinue in such manner and for such time as are therein mentioned the landing and discharging lading or shipping of Goods Wares and Merchandize at the Town and within the Harbour of Boston in the Province of Massachusets' Bay in North America" your Majesty is impowered to assign and appoint the Extent Bounds and Limits of the said Port or Harbour and also to appoint Quays and Wharfs within the said Harbour for the landing discharging lading and shipping of Goods in case it shall appear to your Majesty that full satisfaction hath been made by the Inhabitants of the said town of Boston to the East India Company for the Damage sustained by the said Company by the Destruction of their Goods sent to Boston And when it shall be properly certified to your Majesty that reasonable Satisfaction hath been made to others who suffered by the Riots and Insurrections at Boston in November and December One thousand seven hundred and seventy three and January One thousand seven hundred and seventy four.

That at the time of passing the said Act Advice had not been received in England of the Riots and Disorders committed at Boston in March One thousand seven hundred and seventy four and therefore the same could not be therein particularly taken Notice of But nevertheless your Petitioners humbly conceive that by the said Act it was intended that no such Port Harbour Quays or Wharfs should be appointed at or for the said Town of Boston until it should appear to your Majesty that reasonable satisfaction had been made to all Persons who suffered by the Riots and Insurrections at Boston Wherefore and in regard that the Violence used in destroying the said Sixteen Chests of Tea was not provoked by your Petitioners and did not proceed from any Resentment conceived against them or against their manner of trading but was intended and used by ill affected Persons as an Opposition to and defiance of your Majesties' Government and Authority.

Your Petitioners most humbly pray that your Majesty will be graciously pleased to give your Petitioners such...as their Case may require and...Majesty may seem just.

And your Petitioners shall ever pra....

P. CUST.	DAVISON & NEWMAN.
WM. GREENWOOD.	ROBT. THORNTON.
CHARLES HERRIES.	JAS. BRADLEY.

Notes

This essay by Owen Rutter was originally subtitled *A brief history of the firm of Messrs. Davison, Newman & Company now incorporated with the West Indian Produce Association Limited* (London, 1938). It is reproduced here, with slight modifications, with the permission of Davison, Newman & Company, which continues to operate under the sign of the Three Sugar Loaves and Crown and which owns the brand name "Boston Harbour Tea."

[1] This invitation—the last sentence of which has so modern a flavor—is taken from a Commonplace Book kept by Thomas Rawlinson's son Walter. This book contains much information about the Rawlinson family and is in the Guildhall Library, London.

[2] Neither the *Dictionary of National Biography*—article on Thomas Rawlinson—nor Joseph Foster's *Pedigrees of the County Families of England*—Rawlinson section—mentions this marriage; however, it is proved by Thomas Rawlinson's will and by entries in the Commonplace Book cited in n. 1 above.

[3] This receipt is the first known mention of the firm's sign, the origin of which is lost in antiquity. Such signs were used before it became customary to number houses.

[4] Joseph Aubrey Rees, *The Grocery Trade: Its History and Romance,* 2 vols. (London, 1910); 1 vol. (London, 1935).

[5] In Star Alley, off Fenchurch Street, at the back of the London Tavern.

[6] Rees, *The Grocery Trade.*

[7] This and the previous quotation are from Benjamin B. Thatcher, *Traits of the Tea Party: Being a Memoir of George R. T. Hewes, One of the Last of Its Survivors* (New York, 1835). There is a copy of this work in the Guildhall Library.

[8] Francis S. Drake, *Tea Leaves: Being a Collection of Letters and Documents Relating to the Shipment of Tea to the American Colonies in the Year 1773, by the East India Tea Company* (Boston, 1884).

[9] Drake, *Tea Leaves,* p. 235.

Appendix 2

The Rawlinson Family and its Language Scholars

Richard Rawlinson did not pretend to be a linguist even though he was proficient in Latin and adequate in Greek, normal accomplishments given the academic program of his day. After receiving his M.A. degree, while still living at St. John's College, he took tentative steps toward the study of Hebrew, but, as a young man with world enough and time before him, he decided to go instead in two other directions: topographical studies and collecting. When he journeyed to the Continent in 1720, in addition to his involvement with collecting, he became eager to learn Italian, a study which no doubt was facilitated by his mastery of Latin. He admired the literary language of Siena, and went there to undertake disciplined study with a tutor. The result was that he was able to pass in the crowd as a native (as he reported), and he learned to use the language so effectively that he was able to defend a fellow Englishman in an Italian court of law. While in Italy, he translated into English the text of a book he admired: Langlet du Fresnoy's *New Method of Studying History*, which he later published in England.

Had he not been obligated to shoulder the family debts on his return home in 1726, a burden he bore for nearly thirty years, he probably would have returned to Oxford, moved into his old rooms in Canterbury Quadrangle at St. John's College, and pursued "his beloved studies." As it was, he did the next best thing to advance language study: he founded and endowed the Anglo-Saxon Professorship. The Rawlinson family did, however, produce two outstanding linguists: Christopher Rawlinson (1677-1733), a Saxonist; and Henry Creswicke Rawlinson (1810-95), an Assyriologist.

Christopher Rawlinson

Christopher Rawlinson, born in Essex, was a direct descendant of the Rawlinsons of Cark Hall in Lancashire. He matriculated at Queen's College, Oxford, in June of 1695 at the age of eighteen, and it was there that he became a prominent Saxon scholar under the tutelage of Edward Thwaites

(1667-1711), a man whose teaching so inspired a large group of young men that Queen's College became known as the center for Anglo-Saxon study during the years directly following the Restoration and extending into the early eighteenth century. Prior to this period the center for study had been at Lincoln College where the monumental work of Francis Junius (1589-1677) flourished, where his pupil was Thomas Marshall (1621-1715), and where Marshall's pupil was the famous George Hickes (1642-1715), who later left for service in the Church and private scholarship.

Among Christopher's Saxonist contemporaries at Queen's were William Elstob (1675-1715), divine, translator, and antiquary; Thomas Tanner (1674-1735), Bishop of St. Asaph and ecclesiastical historian; and Edmund Gibson (1669-1748), ecclesiastical writer, editor, and transcriber of historical manuscripts. During Christopher's time at Queen's he must have been acquainted with the remarkable sister of William Elstob, Elizabeth (1683-1756), often referred to as the Saxon Nymph, a phrase which sounds condescending to twentieth-century ears. Her scholarship out-distanced the work of her brother; she published not only a Saxon grammar but also, in 1709, *A Homily on the Birthday of St. Gregory,* the latter dedicated to Queen Anne.

In 1699 Christopher completed and published a translation of Boethius's *Consolation of Philosophy* into Saxon verse. J. A. W. Bennett has said of this work: "Rawlinson improved on Junius by printing the *Metres* of Boethius as verse, in half lines. Hickes and Hearne also print[ed] Anglo-Saxon in half lines, though Gibson [kept] to the older custom in his edition of the Chronicle" ("History of Old English and Old Norse Studies in England," Ph.D. diss., Oxford University, 1938 [Bodleian MS. D. Phil. d. 287]). This work was done while he was still a student at Queen's under Edward Thwaites, and for his publication Rawlinson used the font that Francis Junius had designed.

On 27 January 1733 Thomas Hearne noted Christopher's accomplishments in his diary:

> He was formerly a Gentleman Commoner of Queen's College in Oxford, where he was educated under the celebrated Mr. Thwaites; under whom he improved himself so much in polite Learning, as also in the Saxon Tongue, that in the latter he published, in a most beautiful manner, at his own expence, King Alfred's Translation of *Boëtius de Consolatione Philosophiae*; for which, and his skill in the northern languages, he was much esteemed by that excellent judge of learning and learned men, the late pious and very reverend Dr. George Hickes.

AN. MANL. SEVER. BOETHI

Confolationis Philofophiæ

LIBRI V.

ANGLO-SAXONICE REDDITI

A B

ALFREDO,

Inclyto Anglo-Saxonum Rege.

Ad apographum JUNIANUM expreffos edidit
CHRISTOPHORUS RAWLINSON,
è Collegio Reginæ.

O X O N I Æ,

E THEATRO SHELDONIANO MDCXCVIII.
Sumtibus Editoris, Typis JUNIANIS.

Title Page to an Edition of Boethius's *The Consolation of Philosophy*, Translated into Anglo-Saxon Verse by Christopher Rawlinson. This translation, published in 1698, used the typeface designed by Francis Junius. The shells on the shield are a distinctive feature of the Rawlinson coat of arms. Reproduced by permission of the British Library.

Qui priscas patriæ linguas, linguisq; decorem
Reddidit, ingenuo hoc IUNIUS ore fuit.
Æthereas tranquilli animi sed pingere dotes
Non potuit, quamvis nobilis arte, manus. Ianus Vlitius.

Ad Tabulam Antonij Van Dyk, in Bibliotheca Bodleiana delineavit MBurghers Sculptor Univ. Oxon.

Frontispiece to Christopher Rawlinson's Translation of *The Consolation of Philosophy*.
Portrait of Francis Junius by Anthony Van Dyck. Reproduced by permission of the British
Library.

VERSIONES POETICÆ

è Codice Cottoniano defumptæ.

Cap. 1. Pag. 1. Lin. 1.

Confolationis hujus caput Primum, quod totius opufculi oc-cafionem complectitur, Poetice exequitur codex Cottonia-nus hunc in modum.

Hit pær geara iu.
Ðætte Gotan.
eartan of Sciþþia.
rcelðar læððon.
Ðreate geþrungon.
Ðeoð lonð monig.
retton ruþþeaðer.
rige ðeoða tpa.
Gotene rice.
geanmælum peox.
hæfðan him gecynðe.
cyningar tpegen.
Ræðgoð anð Aleric.
rice geþungon.
Ða pær ofer muntgiop.
monig atyhteð.
Gota gylper full.
guþe gelyrteð.
folc gepinner.
fana hpeanfoðe.
rcip on rceafte.
rceotenð ðohton.
Italia ealla gegongan.
linðpigenðe.

higelærtan.
rpua efne fpom muntgiop.
oþ ðone mæran peanoþ.
ðær Sicilia ræ.
rtreamum in eglonð.
micel eþel mænraþ.
Ða pær Romana rice gepun-
aðnocen bunga cyrt. [nen.
beaðu rincum pær.
Rom genymeð.
Ræðgoð anð Aleric.
fopon on ðæt færten.
fleah Garene.
mið ðam æþelingum.
ut on Grecar.
Ne meahte þa.
reo pea lar.
pige foprtanðan.
Gotan mið guþe.
gio monna gertrion.
realðon unpillum.
eþelpeanðar.
halige aþar.
pær gehpæþerer paa.

Ðeah

Two Plates from Christopher Rawlinson's Translation of *The Consolation of Philosophy*. The Junius typeface is evident, as is the division of the verse into half-lines. Reproduced by permission of the British Library.

Ðeah þær maᵹo þinca.
Mod mid Ᵹrecum.
ᵹif hi leodfruman.
læjtan dojhten.
Stod ðpaᵹe on ðam.
ðeod þær ᵹepunnen.
pintþa mæniᵹo.
oþ ðæt pynd ᵹejcpaf.
ðæt þe þeodþice.
ðeᵹnaj and eoplaj.
heþan jceoldan.
Ɣæj je Hepetema.
Cpijte ᵹecnoden.
cyninᵹ jelfa onfenᵹ.
fulluht ðeapum.
Fæᵹnodon ealle.
Rompaþa beajn.
and him þecene to.
fþiþej þilnedon.
He him fæjte ᵹehet.
ðæt hy eald þihta.
ælcej mojten.
pynþe ᵹepuniᵹen.
on ðæþe peleᵹan byþiᵹ.
ðenden Ljod puolde.
ðæt he Hodena ᵹepeald.
aᵹan mojte.
He ðæt eall aleaᵹ.
þæj ðæm æþelinᵹe.
Apþianej ᵹedpola leofpe.
ðonne Djihtnej æ.
Het Iohannej.
ᵹodne Papan.
heafde beheapon.
næj þ hæplic dæd.
eac ðam þær unþim oþþej
þ je Hota fþemede. [manej.
ᵹodþa ᵹehþilcum.

Ða þær þicþa jum.
on Rome byþiᵹ.
ahefen Hepetoᵹa.
hlafopde leof.
ðenden Cyþejtole.
Cþeacaj þioldon.
Ðæt þær þihtþij þinc.
næj mid Rompaþum.
jincᵹeofa jella.
jiððan lonᵹe he.
þæj foþ peoþulde þij.
peoþþ mynþa ᵹeoþn.
beoþn boca ᵹleap.
Boitiuj.
je hæle hatte.
je ðone hliþan ᵹeþah.
Ɣæj him on ᵹemynde.
mæla ᵹehþilce.
yfel and edþit.
ðæt him elþeodᵹe.
Kyninᵹaj cyðdon.
þæj on Cþeacaj hold.
ᵹemunde ðaþa aþa.
and ealdþihta.
ðe hij eldþan.
mid him ahton.
lonᵹe lufan ך lijja.
Anᵹan ða lijtum.
ymbe ðencean.
ðeaþflice.
hu he ðideþ meahte.
Cþecaj onceþþan.
ðæt je Laþeþe.
eft anpald ofeþ hi aᵹan
jende æþend ᵹeþþit.[mojte.
eald hlafoþdum.
deᵹelice.
and hi foþ Djihtne.

bæd

Later, on 1 May 1735, Hearne again remembers Christopher and his scholarship:

> Christopher Rawlinson, of Queen's Coll. Oxon., whom I well remember, was an honest, plain Gentleman even when young, and much addicted to his studies, which introduced him (by the means of Mr. Edw. Thwaites) into the acquaintance of Dr. John Mill, Principal of Edmund Hall. Which proved of very good service to Mr. Rawlinson who by that means procured the Dr.'s. assistance in his (Mr. Rawlinson's) beautiful Edition of K. Aelfred's Saxon *Boëtius de Consolatione.* Mr. Rawlinson after his retirement from Oxford, erected a monument to his Grandfather and Grandmother at Cark Hall in Lancashire....

Christopher was not only a linguist; he was also a noted antiquary, with large collections of historical papers. His manuscripts (according to Warwick Wroth, F.S.A., in *DNB*) were "disposed of in bundles and were bought for pence by the villagers. Rawlinson had made valuable collections for the history of Lancashire, Westmoreland, and Cumberland, all of which have probably perished." But his Saxon Boethius is extant.

Henry Creswicke Rawlinson

Henry Creswicke Rawlinson, whose father came from the old Lancashire family, was born in 1810 on an estate near Chadlington in Oxfordshire. One of a large family, Henry, with a good solid schooling but no university background, went into military service with the East India Company at the age of seventeen and was immediately sent to India. He was a fine athlete, an excellent horseman, and had an affable disposition. In addition, he was a natural linguist and quickly learned the Indian and Persian languages. He advanced from one position to another, and was so successful in each assignment that by the time he was twenty-three he was employed in Persia, assigned to reorganize the Persian army. While in that country he came under the spell of the undeciphered Rock of Behistun; this and not the military was to be his life's work.

The Behistun Rock is in the Zangers range in Persia on the direct route between Babylon and Ecbatana. Here on the sheer rock face, five hundred feet above the road below, Darius I, King of Persia (circa 500 B. C.), had the rock surface polished and an inscription engraved in three kinds of cuneiform, Old Persian, Babylonian, and Susian. The main text, in the Persian language, narrated the exploits of Darius in defeating the usurpers of his crown; thus it was his monument to himself. When Alexander later conquered the country, the language of Darius had been forgotten, and the inscription remained untranslated for nearly twenty-five centuries.

Rawlinson's athletic skills and his rugged six-foot frame were assets in his task. He had to climb the sheer rock face in order to read the inscribed surface which measured 60' x 23'. Stationed at Kirmanshaw, twenty miles away, he spent all available time at the Rock. During the summer and autumn of 1835 he worked at the task of copying the symbols; then he moved on to a different military assignment. But he returned to the Rock at every opportunity as though drawn by a magnet until he solved the riddle. It should be noted that Rawlinson had earlier had the opportunity to study a smaller stone near Ecbatana, and, assisted by prior work done by the German linguist Grotefend, he was able to assign correct values to a fraction of one of the alphabets used at Behistun; thus initiated, he succeeded in translating the whole of the massive inscription. When he finally did so in 1846, he opened the door of the sealed treasury of cuneiform writing which contained texts as old as the earliest civilizations—the annals of kings, epics of forgotten poets, works of law and science, an entire literature of antiquity. This was the achievement of Henry Rawlinson in his early years, an accomplishment parallel to that of the Eyptologist Jean François Champollion who deciphered the Rosetta Stone. The remainder of his life, in addition to ambassadorial appointments, was spent in the revision and prolific publication of his philological studies. On his return to England with the rank of Major-General he became a member of Parliament, president of the Royal Geographical Society, and, among other honors, a trustee of the British Museum.

We cannot leave Henry without speaking of the scholarship and distinguished career of his brother George Rawlinson, two years Henry's junior; the Blue Plaque on their house honors them both. A skilled linguist, but primarily a historian of ancient civilizations, George demonstrated the Rawlinson family characteristic of showing reverence for antiquities. He was educated at Trinity College, Oxford, where he excelled at athletics as well as academics, and became a tutor at Exeter College. When he married he accepted a curacy near Oxford, but he remained involved with the life of the University and excited the admiration of William Gladstone. His first of many historical works was an English edition in four volumes of *The History of Herodotus* which was dedicated to Gladstone. Henry Rawlinson assisted George with the translation. Besides writing numerous other works on the ancient history of the Middle East, he became Canon of Canterbury and Camden Professor of Ancient History at Oxford.

Appendix 3

Eighteenth-Century Copperplates
Discovered in Richard Rawlinson's Collection

As is detailed elsewhere in this volume, Richard Rawlinson and his elder brother Thomas began collecting manuscripts, rare books, portraits, seals, maps, and prints before their father, Sir Thomas Rawlinson, died. When Richard assumed responsibility for the family fortunes after his brother's death in 1725, he had to preside over the dispersal of Thomas's collection to satisfy numerous creditors. Some of the more desirable items he was able to purchase himself; others he re-purchased later after the creditors had been satisfied and his own financial circumstances had been secured. Before his death he amassed an astonishingly large and varied collection, and in his will he inserted provisions designed to insure that what he had so carefully accumulated would be preserved intact for future generations.

Among the more than seven thousand items which he bequeathed to the Bodleian Library is a remarkable and unique collection of 754 copperplates, eleven of which are now known as the "Americas Series." The existence of two plates was first recorded by the American historian Charles M. Andrews in his *Guide to the Manuscript Materials for the History of the United States to 1783, in the British Museum, in Minor London Archives, and in the Libraries of Oxford and Cambridge* (Washington, D.C., 1908). Andrews noted the existence of the two plates in the Bodleian, though it is not clear that he actually saw them. He may have derived his information from a handwritten list which had been compiled by members of the staff of the Bodleian in 1898-1900 and recorded on slips which were then pasted into a bound volume to form a simple inventory list to the collection. That volume was shelved with the plates in a remote and highly secure area of the library's closed stacks, however, and, thus, both it and the plates were virtually lost to historians.

In 1929, Mary Goodwin, historian of the Williamsburg Foundation, visited the Bodleian Library. The restoration of Colonial Williamsburg was in its early stages; the Wren building at the College of William and Mary, the oldest academic building to be in continuous use in America, was being reconstructed. Among the Rawlinson copperplates Mary Goodwin found one that depicted historic buildings in Colonial Williamsburg. Represented were the Governor's palace, the capital, Brafferton House, the President's house, and the Wren building, the latter of which was shown as having three floors rather than the two that were being reconstructed. Since the details in the copperplate were so relevant and timing critical, Mary Goodwin had a central section of a strike from the plate transmitted to the offices of the Boston architectural firm of Perry, Shaw, and Hepburn via a receiver in New York. Work on the building was altered in light of the new information available, and the authentic reconstruction evident today was thus made possible partly through the efforts of Richard Rawlinson to collect and to preserve. Eventually this "Williamsburg plate" was presented to Mr. John D. Rockefeller, Jr., by the librarian of the Bodleian in gratitude for Mr. Rockefeller's generous support of the New Bodleian Library, and he, in turn, presented it to the library of the Williamsburg Foundation where it resides today.

At the time of her discovery, Mary Goodwin requested that six strikes be made from the Williamsburg plate. Four were sent to her uncle, the Reverend Dr. William A. Rutherford Goodwin, minister of Bruton Parish Church, who had initiated the restoration of Williamsburg; one she presented to the Bodleian with a description of its contents and information about the significance of it to the restoration; and one she retained while she searched in England and Europe for its origins. The plate was of primary importance to the reconstruction of Williamsburg and of scholarly interest to historians, librarians, architects, biologists, engravers, and journalists. In response to immediate demand, thirty additional strikes were made from the plate and sent to the architectural firm. The records of the Williamsburg Foundation indicate that many of these were subsequently given to prominent individuals, libraries, and historical organizations in the United States. Several of these original strikes reside in the Colonial Williamsburg Foundation Library.

Despite the interest it generated and despite publicity here and abroad, no information about the origin or intended purpose of the Williamsburg plate came to light during Mary Goodwin's lifetime. In 1986, however, my efforts to research the origins of the plate led to the discovery of a previously unknown series of at least eleven eighteenth-century copperplates of Colonial America in the Rawlinson collection. Since the plates in the collection are shelved by size, the relationship among them is not immediately apparent either in the handwritten inventory list or on the shelves, but one of them is engraved with a capital A and the others with the numerals I through X. They are as follows:

Plate Number	Catalog Number	Description
A	d.32	Map of the North American continent
I	c.30	Buildings, probably of some town in Virginia or Carolina, with figures of plants and animals
II	c.20	Map of Roanoke, Blackwater, and other rivers in Virginia and Carolina. Currituck Inlet is dated March 6, 1727/8 with figures of plants and animals
III	d.33	Map of Nova Georgia
IV V VI VII		These four plates are not mentioned in the inventory list, but the logic of the numbering indicates that they were planned for if not executed.
VIII	c.31	Plan of Paramaribo with figures of plants and animals
IX	c.32	Figures of [American] plants and insects
X	d.34	Map of Caribee and Virgin Islands with plants and animals

Plate A, the map of North America is reproduced in this volume on p. 204. Plate I is the Williamsburg plate (reproduced on the endpapers in this volume). Plate II, which depicts the dividing line between Virginia and North Carolina, was one of the two noted by Andrews in 1903-04. Correspondence between contemporaries in England and the colonies has been found which suggests to some that Plates I and II were designed to illustrate William Byrd's *Histories of the Dividing Line Betwixt Virginia and North Carolina,* but Byrd's book was not published until 1841 (2nd ed. 1866, 3rd ed. 1901) and neither those editions nor that supervised by the Duke University historian William Boyd in 1929 included the Rawlinson copperplates.

That all of the plates are somehow connected is clear from the letter and number series engraved on them, from the fact that they were all produced in the early eighteenth century, from their presence in the Rawlinson collection, and from their Americas content. Elaborate numbering and lettering is used for illustrations on Plates A, II, III, VIII, and X, for example. Three of the plates—III, VIII, and X—feature forts, with Plate X containing an inset of Antigua and a second inset of its early fort. On plates I, II, and VIII, the detailed drawings of people, plants, insects, and animals are very similar, and trees are drawn alike on Plates A, II, III, VIII, and X. Despite such similarities, no cartographer, artist, copperplatesmith, or author is yet known, although there may be some significance to the facts that the smaller inset on Plate A

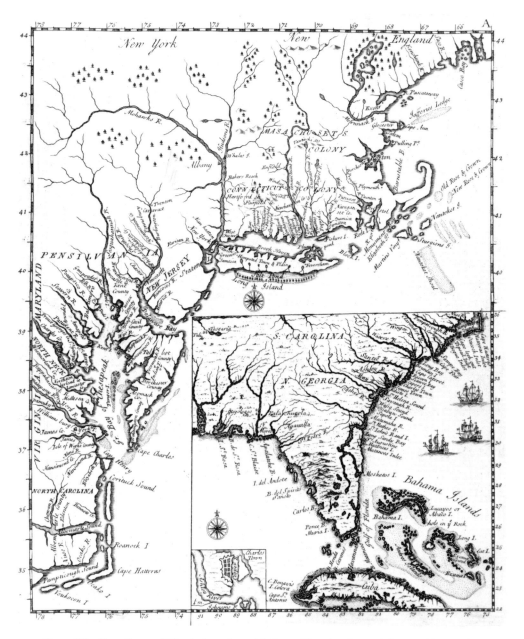

Map of the East Coast of North America with Inset Showing Part of the Caribbean, the Bahamas, and Cuba. Rawlinson copperplate d. 32. Reproduced by permission of the Bodleian Library.

appears to be from an earlier map by Hans Moll and the larger inset from a contemporary map by Henry Popple.

As indicated in the listing above, four of the Plates—Numbers IV, V, VI, and VII—are missing. There is no reference to them in the inventory, and they are not on the shelves of the Bodleian. There is nothing to indicate what they might have contained or even if they ever existed. There are, however, two other unnumbered plates in the Rawlinson collection that pertain directly to Colonial America—shop labels which advertise Virginia tobacco.

The discovery of these plates has generated considerable interest on both sides of the Atlantic. At Colonial Williamsburg, the information engraved on all of the Rawlinson plates has been translated from many languages into English, and an automated database has been created which is indexed by author/artist, title, illustrator/engraver, date, geographical location, and the Bodleian Library's shelf list numbering and lettering system. Such British scholars as Professor Eila M. J. Campbell, editor-in-chief of *Imago Mundi,* and Dr. Helen Wallis, retired Map Librarian of the British Library, have been particularly interested in the Americas Series. They have travelled to Williamsburg to consult with me and with William Cummings of Davidson College, an authority on early American maps. Together we have been able to assemble a few clues but no definite answers to the mysteries surrounding the Series.

In America, slides of the seven plates have been shown at professional conferences—e.g., the Joint Meeting of the Society of the History of Discovery and the Hakluyt Society, the Eastern Historical Geography Association Conference (Savannah, Ga.), the Conference of the Washington Map Society, and the American Society for Ethno-History Conference (Charleston, S.C.)—and scholars have been invited to assist the staff of the Americas Copperplate Series Project at Colonial Williamsburg with information or ideas about the engravings, the original drawings, the collector, the contents of the plates, or any other relationships that might enable us to assess the historical significance of the plates.

Through the generosity of the Bodleian Library and its Librarian, Mr. D. G. Vaisey, the original plates of the Americas Series and also strikes taken from these plates were placed on loan for a year-long exhibit at Colonial Williamsburg (1988-89), thus re-uniting the Williamsburg Plate with the others in the Series. When the National Geographic Society published its Centennial Edition of *The Historical Atlas of the United States of America,* it selected for the front cover illustration the map of North America from the Americas Series, and the editors confessed: "Mystery surrounds this copperplate, discovered in Oxford University's Bodleian in 1986. Its engraver is unknown, but the ships off the coast of 'N(ova) Georgia' date it to the 1730s, when that colony, last of the thirteen, was planted." There was no mention of Richard Rawlinson or his collection.

Still, one suspects that Rawlinson would be pleased to know that once again his benefactions have proved useful to scholarship, especially pleased, perhaps, that in this case it was his copperplates rather than his books and manuscripts that commanded attention. He had great admiration for engravings and for the plates from which they were struck, and collected both. For him and his contemporaries the fact that multiple copies of an engraving could be pulled from plates in future generations made copperplates the eighteenth-century equivalent of the twentieth-century photocopy machine. At times during his life Rawlinson had plates made, and one of his fondest dreams was to commission engravings of the Caedmon *Genesis* (MS. Junius 11), one of the greatest treasures of the Bodleian. Unfortunately, during the years when eighteenth-century enthusiasm for Anglo-Saxon studies was at its height Rawlinson could not afford so expensive a commission, and when he could afford it public interest had swung away from Saxon studies and Rawlinson's dream was never realized. Nevertheless, there remain at Oxford 754 copperplates gathered by Richard Rawlinson and saved from destruction by the Bodleian Library since 1755. They serve as a memorial to their collector and as an example to all who are entrusted with the preservation of the past.

Pearce S. Grove, Director
The Foundation Library
The Colonial Williamsburg Foundation
October, 1989

Appendix 4

Daniel Rawlinson, the Mitre Tavern, and Samuel Pepys

Daniel Rawlinson was born in 1614, the son of Thomas and Susannah Rawlinson of Griesdale in Lancashire. As a younger son not in line to inherit the family lands, he left the north country about 1640 and established himself in London as a vintner and as keeper of the Mitre Tavern which was located in Fenchurch Street near the foot of Lime Street and close to St. Dionis Backchurch.[1] In 1650 he opened a grocery and tea business near the Mitre under the sign of the Three Sugar Loaves and Crown, and this was to make him a wealthy man. History remembers him not so much for his wealth or his public service, however, as for the fact that the Mitre Tavern was very near Seething Lane where the diarist Samuel Pepys had his home. The Mitre, in fact, became one of Pepys's favorite places to dine and entertain, and its keeper, Daniel Rawlinson, was an intimate friend as well as a congenial host. The Mitre, Daniel Rawlinson, or both are mentioned more than forty times in Pepys's *Diary*.

Rawlinson was twenty years older than Pepys, but both were good conversationalists and convivial men who enjoyed the London scene. At the Mitre, Pepys could dine on venison, roast pork, a chine of beef, a dish of marrow bones, or a gammon of bacon. He could drink good ale or sack and secure wine for private consumption at home. On 23 October 1663, for example, he recorded: "Thence to Mr. Rawlinson's and saw some of my New bottles, made with my crest upon them, filled with wine, about five or six dozen."[2] At the Mitre, Pepys could entertain his friends: on 3 October 1661, after signing a bond for "the first money that ever I borrowed...for my own occasions," Pepys took his friends to the Mitre where they "sat and discoursed in matters of religion till night, with great pleasure"[3]; and on 30 December of the same year he entertained "about twelve" old friends from the Exchequer at a dinner at the Mitre that consisted of "a good chine of beef..., three barrels of oysters and three pullets and plenty of wine and mirth...."[4] At the Mitre Pepys sought consolation after the deaths of friends[5] and obtained news of those who had succumbed to the plague.[6] On at least one occasion, Pepys even conducted family business at the Mitre. On 13 August 1661 he reports:

> ...[M]y father and I went forth to Mr. Rawlinson's; where afterward comes my uncle Tho. and his two sons and then my uncle Wright, by appointment of us all; and there we read the Will and told them how things are and what our thoughts are of kindness to my Uncle Tho. if he doth carry himself peaceably; but otherwise if he persist to keep his Caveat up against us. So he promised to withdraw it, and seemed to be very well contented with things as they are.[7]

The relationship between Pepys and Rawlinson was more than just that of valued customer and business man, however; they were personal friends as well. On 25 July 1665, Pepys notes in his *Diary* that Daniel Rawlinson called him in and that the two "dined" and kept "good company" and were "very harmlessly merry."[8] On Sunday, 16 September 1660, they sat together at St. Dionis Backchurch to hear "a good sermon" preached on the occasion of the death of the Duke of Glocester,[9] and on 14 October 1663 Pepys and his wife visited the Jewish Synagogue in Creechurch Lane "by Mr. Rawlinson's conduct."[10]

One wishes Pepys had said more of Daniel Rawlinson than he does, but other sources and public records enable us to sketch the outlines of his career. We know, for example, that he was a royalist[11] and that, as a civic-minded man, he served as Governor of Christ's Hospital in 1662.[12] We know that he was a generous man who endowed his parish church at Hawkshead in Lancashire and founded the library at Hawkshead school.[13] We know that his interest in and support of both church and school continued throughout his life, that he personally donated books to the Hawkshead School library, and that he solicited other donations from no fewer than seventy-five donors, among them William Sancroft, then Dean of St. Paul's and later Archbishop of Canterbury.[14] We know that he left a legacy of £100 to the school

> The interest to be disposed of thus, the first Year to buy Books for Hauxshead School, & for a visiting Master there: the second year to the Master or Usher, or to the Master and Ush[r]. The 3[d]. to the Preaching Minist[r]. of Hauxshead. the 4th. to the Poor of Grekedale and Satterthwaite. the 5th. to a Poor Boy to y[e] university, or to one or more to be apprentices, and so forever beginning as before.[15]

As a family man and as a business man, Daniel Rawlinson struggled through difficult times. In 1665 the Great Plague struck London. The most reliable estimates are that approximately 10% of the population of the city died, some 68,500 people, and included in the toll was Daniel's son, also named Daniel. To protect the remainder of his family, Rawlinson removed his household, including his servants, to Lancaster where they remained until the spring of 1666 when, it was hoped, all danger had passed. Unfortunately, the lingering plague quickly claimed three additional members of the household: a servant, William Chombly; a maid, Elizabeth; and, most tragically, Daniel's wife, Margrett. Pepys notes in a *Diary* entry for 10 August 1666: "So homeward, and hear in Fanchurch Street that now the mayd also is dead at Mr. Rawlinson's; so that there are three dead...."[16]

The rest of the household survived, so far as we know, but the trials of the mid-1660s were not yet over. On 2 September 1666 the so-called "Great Fire of London" broke out in Pudding Lane. It began in a crowded row of unsteady houses built of pitch-coated wood and quickly developed into a conflagration that swept through Thames Street and its warehouses crammed with tallow, oil, spirits, and hemp. Before it ran its course, much of the old city of London—including the Mitre Tavern—had been destroyed. After the fire, Daniel petitioned the Pewterer's Company to request that he be permitted, as tenant, to rebuild the Mitre, return to his former living quarters, and follow his trade as a vintner. The main room of the new tavern was decorated with murals by Isaac Fuller, who had decorated All Soul's Chapel and Magdalen College in Oxford. George Vertue described the drawings: there were "figures being as large as life; over the chimney a Venus, satyr, and sleeping Cupid.... The seasons between the windows, and on the ceiling, two angels supporting a mitre."

Eventually, after the deaths of his older brothers, Daniel returned to his ancestral lands in Lancashire. With profits accumulated from the Three Sugar Loaves and Crown, he purchased valuable estates in Warwickshire, Essex, and Norfolk, as well as numerous holdings in London. On Daniel's death, most of these properties were left to his son, Sir Thomas Rawlinson (1647-1708), but since Sir Thomas was more interested in civic pursuits than in trade, both the Three Sugar Loaves and Crown and the Mitre Tavern were left to Daniel's nephew and namesake, Daniel Rawlinson (1654-1701).

Notes

[1] Kenneth Rogers, "The Mitre Tavern in Fenchurch Street: A Favourite House of Samuel Pepys," *Transactions of the London and Middlesex Archaeological Society* (1925), 1-2.

[2] *The Diary of Samuel Pepys,* ed. Robert Latham and William Matthews, 11 vols. (Berkeley and Los Angeles, 1979-83), 4.346.

[3] *The Diary of Samuel Pepys,* 2.191.

[4] *The Diary of Samuel Pepys,* 2.241.

[5] 26 October 1661: "...in the evening news was brought that Sir R. Slingsby our Comptroller (who hath this day been sick a week) is dead; which put me into so great a trouble of mind, that all the night I could not sleep, he being a man that loved me and had many Qualities that made me to love him above all the officers and Commissioners in the Navy. Coming home, we called at Dan. Rawlinson's and there drank good sack; and so home" (*The Diary of Samuel Pepys,* 2.202).

[6] 14 November 1665: "This day, calling at Mr. Rawlinson's to know how all did there, I hear that my pretty grocer's wife, Mrs. Beversham, over the way there, her husband is lately dead of the plague at Bow, which I am sorry for, for fear of losing her neighbourhood" (*The Diary of Samuel Pepys,* 6.298).

[7] *The Diary of Samuel Pepys,* 2.153.

[8] *The Diary of Samuel Pepys,* 6.168.

[9] *The Diary of Samuel Pepys,* 1.245.

[10] *The Diary of Samuel Pepys,* 4.334-35.

[11] *Remarks and Collections of Thomas Hearne,* ed. C. E. Doble, D. W. Rannie, and H. E. Salter, 11 vols. (Oxford, 1886-1915), 5.296.

[12] Brian J. Enright, "Richard Rawlinson: Collector, Antiquary, Topographer" (Doctoral Thesis, Oxford University, 1955), p. 4 n. 3.

[13] Enright, "Richard Rawlinson: Collector, Antiquary, Topographer," pp. 4-5.

[14] Enright, "Richard Rawlinson: Collector, Antiquary, Topographer," p. 5.

[15] *Remarks and Collections of Thomas Hearne,* 4.215.

[16] *The Diary of Samuel Pepys,* 7.242.

Appendix 5

Rawlinson Family Genealogies

One of Seven Armorial Book Plates (Rawlinson Copperplates g. 107-114) that Rawlinson had made for his own use. Reproduced by permission of the Bodleian Library.

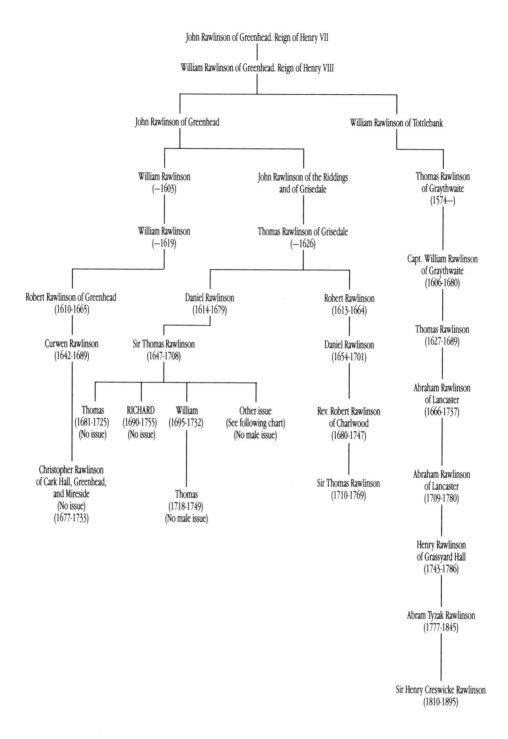

John Rawlinson of Greenhead. Reign of Henry VII

William Rawlinson of Greenhead. Reign of Henry VIII

John Rawlinson of Greenhead

William Rawlinson of Tottlebank

William Rawlinson
(—1603)

John Rawlinson of the Riddings
and of Grisedale

Thomas Rawlinson
of Graythwaite
(1574—)

William Rawlinson
(—1619)

Thomas Rawlinson of Grisedale
(—1626)

Capt. William Rawlinson
of Graythwaite
(1606-1680)

Robert Rawlinson of Greenhead
(1610-1665)

Daniel Rawlinson
(1614-1679)

Robert Rawlinson
(1613-1664)

Thomas Rawlinson
(1627-1689)

Curwen Rawlinson
(1642-1689)

Sir Thomas Rawlinson
(1647-1708)

Daniel Rawlinson
(1654-1701)

Abraham Rawlinson
of Lancaster
(1666-1737)

Thomas
(1681-1725)
(No issue)

RICHARD
(1690-1755)
(No issue)

William
(1695-1732)

Other issue
(See following chart)
(No male issue)

Rev. Robert Rawlinson
of Charlwood
(1680-1747)

Abraham Rawlinson
of Lancaster
(1709-1780)

Christopher Rawlinson
of Cark Hall, Greenhead,
and Mireside
(No issue)
(1677-1733)

Thomas
(1718-1749)
(No male issue)

Sir Thomas Rawlinson
(1710-1769)

Henry Rawlinson
of Grassyard Hall
(1743-1786)

Abram Tyzak Rawlinson
(1777-1845)

Sir Henry Creswicke Rawlinson
(1810-1895)

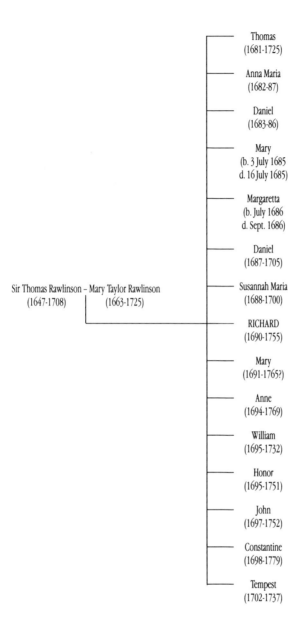

Thomas
(1681-1725)

Anna Maria
(1682-87)

Daniel
(1683-86)

Mary
(b. 3 July 1685
d. 16 July 1685)

Margaretta
(b. July 1686
d. Sept. 1686)

Daniel
(1687-1705)

Susannah Maria
(1688-1700)

RICHARD
(1690-1755)

Mary
(1691-1765?)

Anne
(1694-1769)

William
(1695-1732)

Honor
(1695-1751)

John
(1697-1752)

Constantine
(1698-1779)

Tempest
(1702-1737)

Sir Thomas Rawlinson – Mary Taylor Rawlinson
(1647-1708)   (1663-1725)

Index

Abingdon, Thomas 170
Acton, Oliver 146, 148, 153, 158
Addison, Joseph 2, 39-40
Allestree, Richard 10
Allibone, S. Austin 173, 176
Ames, Joseph 156
Andrews, Charles M. 201, 203
Anne 12, 21, 37, 51, 79, 194
Anstis, John 17, 39, 142, 149, 155
Ashmole, Elias 170, 171
Aubrey, John 26, 123, 171, 173,
    175

Bacon, Montagu 141
Bacon, Sir Francis 1
Baker, Thomas 61, 145, 147, 149,
    150, 155, 158
Ballard, George 61, 63, 64, 65, 67
Ballard, Thomas 145
Barker, Anthony 145, 156
Bayne-Powell, Rosamund 30, 51,
    173
Bedford, Hilkiah 21, 78
Bedford, William 78
Benedictine XIV 34
Bennett, J. A. W. 194
Blackbourne, John 74, 80, 81,
    141, 143
Blacow, Richard 62, 81
Blomefield, F. 173
Bosworth, Joseph 85-86, 88-89,
    92, 93, 96, 102-03

Bowdler, Thomas 126-27
Boyd, William 203
Bradley, James 189, 190
Brett, Thomas 21, 71, 80, 121-22,
    124, 129, 157
Brome, William 61, 77, 149, 156
Browne, Sir Thomas 18, 122
Broxap, Henry 71, 173
Bryant, A. 173
Buckley, William Edward 92-93,
    96
Byrd, William 203

Campbell, Alistair 95, 96, 107-08
Campbell, Eila M. J. 205
Carlyle, E. Irving 92
Carpenter, Edward 174
Carpenter, Humphrey 174
Carte, Thomas 128, 156
Carter, John 174
Casaubon, J. 149
Champollion, Jean François 200
Charles I 70, 120
Charles II 7, 21, 37, 75, 126, 127
Charlett, Arthur 128
Cherry, Francis 77
Chombly, William 209
Churchill, Sarah 37
Clark, Andrew 174
Clark, Donald Lemen 174
Clarke, Richard 186
Clavell, Walter 39

Clement XI 23, 32
Cole, William 63
Coleraine, Lord Henry 141, 156
Collier, Jeremy 70, 73, 79, 80
Compton, Bishop Henry 37, 59, 80, 125, 174
Conybeare, John 85, 91, 95, 100
Conyers, Samuel 181
Cooke, Sir John 125
Craigie, Sir William A. 89, 94, 96, 105-06
Craster, Edmund 174
Cromwell, Richard 122
Crynes, Nathaniel 142, 145, 151, 154, 155, 160
Cummings, William 205
Cunliffe, Lynette Rawlinson 174
Curll, Edmund 18, 122
Cust, Peregrine 189, 190

Dadichi, Theocharis 155
Danyall, A. Johnson 91
Darius I 199
Davenport, C. 174
Davis, Charles 143, 144
Davison, Isaac 182
Davison, Mainplaise 182
Davison, Monkhouse 182, 185, 189
Deacon, Thomas 136, 151
Defoe, Daniel 174
de Ricci, S. 133, 174
de Spira, J. 142
Dibdin, Thomas Frognall 3, 133
Doble, C. E. 174
Dobson, A. 174
Dodwell, Henry 73, 77
Doughty, Henry 80
Douglas, David C. 70, 77, 174

Downes, Theophilus 79, 172
Dryden, John 22
du Fresnoy, Nicholas Lenglet 32-33, 54, 172, 193
Dugdale, Sir William 173
Dyson, Charles 91, 95

Earle, John 87, 93, 96, 101-02
Edward VI 35
Elizabeth I 35, 59
Elstob, Elizabeth 192
Elstob, William 192
Elton, C. I. 174
Elton, M. A. 174
Emden, Alfred B. 174
Emmison, F. G. 174
Esdaile, Katherine A. 174
Evans, Dame Joan 57, 175
Evelyn, John 2
Evelyn, Richard 9

Faneuil, Benjamin 186
Finch, William 91
Firth, Sir Charles 85, 175
Fitzgerald, Percy 60, 175
Fitzwilliam, John 73
Fleming, Robert 124
Fletcher, of the Turl 124
Fletcher, W. Y. 133, 175
Flower, C. T. 175
Folkes, Martin 64, 125
Ford, William 2, 39, 41, 135-36, 151
Foster, Joseph 175
Frampton, Robert 73
Frewin, Amy 3, 4, 7, 33, 41, 43, 134-36
Fuller, Isaac 209
Fussner, F. Smith 175

Gale, Roger 21, 55, 56

Gandy, Henry 21, 80, 81, 122

Gardner, William 172

Garnier, Paul 181

George I 21, 29, 52, 53, 70, 79

George II 53

Gibbon, Anthony 125

Gibson, Edward 85, 194

Gladstone, William 200

Goodwin, Mary 201-02

Goodwin, William A. Rutherford
   202

Gordon, John 126

Goreham, Benjamin 189

Gough, Richard 85

Grascome, Samuel 79

Green, J. R. 72, 175

Greenfield, Stanley B. 99, 175

Greenwood, William 189, 190

Griffin, John 39, 43, 151

Habakkuh, H. J. 175

Hake, Henry M. 175

Halley, Sir Edmund 9, 21

Hannam, John 49

Hardcastle, Thomas 91, 95

Harley, Robert (Lord Oxford) 49,
   59, 61, 124, 140, 146, 150, 152,
   177

Harrison, Charles 152

Harte, Henry 79

Hay, John 32

Hayes, Christopher 171

Heal, Sir Ambrose 182

Hearne, Thomas 3-4, 5, 10, 14,
   16-18, 19, 20, 21-22, 23-25, 26,
   29, 33, 34, 39, 40-41, 42, 43-44,
   49, 54-55, 59, 65, 70, 75, 77-79,
   122-24, 129, 133, 134, 136,

   137-39, 141, 142, 143, 144,
   146, 147, 148, 149, 150, 151,
   152-53, 154, 155, 156, 157, 158,
   160, 174, 194, 199

Heber, Reginald 159

Henry V 83

Henry VI 9

Henry VIII 35, 59, 128

Herries, Charles 189, 190

Hickes, George 23, 70, 73-74,
   75-77, 79, 194

Hoefer, J. C. F. 175

Hogarth, William 121, 174

Hollis, Christopher 175

Holman, William 122

Holmes, Geoffrey 175

Hopkinson, M. R. 176

Howell, Lawrence 75

Hunt, Thomas 125-26

Hunter, Michael 175

Hutchinson, Elisha 186

Hutchinson, Stephen 18

Hutchinson, Thomas 186

Hutton, W. H. 40

Hyde, Henry 73

Ingram, James 85, 91, 95, 99

Innocent XIII 32

Ironside, Edward 183

Jackson, Frederick 92

Jackson, J. M. 92

James II 8, 15, 22, 31, 37, 39, 51,
   69, 71-72, 73, 76, 79, 81, 126,
   127

James III 22-23, 28, 32, 52, 53, 90

Jarvis, Leonard 187

Johnson, Anne 25

Johnson, Arthur 91, 96

Johnson, Dr. Samuel 1, 51
Junius, Francis 194, 195, 196

Ken, Thomas 73, 79
Kennett, White 26, 76, 79, 170
Kent, Henry 181
Ker, John 172
Kettlewell, John 79
Kirby, Paul F. 176
Kirk, John Foster 176
Kneller, Sir Godfrey 6, 12

Ladbroke, Sir Robert 183
Lake, John 73
Lambarde, William de Wescomb
  20, 177
Lang, A. 177
Latham, Robert 176
Lathbury, Thomas 71, 77, 176
Laud, Archbishop William 14, 54,
  55, 153, 172
Layer, Christopher 52-53
Lemprière, John 14
Le Neve, Peter 21, 55, 154, 155
Lewis, John 61
Lilly, William 9, 170
Lindsey, Phillip 176
Lister, Michael 18-19, 20, 25,
  28-29
Lloyd, Henry 187, 189
Lloyd, Nicholas 123
Lloyd, William 70, 73, 74
Lovelace, Richard 35, 177
Lowndes, Samuel 152

Macauley, Thomas B. 51, 176
Macray, W. D. 121, 176
Maffei, Scipio 34

Maittaire, Michael 39, 61, 141,
  146, 152, 155, 159-60
Markham, John 47, 62, 67
Marshall, Dorothy 176
Marshall, Thomas 194
Mary of Modena 23, 31, 72
Mary Tudor 35
Matthews, John 7
Matthews, William 176
Mayo, Charles 85, 91, 95
McLynn, Frank 69, 176
Mead, Dr. Richard 3, 21, 28, 40,
  55, 61
Meredith, Edward 126
Merryman, Charles 152
Middleton, Conyers 149
Mill, John 199
Milton, John 8, 9
Minshull, R. 7, 140-41
Mirrlees, Hope 176
Moll, Hans 205
Mores, Edward Rowe 62, 85
Murray, John 142

Napier, Arthur Sampson 87,
  93-94, 96, 103-05
Newborough, John 10
Newman, Abram 183, 185, 189
Newton, Sir Isaac 21, 55
Nichols, John 52, 176
Norden, John 171, 172
North, Roger 73

Ogle, Octavius 92
Oldisworth, William 39
Oldys, William 158, 160, 177
Ollard, Richard 176
Orme, Robert 126

Overton, J. H. 71, 157, 176
Owen, Humphrey 61

Palmer, David J. 176
Palmer, Thomas 154
Parker, Matthew 5, 49, 59, 146, 150
Parkes, Joan 176
Parr, Samuel 91
Pepys, Samuel 7, 22, 50-51, 59, 70, 123, 126-28, 181, 207-10
Perrott, Sir John 172
Petre, Sir William 35, 174
Philip, Ian 177
Phillipps, Thomas 122
Pinkham, Lucille 177
Pope, Alexander 121, 122
Popple, Henry 205
Porteus, Mr. 7
Powell, J. Enoch 69

Radcliffe, John 40, 121, 170
Rannie, D. W. 174
Rawlins, Thomas 125, 126, 127, 128, 129, 136
Rawlinson, Anne 11, 19, 25, 45
Rawlinson, Christopher 43-44, 83, 193-99
Rawlinson, Constantine 11, 19, 25, 28, 31, 33, 34, 48, 90
Rawlinson, Daniel (1614-79) 7, 11, 27, 50, 69-70, 126, 179, 180, 181, 207-10
Rawlinson, Daniel (1654-1701) 179, 181, 209
Rawlinson, Daniel (1687-1705) 10-11
Rawlinson, George 200

Rawlinson, Henry Creswicke 193, 199-200
Rawlinson, Honor 11, 19, 25, 45
Rawlinson, John 3, 11, 20, 25, 45, 46-48, 49, 60
Rawlinson, Lady Mary *See Taylor, Mary*
Rawlinson, Margaret 181, 209
Rawlinson, Mary 11, 18, 19, 25, 45, 50
Rawlinson, Richard
  And the Chandlers 121-32
  Anglo-Saxon Professorship 61, 83-98
  Auctions of brother's library 5-7, 42, 133-67
  Copperplates 201-05
  Education
    Eton 9-10
    Oxford 12-22
    St. Paul's School 8-9
  Financial difficulties 4-7, 40-50
  Freemasons 55-56
  Grand tour 1-2, 28, 31-34
  Hospital boards 21, 55
  Non-jurors 21-23, 50-53, 69-81
  Publications 17-18, 26-27, 53-55, 169-73
  Royal Society 21, 55, 90
  Society of Antiquaries 55-58, 61-65, 81, 90
  Topographical Interests 19-20, 26-27
Rawlinson, Robert (of Charlwood) 179, 181
Rawlinson, Susannah (1688-1700) 11
Rawlinson, Susannah 183, 207

Rawlinson, Tempest 10, 11, 18, 19, 25, 34, 49

Rawlinson, Thomas (of Grisedale) 207

Rawlinson, Sir Thomas (1647-1708) 6, 7-8, 10, 11-12, 13, 18, 19, 21, 25, 39, 49, 181, 201, 209

Rawlinson, Thomas (1681-1725) 2, 3-4, 9, 10, 16, 17, 18, 20, 23-26, 27, 29, 31, 33, 34-43, 45, 49, 54, 59, 60, 65, 78, 83, 90, 123, 124, 133-67, 172, 201

Rawlinson, Thomas (1718-49) 27, 45-46

Rawlinson, Sir Thomas (1710-69) 179, 181, 182, 183

Rawlinson, Sir Walter 183

Rawlinson, William 11, 19, 25, 27, 45, 90

Rawlynson, Henry 83

Rawlynson, Walter 83

Ray, Dorothea 181

Ray, Walter 181-82

Reynolds, Rev. John 152

Richardson, Dr. Richard 128

Ridley, John Charles 91, 96

Risdon, Tristram 169

Roach, Richard 123

Robinson, Bishop John 59, 125

Robinson, Fred C. 99, 175

Rockefeller, John D., Jr. 202

Roscoe, E. S. 177

Rosenbach, A. S. W. 177

Rossi, Guilio 152

Rotch, Francis 186, 187

Rutter, Owen 179

Sacheverell, Dr. Henry 15-16, 175

Salter, H. E. 174

Sancroft, William 73-74, 79, 81, 124, 208

Saville, Sir Henry 10

Sebright, Thomas 49

Shadwell, Thomas 22

Shield, A. 177

Silver, Thomas 91, 96, 100

Sloane, Sir Hans 21, 40, 55, 141

Smith, George 78

Smith, Samuel 13, 16

Smith, Thomas 149

Sobieski, Maria Clementina 23, 31, 53

South, Robert 170, 171

Spinckes, Nathaniel 80

Stanhope, Philip H. 177

Stanley, Eric Gerald 95, 96, 108-11

Stillingfleet, Edward 79

Stow, John 121

Strangeways, Giles S. H. F. 175

Strype, John 24, 59

Stuart, William 158-59

Stukeley, Dr. William 56, 58, 177

Sunstead, Daniel 183-84

Tabor, John 7, 41, 42, 49, 136-37, 139, 143-44, 151, 152, 159

Tanner, Thomas 60-61, 62, 121, 124, 194

Taylor, Mary 7, 16, 18, 19, 25, 28-29

Taylor, Richard 27

Taylor, Susanne 48

Thompson, Richard P. 72, 177

Thoresby, Ralph 21, 55

Thornton, Robert 189, 190

Thurloe, John 59, 122

Thwaites, Edward 84, 193-94, 199

Thwaytes, William 185
Tillotson, John 74
Tireman, Mr. 146, 157
Tolkien, J. R. R. 94, 96, 106
Trease, Geoffrey 177
Turner, Francis 73, 80

Umfreville, Edward 121

Vaisey, D. G. 205
Van Dyck, Anthony 196
Vertue, George 6, 59, 128, 209

Wagstaffe, Thomas 74, 153
Waite, A. E. 35
Wake, Archbishop William 125
Walesby, Francis Pearson 91-92, 96
Wallis, Dr. Helen 205
Walpole, Horace 2
Walpole, Robert 53
Wanley, Humphrey 21, 55, 56
Warnicke, Retha M. 177
Weidhorn, Manfred 177
West, James 44, 146, 156, 157

Weston, Stephen 10
Wheatley, A. B. 177
Wheeler, Edward 187
White, Robert Meadows 92, 96, 101
White, Thomas 73
William III (of Orange) 22, 51, 69, 70, 71, 72-73, 74, 79, 90
Willis, Browne 44, 156
Wilson, Henry Bristow 92, 96
Winslow, Joshua 186
Witham, Thomas 157
Wood, Anthony 15, 17, 35, 59, 122, 124, 169
Worde, Wynken de 152
Wordsworth, William 12, 83
Wren, Sir Christopher 7, 9
Wrenn, C. L. 94, 96, 106-07
Wright, Samuel 153
Wroth, Warwick 199
Wyatt, Sir Thomas 152

Yeowell, J. 177

Zetzner, J. E. 9, 51